# Ludomusicology

**Genre, Music and Sound**

Edited by Mark Evans, Macquarie University

Over the last decade Screen Soundtrack Studies has emerged as a lively area of research and analysis mediating between the fields of Cinema Studies, Musicology and Cultural Studies. It has deployed a variety of cross-disciplinary approaches illuminating an area of film's audio-visual operation that was neglected for much of the mid-late 1900s. Equinox's *Genre, Music and Sound* series extends the emergent field by addressing a series of popular international film genres as they have developed in the post-War era (1945–present); analyzing the variety and shared patterns of music and sound use that characterize each genre.

**Published**

*Terror Tracks: Music, Sound and Horror Cinema*
Edited by Philip Hayward

*Drawn to Sound: Animation Film Music and Sonicity*
Edited by Rebecca Coyle

*Earogenous Zones: Sound, Sexuality and Cinema*
Edited by Bruce Johnson

*The Music of Fantasy Cinema*
Edited by Janet K. Halfyard

*Sounding Funny: Sound and Comedy Cinema*
Edited by Mark Evans and Philip Hayward

*Movies, Moves and Music: The Sonic World of Dance Films*
Edited by Mark Evans and Mary Fogarty

**Forthcoming**

*The Singing Voice in Contemporary Cinema*
Edited by Diane Hughes and Mark Evans

# Ludomusicology

Approaches to Video Game Music

Edited by
Michiel Kamp, Tim Summers and Mark Sweeney

Equinox Publishing Ltd

Sheffield, UK Bristol, CT

Published by Equinox Publishing Ltd

UK: Office 415, The Workstation, 15 Paternoster Row, Sheffield, South Yorkshire S1 2BX
USA: ISD, 70 Enterprise Drive, Bristol, CT 06010

www.equinoxpub.com

First published 2016

British Library Cataloguing-in-Publication Data
   A catalogue record for this book is available from the British Library.

ISBN-13   978 1 78179 197 4   (hardback)
          978 1 78179 198 1   (paperback)

Library of Congress Cataloging-in-Publication Data
Names: Kamp, Michiel. | Summers, Tim, 1987- | Sweeney, Mark, 1988-
Title: Ludomusicology : approaches to video game music / edited by Michiel
      Kamp, Tim Summers and Mark Sweeney.
Description: Sheffield, UK ; Bristol, CT : Equinox Publishing, 2016. |
      Series: Genre, music and sound | Includes bibliographical references and
      index.
Identifiers: LCCN 2016002616| ISBN 9781781791974 (hb) | ISBN 9781781791981
      (pb)
Subjects:  LCSH: Video game music--History and criticism.
Classification: LCC ML3540.7 .L83 2016 | DDC 781.5/4--dc23
LC record available at http://lccn.loc.gov/2016002616


Typeset by Atheus
Printed and bound in Great Britain by Lightning Source UK Ltd., Milton Keynes
and in the USA by Lightning Source Inc., La Vergne, TN

# Contents

# 1 Introduction

## Michiel Kamp, Tim Summers and Mark Sweeney[1]

The last half-decade has seen the rapid and expansive development of video game music studies. As with any new area of scholarship, this sub-discipline is still tackling fundamental questions concerning how video game music can be investigated. This book suggests a variety of new approaches to video game music, but collectively we are more broadly concerned with the relationship between music and play – a domain of research that is now commonly referred to as "ludomusicology". A term coined by Guillaume Laroche and taken up by Roger Moseley (2013), ludomusicology, at its broadest, attempts to see our engagement with music, any kind of music, in terms of play. While our interests in this volume are confined to music in digital games, they are for a large part informed by the idea that there is a special relationship between playing video games and engaging with their music. Whether we are descending down a dark corridor in *Dead Space* and hearing dissonant strings swell up, or reconstructing Björk's songs in the *Biophilia* app, gaming involves more than passive listening. This book presents a variety of approaches to video game music through the lens of ludomusicology's emphasis on play.

## A Short History of Video Game Music Scholarship

Two important and often-cited pioneering articles on video game music were penned by Zach Whalen (2004; 2007), but the true establishment of the field came in 2008 with Karen Collins's *Game Sound: An Introduction to the History, Theory, and Practice of Video Game Music and Sound Design*. As the title suggests, *Game Sound*'s scope is broad, including discussions of technological developments, compositional techniques, and more game-theoretical concepts such as immersion and interactivity. The same year saw the publication of *From Pac-Man to Pop Music*, a collection of articles edited by Collins, which integrated game music discourse into wider discussions of interactive audio, including studies on ringtones, music marketing and chip music. Another milestone collection, Mark Grimshaw's *Game Sound Technology and Player Interaction* (2011) more broadly covers sound effects and technology, but also examines soundscapes, diegetic music and procedural audio.

By 2012, an increasing number of students were pursuing higher education degrees in the field, and alongside this, a new current of musicological interest in video games began to emerge. Kiri Miller's *Playing Along: Digital Games, YouTube, and Virtual Performance* looks at video game music cultures, and contains two major case studies of music games (*Guitar Hero/Rock Band* [2005-]) and the *Grand Theft Auto* (1997-) series. Both cases heavily rely on player interviews and participant observation and, together with studies of players of *Dance Dance Revolution* (1998) by Jacob Smith (2004) and Joanna Demers (2006), should be seen as the first ethnographic forays into the field. Also in 2012, we founded the Ludomusicology Research Group and held an international symposium dedicated to video game music at St Catherine's College, Oxford. It has since become an annual conference. In 2014, the inaugural North American Conference on Video Game Music took place at Youngstown State University, and has also become a regular event.

In the last few years, the study of video game music has come into its own. Chapters and articles have started appearing in general music and media journals and volumes (e.g. Gibbons, 2011; Moseley, 2013; Lerner, 2013; Bridgett, 2013). Collins's second key contribution to the field, *Playing with Sound: A Theory of Interacting with Sound and Music in Video Games* (2013), is an attempt to offer an overarching theory of sound and music in video games through the central notion of interaction. Drawing in part on psychological and phenomenological approaches to sound in general, and in part on discussions of the role of music in broader gaming culture, it provides a theoretical bridge between sound studies and musicological approaches on the one hand (such as Collins's earlier work), and ethnographic approaches on the other, as used by both Miller and Demers, but also in William Cheng's more recent *Soundplay: Video Games and the Musical Imagination* (2014). Cheng's own (partly ethnographic, partly hermeneutic) contribution to the field is to embed musical engagements with video games in a larger musical culture.

Two recent edited collections serve as precursors to our project in this volume. Contributors to Peter Moormann's *Music and Game* (2013) map out the game music territory with particular focus on game music traditions, both historical and genre-based. *Music and Game*'s often survey-based approach is valuable for providing contextual understanding of game music. More traditionally analytical musicological approaches can be found in the collection of essays edited by K. J. Donnelly, William Gibbons and Neil Lerner, entitled *Music in Video Games: Studying Play* (2014). It addresses video game music aesthetics, music analysis and hermeneutics through a series of focused case studies. The present volume takes a theoretical "step back", taking an interest in methodology and the idiosyncrasies of video game music. Issues of modularity, textuality, interactivity, aesthetics and immersion have been implicit in many if not all video game music scholarship, but the contributions to *Ludomusicology* are united in their explicit aim to address these thorny, underlying concepts. Taken alongside the recent developments in game music scholarship, this book is part of a coalescing body of research that is evolving into a fully-fledged sub-discipline with its own conventions, theories and debates.

## Challenges and Approaches

In this context, certain significant issues loom large in the scholarly landscape, the most crucial of which are addressed by authors in the present volume:

1.  conceptualizing and analysing game music (Chapters 2, 3 and 4)
2.  how notions of diegesis are complicated by video game interactivity (Chapter 5)
3.  video game musical culture and literacies (Chapter 6)
4.  the distinction between game play and music play (Chapters 7 and 8)
5.  the technicalities of game music production (Chapter 9)
6.  the relationships between game music and art music traditions (Chapters 10 and 11).

The chapters in this book trace a course from broad models and methods to more specific cases. Both **Tim Summers** and **Isabella van Elferen** offer basic methods and models for game music research. Summers starts out from a very straightforward question: How does one go about analysing video game music? With any youthful field, certain vital issues concerning the practicality of conducting research into the topic quickly arise. Games demand that researchers engage with the text (playing and reading both with and against the grain) and video game scholarship challenges scholars to embrace and make obvious their personal engagement with the texts under scrutiny. The aim of van Elferen's chapter is to outline a research model for analysing game music through a systematic theorization of musical immersion. The chapter proposes three overlapping, music-specific concepts that lead to a comprehensive framework that charts the conditions for and mechanics of musical player involvement. This framework, the ALI model, shows how musical affect, literacy and interaction cooperate in a process of signification, identification and play leading to game musical involvement. The ALI model enables investigations of the separate areas of musical game involvement, but also offers room for their integration: player involvement is likely to be most intense where the three areas of the framework overlap.

**Elizabeth Medina-Gray** considers the dynamic qualities of video game music by placing it within a larger conceptual context of modularity. Medina-Gray's chapter provides the first thorough examination of modularity in video game music. Two aspects of game music, in particular, distinguish it from other types of modular music: (1) a *usability* function and (2) a concept of *smoothness* (or lack thereof) between modules as they combine during gameplay. This chapter argues that by attending to the dynamic and modular aspects of video game music, we gain a more complete understanding of this music within the context of games and gameplay. **Michiel Kamp** asks what role video game music plays beyond gameplay. Drawing on narratology theory, Kamp describes how nondiegetic music has the unique ability to overarch game menus, cutscenes and other peritexts, and by doing so can affect our understanding of games as a whole. Kamp and Medina-Gray both examine how the smoothness and rupture of dynamic music can serve to de-emphasize or emphasize transitions both during gameplay and surrounding it. **Melanie Fritsch** goes one step further than a game's menus, presenting the argument that game musical literacy involves fan cultural discourse as well. Through a case study of *Super Mario Bros.: The 8-Bit Opera*, she shows that an understanding of video games and their music is a crucial component in the analysis of gaming culture as a whole.

In "Game and Play", **Anahid Kassabian** and **Freya Jarman** consider the ways that music as a central activity is represented in video games and smartphone apps, specifically those labelled "music games" or "music apps". Games present music as a task to be achieved, a disciplinary activity in which the player should "play" again and again until the game (and thereby music) is mastered, while apps allow for dipping in and out, for casual engagement as well as more intensive devotion, and for experimentation and creativity. While it is clear to any practising musician that the two styles of musical activity are inextricably intertwined, and cannot be pulled apart, music in virtual worlds seems only to be able to appear – or perhaps sound? – as one or the other, but not both. **Samantha Blickhan**'s case of Björk's digital album *Biophilia* (2011) perhaps best fits Kassabian and Jarman's "app" category. Due to the ambiguous presentation of player agency in the interactive versions of the *Biophilia* songs, the line between game play and music play can at times become blurred. By recognizing their own presence within a song as a collaborator, the listener engages the music on a strongly personal level, but do the varying results of interaction cause Björk's own recorded "fixed" version of each song to somehow matter less? This chapter facilitates discussion about where the line between creation and interpretation should (or even can) be drawn, and the possible challenges of presenting the manipulation of an original piece of musical art as a game. Blickhan ultimately asks how interactivity might affect the way we listen to music.

The final three chapters of this volume deal with aesthetics, both the aesthetics of game music and game music's relation to music-historical aesthetics. Composer and audio director **Stephen Baysted** focuses on the former in his discussion of the compositional processes behind *Need for Speed Shift 2: Unleashed* (2011). He provides unique insights into the commercial tensions inherent in the production of a high-budget game franchise and their impact on creative musical interventions. **Mark Sweeney** provides a case study of Jason Graves's soundtrack for *Dead Space* (2008). He investigates a particular set of relationships between video game music, film music, and modernist avant-garde music, tracing the origins of the aleatory sound-world employed in *Dead Space*, back, via Hollywood, to the avant-garde music prevalent since the 1950s. **William Gibbons** continues the discussion of art music traditions in games through an examination of instances of remixed classical music in games. After theorizing about the remixing process, Gibbons describes how "reflexive remixes" serve as musical transgressive play. Through case studies of several games, including *Gyruss* (1983), *Boom Boom Rocket* (2007) and *Catherine* (2011), Gibbons reveals the way that the classical music remixes utilize and problematize the more general art versus entertainment discourse that exists both with respect to music and with respect to games.

This volume has been made possible through the generous support of many institutions and individuals. We are particularly grateful to the institutional hosts of the Ludomusicology Easter conferences, Peter Franklin, Anahid Kassabian and Stephen Baysted. While several conference keynote speakers have contributed to this volume, we also wish to thank those who have not directly written for this book, but whose work and involvement with the field has distinctly informed the scholarship presented within these pages: Mark Grimshaw, William Cheng, and particularly Kevin Donnelly, for their help, advice and advocacy on the part of the Ludomusicology project. Additional thanks are also due to James Barnaby, Huw Catchpole-Davies and Jemima Cloud for their efforts in organizing the events that led to the body of scholarship represented here.

## Notes

1.  Michiel Kamp is Junior Assistant Professor of Music at Utrecht University, where he specializes in teaching music in film and digital media. Michiel completed his AHRC-funded PhD in Music at Cambridge University with his thesis, "Four Ways of Hearing Video Game Music", which focused on phenomenological approaches to listening. As well as presenting his research at international conferences, he has also written for journals including *Philosophy and Technology*. He has co-edited a special issue on video game music for *The Soundtrack*.

    Tim Summers is a Teaching Fellow in Music at Royal Holloway, University of London. He has written on music in modern popular culture for journals including the *Journal of the Royal Musical Association*, *Journal of Film Music* and *Music, Sound and the Moving Image.* He is the author of *Understanding Video Game Music* (CUP, 2016).

Mark Sweeney completed his D.Phil. thesis (entitled "The Aesthetics of Videogame Music") in Musicology at Hertford College, Oxford. His primary research interest is on aesthetic theory and video game music. He was previously a lecturer in Music at St Catherine's College, Oxford.

## References

Bridgett, R. (2013) "Contextualizing Game Audio Aesthetics." In *The Oxford Handbook of New Audiovisual Aesthetics*, edited by J. Richardson, C. Gorbman and C. Vernallis, pp. 563–71. New York: Oxford University Press.

Cheng, W. (2014) *Sound Play: Video Games and the Musical Imagination.* New York: Oxford University Press.

Collins, K. (2008a) *Game Sound: An Introduction to the History, Theory, and Practice of Video Game Music and Sound Design.* Cambridge, MA: MIT Press.

Collins, K. (ed.) (2008b) *From Pac-Man to Pop Music: Interactive Audio in Games and New Media.* Aldershot: Ashgate.

Collins, K. (2013) *Playing with Sound: A Theory of Interacting with Sound and Music in Video Games.* Cambridge, MA: MIT Press.

Demers, J. (2006) "Dancing Machines: 'Dance Dance Revolution', Cybernetic Dance, and Musical Taste." *Popular Music* 25(3): 401–414.

Donnelly, K. J., W. Gibbons and N. Lerner (eds) (2014) *Music in Video Games: Studying Play.* London and New York: Routledge.

Gibbons, W. (2011) "Wrap Your Troubles in Dreams: Popular Music, Narrative, and Dystopia in *Bioshock.*" *Game Studies* 11(3). http://gamestudies.org/1103/articles/gibbons

Grimshaw, M. (ed.) (2011) *Game Sound Technology and Player Interaction: Concepts and Developments.* Hershey: Information Science Reference.

Lerner, N. (2013) "The Origins of Musical Style in Video Games, 1977–1983." In *The Oxford Handbook of Film Music Studies*, edited by D. Neumeyer, pp. 319–47. New York: Oxford University Press.

Miller, K. (2012) *Playing Along: Digital Games, YouTube, and Virtual Performance.* New York: Oxford University Press.

Moormann, P. (ed.) (2013) *Music and Game: Perspectives on a Popular Alliance.* Wiesbaden: Springer.

Moseley, R. (2013) "Playing Games with Music (and Vice Versa): Ludomusicological Perspectives on Guitar Hero and Rock Band." In *Taking It to the Bridge: Music as Performance*, edited by N. Cook and R. Pettengill, pp. 279–318. Ann Arbor: University of Michigan Press.

Smith, J. (2004) "I Can See Tomorrow in Your Dance: A Study of *Dance Dance Revolution* and Music Video Games." *Journal of Popular Music Studies* 16(1), 58–84.

Whalen, Z. (2004) "Play Along – An Approach to Videogame Music." *Game Studies* 4(1). http://www.gamestudies.org/0401/whalen/

Whalen, Z. (2007) "Film Music vs. Video-Game Music: the Case of Silent Hill." In *Music, Sound and Multimedia: From the Live to the Virtual*, edited by J. Sexton, pp. 68–81. Edinburgh: Edinburgh University Press.

# 2 Analysing Video Game Music
## Sources, Methods and a Case Study

## Tim Summers[1]

The academic study of video game music is at a transitionary phase in its life
– it is developing from a punky juvenile scholarly newcomer into an adolescent
marked by self-reflective critical angst about purpose, terminology and
methodology. Polemic pleas for attention ("Why is this music being ignored?")
have given way to more mature questions concerning how such investigation
might proceed ("How can game music be examined?"). To continue the work
of opening up the topic of video game music for analysis, this chapter will
outline some answers to the question "How does one go about analysing video
game music?" The purpose of this essay is not to prescribe a single solution
of how video game music analysis should be conducted, and neither do the
observations and suggestions offered here represent the entirety of the sources
and methods available for analysts. Instead, what follows is intended to provide
a starting point for those wishing to engage with game music.

The most straightforward approach to understanding how video game music
might be analysed is through a consideration of the materials available to
analysts, and how these may be used and interrogated. Traditional musicology
has been justly taken to task for relying too much on the written score as the
ultimate authoritative incarnation of a musical "work", but this legacy has not
been inherited by game music studies. While such a state of affairs may be
considered a generally positive aspect of the new field of inquiry, it has an
unnerving effect upon those of us whose normal mode of analysis is very much
score-focused. We may be at something of a loss when, in the absence of a
score or a fixed sonic output, our familiar tools of the trade are not available
to us. The analyst is thus left to ask, "What is the object of analysis to be and
how is it to be analysed?" This chapter will outline some of the main sources
of game music, the methods by which these sources may be interrogated, and
some of the issues that analysts face.

In order to keep this analytical discussion grounded, I will be using a
recurring example within this chapter and enact an instance of game music
analysis. Much of this chapter will be written in the first person. This has the

advantage of allowing me to narrate my decisions and processes, hopefully illuminating the activity of analysis as much as the materials that are being studied. The game that I have selected for this chapter is a well-known one: *Halo: Combat Evolved* (2001), a first-person shooter (FPS) in which the player controls a cybernetically-enhanced space marine (Master Chief), who must battle aliens and investigate a mysterious, ancient, planet-sized, ring-shaped, artificially constructed world (Halo). The game was originally released as a flagship launch title for Microsoft's Xbox console (2001), and later adapted for PC Windows and Mac platforms in 2003. In 2011, to celebrate ten years of the *Halo* franchise, a remake of the game, *Halo: Combat Evolved Anniversary* was produced. The 2001 *Halo: Combat Evolved* launched a multimedia franchise (encompassing films, comics, toys and board games) that continues to be an important part of the cultural landscape of video games. As well as being positively remarked upon by reviewers of the game (Boulding, 2001; Fielder, 2001), *Halo*'s music has been taken to heart by gamers as a significant component of the experience of playing the *Halo* game. The score is firmly part of the canon of game music performed and re-recorded outside the game: music from *Halo* is a staple of game music albums and *Video Games Live* concerts.[2] *Halo* is a useful example for discussions of video game music analysis since, as a conventional mass-audience game, it illustrates many of the challenges that often come with investigating game music.

One of the first questions we have to answer is, "What is it that we examine when we analyse game music?" Video games are complex, multidimensional texts. As with most subjects of musical analysis, there are a variety of ways that any one text (game/piece of music/artefact) may be interrogated. The sources for video game music may be considered in two domains – those generated from within the game text and technology (in-game sources), such as game code and music data, and those that are outside the boundaries of the particular video game object (satellite sources) such as interviews, production documents, and so on. Each of these sources has the potential to provide information of a certain type about the game's music, subject to the advantages and shortcomings of the particular source, and approach, in question.

## In-Game Sources

### Versions and Editions

Video games are slippery texts. Quite apart from the differences of musical output between play sessions, it is common for games to be produced in multiple divergent editions and versions. For what is ostensibly the same game, the audio experience of the player can vary significantly depending on the computer system (platform) and sound technology that is used to play the game. The player of the PC CD-ROM version of *Quake* (1996), with a score by Nine Inch Nails, hears different music to the gamer who plays the Nintendo 64 (1998) version, which features music by Aubrey Hodges. In early sound-era PC games, the way that the music was rendered depended upon the particular sound hardware that the player owned. Game music can change between platforms, versions and regional localizations of the same title across the globe. Even software emulators of older consoles cannot always be relied upon to replicate the original audio with complete accuracy.

In the case of *Halo*, once the decision has been taken to analyse this particular game, the analyst must answer a question: which *Halo* should be analysed? Even after leaving aside sequels, I must consider which version I will use for my analysis, and through what sound technology to listen to the game. Should I use the version that represents the game experience of the largest number of players? If this is the metric to be used, then the Xbox version, with over 5 million copies sold (Bungie, 2005) is clearly the preferable choice, rather than the far less popular PC version. Given the game's sales and the relatively recent discontinuation of the Xbox console, the hardware and software are inexpensive and readily available.[3] However, if I believe I should use the version that most fully represents the producers' creative ambitions for the game (and its music), perhaps I should use the *Anniversary* edition, which includes re-recorded music and an improved sound programming. Despite these choices, I shall instead be using the rather less popular Windows PC version for this analysis.[4] My justification for this is based upon the greater ease with which the PC version of the game may be recorded and dissected (of which more later). As a result of this choice, it should be borne in mind that some of my conclusions may not always hold true for every other edition of the game. Much like the so-called "Bruckner Problem" (the hand-wringing by analysts about different multiply-valid versions of Bruckner symphonies; see Cooke, 1969), this issue highlights the fluidity of these musical entities.

## Analytical Play

It is important to recognize that these texts and objects are games. Putting aside our anxiety about investigating what is supposedly "low culture", it is entirely necessary for the analyst to *play* the games and engage with them as a player and analyst simultaneously. It is not possible to be one and not the other when investigating this topic in an academic way. In order for the music to be sounded from this interactive media, the game must be played.

For this analysis of *Halo*, I have chosen not to use a bedroom-style television of the kind familiar to many an adolescent gamer, nor a large, high-quality television in a "home cinema" setting, but instead to use my Windows laptop's in-built sound and graphics drivers, and to listen through headphones. Here, I am able to easily record my gameplay, using screen recording software. There are several excellent free open-source screen recording applications, such as Open Broadcaster Software.[5] I might choose to record the output of my soundcard while playing the game, by using a freeware wave sound recorder like Audacity. The recordings allow me to avoid the difficulty of attempting to both analyse the music and progress through the game at the same time. In order to investigate the different possibilities of play, multiple play sessions are necessary, which then can be easily compared using the recordings.

I have elected to concentrate on the first level of *Halo*, "Pillar of Autumn". I have selected this level as a case study primarily because of the interesting diversity of musical material heard in the level and the way that it sets up the musical associations and processes that are used throughout the game.

After playing the game for even a short while, the fundamental programming mechanic of the game becomes clear: the player's in-game actions and movements trigger programmed occurrences that facilitate progression of the storyline and mission – perhaps moving through a certain door will set off an alarm, or vanquishing enemies will prompt plot progression. By noticing the fundamental ways that the game's musical output changes with the gameplay (i.e. when music starts, stops and obviously changes), the basic programming of the music usually becomes clear. Karen Collins calls this kind of "changeable" music "dynamic music" (2008: 184) because it anchors musical prompts to events within the gameworld, which may be to begin or end a cue, or prompt a musical change. Quite where and how these musical changes and transitions are specifically anchored requires more investigation.

The level begins with a cutscene (non-interactive video clip) showing the titular Halo ring. A spaceship of human marines, led by Captain Keyes, is approaching the Halo, fleeing from an as-yet-unseen enemy. In a hanger of the ship, a Sergeant briefs a platoon of marines – aliens are expected to board the human vessel and the marines must be prepared to repel the invaders. Meanwhile, in another part of the ship, two crewmen are given an order to bring the Master Chief, the player's character, out of hibernation. After this video clip, the player gains control of the avatar, and is given instruction by one of the other soldiers about the basic game controls. As the aliens attack, the player must reach the bridge of the ship and then battle through the besieged vessel towards the lifeboats. Boarding a lifeboat prompts the end-of-level cutscene, which depicts the Master Chief travelling to the Halo, where the next level of the game will take place.

The duration of this level changes considerably based on the player's proficiency and familiarity with *Halo*, and first-person shooters more generally. Some players may complete the level in about ten minutes, but a more typical duration of play, judging by my own performance, is closer to half an hour. While playing the game as the programmers expected is a representative way of experiencing the game, it is common (usual even) that gamers also sometimes play "against the grain" by deliberately subverting the game's instructions to, and expectations of, the player's actions. Gamers test the game construct in a playful and exploratory way: "What happens if I go the 'wrong' way?"; "Will the game let me do the opposite of my task?"; "Can I put my avatar where it is clearly not supposed to be?"; "When I am urged to move quickly, what happens if I don't move?"; "Can I shoot my comrades?" In the context of game analysis, this kind of "reactionary play" is useful since it has the potential to reveal much about the game construction that is otherwise less obvious – at moments when game rules are tested, the architecture may be revealed.

Playing *Halo* against the grain can reveal aspects of the game's music programming. Since the changes to the repeating musical material are apparently triggered depending on events in the gameworld, by progressing through the level slowly and listening to the audio output, it is possible to isolate the game activity that prompts changes to the musical material (start, stop, change loops, trigger ending segment, etc.). At the same time, if no musical or dramatic triggers are engaged for a long period of time, the music fades out, rather than risk annoying the player with continuous repetition. Thus the analyst-player has to play in particular ways to investigate the musical system in the game. Comparisons of multiple play sessions can be used to isolate the mechanics of the music programming. YouTube hosts a plethora of videos of recorded playthroughs of games – these may also be useful as additional evidence for other players' experiences of the game.[6]

In playing and analysing the game, we can begin to identify the musical material used in *Halo* and the situations in which it is heard. Listening to the game, I am struck by the markedly different stylistic features contained within the musical score. From this, I am led to a kind of informal topic analysis to understand the components of the score. *Halo* contains what I regard as three distinct musical elements: Gregorian chant (and other Western *religioso* materials), Hollywood-style underscore and action music, and exotic/"alien"-signifying musical elements, which includes a female solo voice singing what sounds like improvised non-Western music. The majority of the "Pillar of Autumn" level is accompanied primarily by the "action music" topic – score elements that consist of a variety of repeated drum patterns, fast-moving string ostinati and rising/falling melodic sequences. These elements are typically written in distinct musical layers, with instrumental choirs introduced in turn, playing in dotted dance rhythms in compound time, approaching a jig-like topic. The non-Western singing and the Gregorian chant are heard either in sections of music solely written in those styles (such as the "chant" menu music) or as pronounced unusual inclusions in the Hollywood-style "action music".

What we might call "analytical play" (repeated play and reactionary play) also allows the discovery of glitches in the game's music system. Midway through the level, upon reaching the bridge of the ship, a cutscene is shown during which the ship's captain provides further details of the plot backstory and instructs the player's avatar to try and escape the ship. As the cutscene ends and the gameplay resumes, a low string drone is heard. This loop is programmed to fade out once the player's avatar passes a subsequent location in the level. During many instances of play, however, the drone does not fade out as it should, but instead is abruptly and immediately silenced.[7] While this is obviously a misfiring of the system, it nevertheless clearly indicates the trigger-point and demonstrates conclusively that musical changes are sometimes anchored to the avatar's position in the virtual world.[8]

Analytical play is a way of allowing analysts to determine how the music is encountered by players and it usually gives a good indication of how music is programmed and deployed. In essence, it reveals the musical mechanics and material of the game. Through repeated play of the "Pillar of Autumn" level, I can work out (to a reasonable degree of accuracy) where the trigger-points for musical transition are located. I can investigate how far I progress through the level, in terms of virtual geography and events, before a new piece of musical material is heard. I now know the contexts in which particular pieces of musical material are heard by players. I have also ascertained how long the music will continue to sound without a player-triggered change, before it fades out (five minutes). These conclusions help me to form a mental musical model or map of the level, to understand the common processes that unite the individual play sessions. Like many players, I can learn to predict the moments of musical change and the stages of the musical experience of the level.

Analytical play, while an excellent way of investigating the musical experience of a game, can often not reveal the particulars of the music programming, especially in very complex systems. At this stage, I am uncertain whether *Halo's* music is stored as MIDI-style "note data" files, recorded audio files, or another format. From the loop glitch, the smooth musical changes, and the inclusion of sung material, my suspicion is that the score consists of fragmented audio files that are looped and silenced by the music programming, but I must try another mode of investigation to support this hunch.

## Code and Engine

Video games are programmed using machine-interpretable code of one kind or another, but rather than programming every game from scratch, developers produce "engines", which create the architecture of the gameplay – effectively a programme for controlling the game construct. While types of engine vary greatly, a typical engine might contain components for generating 3D/2D graphics and textures, calculating in-game physics and generating artificial intelligence. Engines may include, or be exclusively concerned with, controls for sound and music. The engine does not create the content of sounds or art, but provides the framework for these to be used in the game. Just as a game artist can design a texture that the engine will apply to a surface, so a musician can create music the engine will control. The (music) engine starts, stops and changes this music, as and when appropriate, depending on the gameplay. Game engines create particular gameplay conditions, and, similarly, each sound engine presents different possibilities for game music. Engines are often customized to achieve particular musical-interactive functionality. Engines dedicated only to music are more properly called "middleware". Certain music middleware systems have become particularly widely used, such as the Miles Sound System, Microsoft DirectMusic, FMOD and Wwise. These tools allow great flexibility in the way in which the music is formed and deployed within the game.

For the analyst, understanding the music middleware/game engine or the programming of the game can be essential to the work of predicting the musical outputs. Rather than working from play instance to play instance and attempting to differentiate out the processes behind the musical output in each example, the rules that govern the deployment and sound of music can be discovered by investigating the game engine and music code. The difficulty of interrogating the music code of a game can vary significantly, depending on the programming of the game. In *Rome: Total War* (2004), which uses the Miles Sound System, for instance, the music code is stored in a text file, "descr_sounds_music.txt" and one can plainly read the coded instructions that explain the game mode (e.g. "BATTLE MAP"), game state (e.g. "state MUSIC_BATTLE_MOBILIZE") and the list of .mp3 sound files (e.g. Mobilize2-Warrior_March.mp3) that should be played during that state. Not all games have such clearly accessible and interpretable code. Nevertheless, the widespread culture of modding games (the practice of modifying commercially-released software) has resulted in a large number of fan-made tools for deconstructing games. For the analyst, these allow extraction of music data and programming. Unfortunately, the legal status of modding is ambiguous. Most games, including *Halo*, demand that the user does not decompile or disassemble the game as part of the licence agreement. While this contract clause is less concerned with modding activity than with pirating and the replication of proprietary software engines, nevertheless, this kind of investigation is legally unclear. Should one wish to deconstruct a game, however, a plethora of applications quite often make this activity straightforward. Some of these programmes may be created for use with a certain game, while others are more general tools for extracting data from video games. The mined musical material might then be matched to the recorded gameplay, so that the specific musical cueing of the game (and the particular level) can be accurately understood.

Some game companies actively encourage adaptation and customization of games. In the case of *Halo*, Gearbox Software, which adapted *Halo* for the PC, did just this by releasing a version of the game called *Halo: Custom Edition* (2004), together with a toolkit for editing the levels. These tools, which include the option to control how music is deployed in the game, allow analysts a way to understand the game through experimenting with the programming architecture. By using the software tools developed by gamers and the *Halo* fan community, I can find a large list of audio files in the *Halo* programme. While the audio files contain speech and sound effects as well as music, in the case of *Halo* it is easy to discount the irrelevant sounds, leaving me with the music. Listening to the files, I may identify the music used in the "Pillar of Autumn", and begin to reconcile how these fragments of music are deployed by the game through a comparison with the recordings I made of the game being played, leading me to draw conclusions about *Halo*'s programming.

The music that accompanies the main gameplay in *Halo* is stored in brief audio files (some only a few seconds in length) that can be repeated or cued to play, based upon the player's actions. The majority of in-game cues are assembled by the randomized ordering of a selection of short musical fragments. This results in a very flexible music system. The large-level cues are usually formed in three sections: starting and ending musical sections bookend a set of repeating fragments. A set of variations on the main repeating fragments may be triggered at a certain point in the level. By listening to the musical output, reviewing the recordings I made earlier, and examining how the audio files are cued by the game, the musical architecture and its relationship to the gameplay may be specifically divined. What we have not been able to glean from this programming analysis are the motivations of the programmers and composers. For this information, we must turn to satellite sources such as interviews and statements from the game's producers (examined below).

## Musical Material

So far, the analytical processes I have discussed have focused on the deployment of the musical material, rather than the sonic contents of these units. Now that I have started to understand how the audio files are triggered by the game, I can examine what musical material is heard and in what circumstances. Such analysis comes hand in hand with interpretative considerations. In tandem with understanding when the music sounds, we should also consider how these musical elements are heard to "mean" in the context of the game. What interpretations can be readily drawn from the deployment of the musical material?

Upon starting the game, after the company logos, the player hears what stands as *Halo*'s main musical identity: a vocalizing male choir singing what sounds like *a cappella* Gregorian chant. Behind the menu is an image of Halo, and the chant theme recurs most often in the game when the mystery of Halo is being discussed by characters, or discoveries are made about the object's origin and purpose. Gregorian chant seems an unusual way to begin a science fiction FPS, but this startling musical material is fundamental to establishing the focus of the game. To interrogate the construction of this chant, transcription seems like a good way to represent and examine this material. Because of the randomization processes in the score and the temporal uncertainties related to triggering, it is obviously not possible to create a straightforward transcription of the entire score, or even a single recorded soundtrack that holds for all cases (see Elizabeth Medina-Gray's chapter in this volume). Nevertheless, transcribing excerpts or motifs from the score that form part of the modular construction of the audio output may be useful. Working from an audio capture of the game's audio output, I can transcribe the motif, as shown in Figure 2.1. Since this is obviously presented to the player as significant musical material, and is used as the basis of musical variation later in the game, it seems wise to make a record of this subject.

*Figure 2.1 Halo*'s "chant" theme, male chorus

Traditional Western notation may be only able to signify certain limited dimensions of musical material, but it is well-suited to representing melodic relationships. Figure 2.1 reveals the motif's chant-like phrase structure, modal tonal design (dorian mode) and an ambiguous metre that serves to invoke medieval religious practice. From this transcription, I can input the notes into the Global Chant Database's musical search engine to give an indication as to whether this is a chant quotation, or a stylistic emulation. The search did not find any specific results, but several gesturally similar phrases. Either the phrase is not a genuine chant, or it is taken from a source sufficiently obscure so as not to be covered by the database. In all likelihood, the chant is a new composition, though it is a successful imitation of the style.

The quasi-mystical Halo object needs to be described as appropriately ancient and mysterious. While Gregorian chant is not "ancient" in the prehistoric sense (as is the Stonehenge-like Halo) it is nevertheless a useful signifier for traditional religion and, for the majority of listeners, sounds indeterminately old.[9] As Western recorded musical history is mapped onto human history, this oldest of preserved Western musical traditions (religious chant) is aligned with undefined ancientness. The chant topic is not marked as geographically alien; it is historically-othered. (Exotic/geographical alterity is reserved for the present-day alien antagonists.) These chanting voices may evoke the mythic past, or the oral tradition of the telling and retelling of epic tales. Gregorian chant has not been extensively appropriated by Hollywood or games, so the use of this type of music helps to create a distinct and unusual identity that differentiates the game from its genre siblings.

The *Halo* score engages in both musical topic-based connections and more specific motivic relationships. In the "Pillar of Autumn" level, the unusual musical elements are included as markedly "different" to the Hollywood-style underscore. One variation, as briefly described above, adds a female singer vocalizing in a non-Western style (rhythmically free and improvisation-style gestures, pitch-bends, limited scale) over the looping drum patterns. This most obviously "exotic" musical material is associated with the alien creatures and environments. While it is heard only fleetingly in this level, the signification is more clearly cemented when the Master Chief encounters creatures and alien environments with this musical topic later in the game. The Western religious topic is associated with the Halo object and the heroic Master Chief through the inclusion of male voices or a pipe organ. This is appropriate, not least because of the religious overtones of the character – the resurrection-like sequence in which Master Chief is revived from cryogenic sleep almost implies immortality. The reverential presentation of the superhuman character, who is legendary, heroic, ageless, timeless and summoned to save the (mere mortal) humans, invokes messianic narratives. Reverential, religious music positions the Master Chief as a demigod, asserting the epic/heroic element of the character/role.

The religious topic is heard in the "Pillar of Autumn" level, with male voices sounding both the "Halo motif" from the main menu, and new chant-like material. The "Halo motif" from the menu recurs in voices during the cutscenes when the Halo ring is discussed and/or the Master Chief is the focus of attention. Material clearly derived from the "Halo motif" is heard in both instrumental and vocal parts during the gameplay, connecting the cutscenes and the main gameplay. Indeed, rather than signifying one entity, the motif serves to create connections between entities, binding together the disparate elements of the game: it is heard in association with the presence of the Halo object, plot exposition about the Halo, the Master Chief, and the game identity itself. To analyse the way that the Halo motif is developed and woven into the musical fabric of the game, we can make use of the thematic transcription prepared earlier. Using Figure 2.1, I can identify when rhythmically augmented versions and fragments of the theme are used. Towards the end of the "Pillar of Autumn", a horn variation uses the "Halo motif" at the original pitch, first rhythmically augmenting the opening phrase, before using fragments of the third phrase in rhythmic diminution to create a descending sequence. For less clear musical processes, further transcriptions are needed. Figure 2.2, for example, shows a choral variation that sounds during the first gameplay stage. When I heard it as a player, it seemed familiar, but it is only when I analyse the variation with Figure 2.1 that I identify how this similarity with the "Halo motif" is generated: the variation uses the opening two pitches of the motif as an alternating accompaniment to a rising gesture that maintains the dorian mode and stepwise contour of the chant theme. We can thus see the musical-developmental processes used in the composition of the game's music.

*Figure 2.2* Variation on *Halo*'s "chant" theme, male chorus

Examining topic deployment, recurring materials and motivic development, in tandem with an understanding of the musical mechanics of the game, allows grounded, sophisticated interpretative connections about the game's use of music – not least the signification of "otherness" in the non-Western musical material which serves as a counterpart to the faux-Gregorian chant.

We have seen that we can glean information from analytical play, investigating the game's programming and transcription/analysis of the musical material. To develop this analysis further, we can draw upon materials outside the boundary of the game text. We can find information from the musicians and programmers who created the game. Like many high-budget games, *Halo* received an extensive marketing campaign that included a considerable number of interviews. Even for lower-profile games, it is common for composers and audio directors to give interviews or report their experiences working on the game (such as in production blogs or through presentations at industry conferences). Such interviews can be found through simple internet searches or on composers'/game developers' websites.

## Satellite Sources

### *Interviews and Presentations*

Interviews about *Halo* are particularly useful in two dimensions – first, they shed light on the production and construction of the game's music. Secondly, they often reveal the aesthetic goals of the game's music producers. Martin O'Donnell, as audio director, had ultimate responsibility for the audio of the game, and composed *Halo*'s score (along with Michael Salvatori). O'Donnell has given interviews and presentations that explain the thinking and implementation behind *Halo*'s audio.

While corporate confidentiality agreements typically limit the detail with which composers can discuss or demonstrate the technologies they use, O'Donnell has described *Halo*'s engine in some depth. He has discussed the engine in interviews and lecture-style talks, and he has co-authored a book chapter on the use of the Microsoft DirectMusic engine in the game (O'Donnell and Weinland, 2004). Figure 2.3 is taken from a presentation about *Halo* audio given by the game's audio team (Johnson et al., 2008). This diagram matches the model of *Halo*'s audio that was deduced from the investigative play and the examination of the game content. In particular, notice the alternative layer of musical material (alt), which allows variation passages to be used. The selection of properties attached to the "tag" (read cue fragment) along the bottom of the diagram illustrates the flexibility of the system, from the "bored now" command, which fades out the music after a fixed period, to the "crossfading" from one music element to another. If we had found that we had mis-interpreted the engine from analytical play or the investigation of the engine, these kinds of documents can help to set us right.

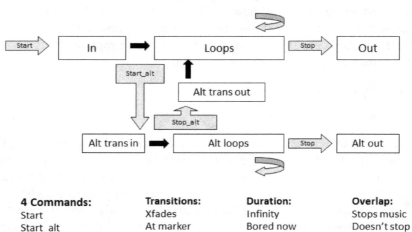

*Figure 2.3* O'Donnell's diagram of *Halo*'s music implementation system (source: Johnson et al., 2008)

As noted above, even if we can accurately investigate the music engine, we are not always able to reliably predict the motivations and aesthetic goals of the creators. Interviews give us an insight into this aspect of the game's music production. O'Donnell explained that *Halo*'s audio was designed to

> give the player information about what is happening (especially things that can't be seen) and make the world seem more alive and real. Music should provide a dramatic component to game play . . . in addition to underscoring story and cinematic sequences. (O'Donnell, 2002a)

O'Donnell here describes his ambition for the music to convey information about the context of play and contribute to the creation of the fictional universe, as well as supplying dramatic import. *Halo* seeks to create what might be referred to as a "retrospectively-scored" aesthetic – the music should be so carefully and seamlessly matched to the gameplay that it gives the illusion of being scored like a film, after the fact, with a fixed score, rather than music reacting to the player's actions: "When [the players] look back on their experience, they should feel like their experience was scored, but they should never be aware of what they did to cause it to be scored" (O'Donnell, c. 2007). O'Donnell is concerned that a music system in which gameplay-directed music changes are obvious could be distracting for the player (Waugh, 2005), jeopardizing player immersion. O'Donnell implements strategies so that even if the start and end of cues are obviously synchronized to in-game events, triggers for the development of material are hidden. In being less directly predictable, and programming score transitions to occur at musically appropriate moments, O'Donnell creates the quasi-magical effect of music that "just happens to fit" the game action.

The interviews also allow insight into the influences of composition. The non-Western vocal topic that was identified earlier, for example, O'Donnell describes as "an improvised Qawwali chant voice over the top to help reinforce the 'alien' nature of the environment" (2002a).[10] It seems as though my hypothesis concerning the Western/non-Western othering of the score was similar to O'Donnell's own thinking about the music. While we should not always defer to the author's intentions when analysing a piece of music, it is nevertheless useful to at least consider their own reports on the work in question. Here, we could interrogate the extent to which the "Qawwali chant" in the *Halo* score is an accurate replication of that musical tradition, we could hermeneutically investigate how this music inflects the representation of the aliens in the game, and we could compare this example to other media texts that use non-Western music to signify alien otherness.

## Recordings, Liner Notes, Scores

Game soundtracks are a significant part of the promotion and marketing of a game. Audio CDs are still produced for high-budget games, but digital music platforms even more readily disseminate game music recordings for consumption outside the game. The usefulness of game music soundtrack recordings varies on a case-by-case basis. For *Halo*, the "score" as presented on the soundtrack CDs lacks one of the central aesthetic goals of the game: O'Donnell's dynamic post-scored implementation system. At the same time, the soundtrack CDs may be useful satellite texts for *Halo*. As noted earlier, these recordings represent a significant mode of encounter with the game's music: the music as formulated on the CD is the main way that players hear the music when it is encountered outside the game – it is usually the case that YouTube videos of game music are taken from soundtrack albums, where such albums exist. *Halo* players reflect and reminisce about their time playing the game with these recordings, which may come to stand for the game soundtrack in a concrete way. As we are here primarily concerned with the music in the game (as opposed to the broader cultural life of this music), the usefulness of the soundtrack CDs as musical representations of the game is limited.

Many soundtrack albums include liner notes that can provide useful insights, similar to interviews. From the *Halo: Original Soundtrack* CD liner notes we learn the histories of particular themes: The original Halo chant was written in 1999 for a Macworld industry trade show, while much of the music from the "Pillar of Autumn" level was written in 2000 and 2001. From the credits, which name the vocalists performing on the soundtrack, I must conclude that at least some (but probably not all) of the vocal material in the game is non-synthesized. This factual information is interesting, but does not enlighten us about the musical experience of the game. However, O'Donnell also writes,

> Themes, moods and even the duration of these pieces will change and adapt with each player's *Halo* experience ... Perhaps a piece of music that you remember hearing won't be found here [on the CD]. That might be because you played *Halo* in a way I never anticipated. (O'Donnell, 2002b)

Using the playthrough recordings and the extracted data, we could use this comment to identify the themes that are not included in the CD recording. This would not only reveal the themes and motivic material that O'Donnell deems to be most significant, but also tell us about the way that the game was anticipated to be played by the majority of players. Analysing game music (both soundtracks and music heard in the game), therefore, may inform under-standing of more general aspects of the game's design.

Another interpretive stimulus might come from the *Halo: Anniversary Edition* soundtrack liner notes. Remake audio director Paul Lipson explicitly states that *Halo*'s music should be understood in a post-9/11 context. He argues that this "sound of hope" (he uses the phrase twice) defined a post-2001 heroic identity:

> While the tragic events of September 11th lingered, the visage of a new hero marked America's return to the next generation console landscape. Master Chief had arrived, not with the sound of bright trumpets and fanfare, but with tribal cellos and the solemn chanting of monks in space. Nothing would ever be the same in the wake of this powerful, noble new music ... [This album] is a tribute to that first sound of hope; and a reminder of what connects our community as we move forward. (Lipson, 2011)

This rather surprising and impassioned perspective on the score could lead us to any number of hermeneutic investigations: we could compare *Halo*'s musical construction of heroism with more traditional musical signifiers of heroism, or other contemporary post-9/11 popular military-themed games or films. This highlighting of the historical/geo-political context of the game's music suggests an uncomfortable allegorical aspect to the musical "othering" of the aliens that attack the humans, particularly when the composer identifies the material as an Islamic musical style. Of course, critical-interpretive investigations do not demand reports from the musical authors or producers, but nevertheless, these kinds of comments open "hermeneutic windows" (Kramer, 1990: 6) for us. Such activity is particularly significant when academic critical interpretations of game music are only beginning to be in evidence (see Cheng, 2014).

Soundtrack recordings arrange the music from the game into suites or long cues for pleasurable listening. Fans in the game music community, however, sometimes extract (and distribute) the music from the game in its raw, unarranged format. This music data is shared between fans and frequently applied to a video and uploaded to YouTube. Despite its ubiquity, this activity represents copyright infringement, even if taking steps to inhibit this action seems to be a low priority for games companies.

Apart from the recordings of music from games, it is sometimes possible to access musical scores. Occasionally, sketches and scores from recording sessions may be made public by game composers, as in the case of music for the *Halo 3* trailer, which was made available on the now-defunct *Halo 3* soundtrack website. More commonly, however, printed scores are either produced by music publishers or by the ever-industrious fan communities. Alfred Music Ltd publish a range of game music, including music from *Halo*, arranged for amateur performance, while fans of *Halo* have spent considerable time and effort transcribing the game's music (see, in particular, rampancy.net/sheetmusic). These sources must be treated very carefully: Both are usually second-degree derivatives from the soundtrack records of the game music, rather than from the primary source of the game, and both may deviate from the "as-heard" original without any indication. Still, since transcription can be a laborious task, having other examples with which to compare can be useful.

## Reviews

Reception studies have had a long tradition in musicology, and, with the proliferation of game review websites and blogs, a huge wealth of popular criticism created by professional and amateur reviewers is available for analysis.[11] As well as investigating reviews specifically concerned with the music of a game, it can also be valuable to notice when general game reviews make special mention of the music and the terms in which they discuss their experience of the score. We can tell that, for example, the chant material was particularly striking, and reviewers identified it as "Gregorian-ish" (Ahearn, 2001), or "Gregorian Chant-style" (Boulding, 2001). O'Donnell seems to have been successful in his aims for the music system. While reviewers were not able to easily understand the process behind the dynamic engine (Ahearn, 2001),[12] they found it to be well-matched to gameplay ("E Nomini Patri", 2002),[13] and communicatively significant (Boulding, 2001; Peters, c. 2001).[14] It is possible to use these kinds of reviews (and perhaps even informal reviews such as YouTube comments) to reveal how gamers listen to music in games, including how music is used to aid gameplay, and the assumptions that players hold about the conventions of video game music.

## Presenting/Representing Analysis

Representing video game music is tricky. While written descriptions may be vivid and notated examples precise, the new media format provides the opportunity for experimentation with new forms of reporting game music analysis. Other chapters in this volume include enhanced online media and this kind of material might easily give way to video demonstrations or interactive models and simulations. As both a way of reporting music-game interactions, and as an analytical tool itself, I offer here a diagram of the "Pillar of Autumn" level, inspired by the diagrammatic film music analyses of John Huntley and Roger Manvell (1957). The full diagram is available as part of the online supplementary materials for this volume, available via the publisher's website and the Ludomusicology UK Research group website. A sample is presented below as Figure 2.4. This diagram attempts to connect the game action with the musical changes and the description of the music in a way that is flexible enough to accommodate notes about unusual or interesting musical features. I found that this diagram was a useful way to structure my self-reporting of the game experience, record notes about the music of the level, and force myself to be specific in the dissection of the level. This architecture could easily be adapted to include written notation, or in an interactive format, video clips and samples. I have also utilized this format as a way to direct readers of my analyses to specific sections of a cue or level without the need for long descriptions.

Each of the sources discussed below is able to provide particular information about the music of *Halo* (Table 2.1). Of course, there are a limitless number of analytical possibilities for any one game, and what is presented here sits alongside methods deployed by game music analysts in the other chapters of this book and elsewhere (see Donnelly, Gibbons and Lerner, 2014 and Moormann, 2013). However, whereas most authors tend to keep their analytical processes implicit, rather than explicit, this chapter has sought to interrogate methods of game music analysis by bringing them into the light for justification and critical evaluation. It is for this reason that I have narrated my activity (mostly in the first person), emphasizing the personal and performative nature of musical analysis.

| | | | |
|---|---|---|---|
| **TRIGGER** | The player walks towards the doorway to trigger the other character to react. This character's reaction, in turn, causes a 'scripted moment' of explosions, with which music begins. | As player approaches door in the darkness, it opens, revealing a mysterious monster that is only partially visible. Once the monster is defeated, the player may move beyond the doorway to the next area and continue through the level. | Arriving at the spaceship's bridge is the objective of this part of the mission. As the player approaches the safe area of the bridge, the music fades out. |
| **MUSIC STRUCTURE** | Intro ‖: Fragment Set :‖ | Second Fragment Set    Choral Variation (one fragment) ‖: :‖    String Stinger Chord | Ending (fade out) |
| **MUSIC DESCRIPTION** | *Halo*'s engine selects cue fragments from a sample library, played in a randomized order. The cue uses a drum loop as the basis of variation. Timpani accentuate the compound metre, playing tonic and flattened 7th pitches. Cymbal crashes and a struck metallic sound are added in some fragments. One fragment interrupts the drums with a gong and low string pedal notes. The music provides propulsion and a sense of urgency. | At whatever point the door opens to reveal the monster, the high, dissonant string stinger chord will immediately play, superimposed upon the background musical material. This moment also serves as a trigger point that commands the music system to move to the next set of fragments. The new fragment set maintains the underlying drum architecture of the previous loop, but adds a female vocalist singing in an improvisatory style that mimics Qawwali chant singing. The effect for the player is that this musical element is 'added' to the score. The choral variation fragment maintains some of the 6/8 rhythms, but removes the more abrasive sonorities. Above this percussion ostinato, male voices sing open-vowel vocalizations in a reprise of a choral figure from the 'thaw' cue heard earlier. This chant would seem to relate to the Master Chief, while the Qawwali refers to the aliens. | |

*Figure 2.4* Diagrammatic representation of part of the "Pillar of Autumn" level

*Table 2.1* Sources, data, analysis and conclusions from *Halo*

| Source | Raw Data Format | Analysis Methods | Examples of Conclusions Drawn |
|---|---|---|---|
| Analytical Play | Experience of play; captured play recordings | Playing with and against grain; critical listening of musical material | Topic-based scoring significant (esp. alien and hero characterization); complex dynamic music system based upon trigger-point programming; recurring thematic material and motivic development |
| Code and Engine | Music deployment code; programming tools; technical data | Find trends of musical material and game deployment; consider rationale of musical-dynamic processes | Music anchored to gameworld locations/event triggers; variation possibilities of cues; start/loop and variation/end structure; even some cutscene cues not entirely fixed duration – allows flexibility |
| Music Data | Audio wave files; note-data files; samples | Comparison with deployment in captured play; survey of musical material used in game; traditional musical-analytic techniques (see also below) | Storage in small clips to allow variation |
| Notated Transcriptions | Staff notation (via transcription of audio material, perhaps converted directly from music data) | Raft of traditional musical-analytic techniques (motivic, harmonic, topic analysis, etc.) | Motivic repetition links cutscenes with in-game music through recurring themes; textual elements connected by repeated themes that accompany more than one character/object; some motivic processes in evidence |

| Source | Raw Data Format | Analysis Methods | Examples of Conclusions Drawn |
|---|---|---|---|
| Interviews/ Presentations | Transcriptions; presentation files; audio/video recordings (autobiographical, historical, technical information) | Identify composers' intentions (compositional ideology); extract technical information about game; integrate historical information | Dynamic music system deliberately obfuscatory; DirectMusic programming; straightforward leitmotivic scoring rejected; concern with emotional-communicative dimension of music; complex randomization procedures; attempt at "retrospectively-scored" aesthetic effect; inspiration for non-Western vocal music from Qawwali tradition |
| Recordings | Audio data (often assembled into cues, rather than as heard in-game) | Comparison of recordings with music as heard in-game; trace after-game life of music; identification of main themes | Assumes quick player progression through "Pillar of Autumn" level; popularity of *Halo* music listening outside the game |
| Liner Notes | Written prose (technical information; historical-biographical information) | Interpretive prompts; identification of important factual information | Historical progression of musical material – some themes predate majority of game content; some vocal material performed by live musicians; *Halo* can be read in terms of post-9/11 heroic identities |
| Scores | Staff notation or other representation | Raft of traditional musical-analytic techniques (motivic, harmonic, etc.); comparisons with transcriptions; identification of significant themes/cues | Musical material popular enough to prompt commercial and amateur arrangements – especially "Gregorian" topic and certain other cues, including menu music and "Lament for Pvt. Jenkins" cue; transcriptions generally accurate |

| Source | Raw Data Format | Analysis Methods | Examples of Conclusions Drawn |
|---|---|---|---|
| Reviews | Written prose | Reception (meta-) analysis; identification of trends; major interpretive themes; positive and negative criticism; reporting of how players' interpretations match composers' intentions | Music structures the game and creates the rhythm of gameplay; "Gregorian" topic commonly identified; musical identity unusual for FPS games; specifics of musical-dynamic engine remains ambiguous to players |

I began this chapter by discussing the development of video game music studies: a domain of scholarship undergoing an exciting period of growth. It is an essential part of the maturation of this discipline that we begin to discuss the methodologies and scholarly techniques underpinning our research. This chapter has been an attempt to begin that discussion. It is important that these considerations occur in an explicit way; it improves accessibility to the field, facilitating engagement by new researchers, providing a "way in" to game music studies, and simultaneously, it prompts us to be critically reflective about our research methods and to ensure we are aware of what precisely it is that we do when we analyse video game music.

## Notes

1. Tim Summers is a Teaching Fellow in Music at Royal Holloway, University of London. He has written on music in modern popular culture for journals including the *Journal of the Royal Musical Association*, *Journal of Film Music* and *Music, Sound and the Moving Image*. He is the author of *Understanding Video Game Music* (CUP, 2016).
2. Music from *Halo* games features on *The Greatest Video Game Music* (X5 Music X 5CD114, 2011), *The Greatest Video Game Music 2* (X5 Music X 5CD118, 2012), *Video Games Live: Volume 1* (EMI/Angel #5087302, 2007) and *Video Games Live: Level 2* (Shout! Factory 12324, 2010).
3. The Xbox's successor console, the Xbox 360 (2005–) is selectively backwards compatible. In the case of the *Halo* games, certain regions and copies of the game will work on the Xbox 360, though glitches and problems are rife.
4. The game sales website Vgchartz (2015) estimates the PC sales of *Halo* to be in the region of 20,000 copies.
5. There are also many widely-available options for recording console output. The popularity of YouTube videos of game footage has provided a market for a plethora of commercial hardware and software products for capturing console

play using a PC. Manufacturers including Elgato, Nvidia and Roxio have produced technology specifically for this purpose.

6. YouTube videos may be useful sources for a great variety of game music analysis, such as, for example, documentation of different types of play and musical reaction, players' reception of the music, and so on. Relying only on player-uploaded videos as evidence of a game's musical mechanics may be dangerous, since, to cite just one reason, these videos do not afford the ability to experiment and test musical reactivity with the same precision as playing the game oneself, opening up the possibility of erroneous conclusions such as misinterpreting co-incidental musical changes as casual events.

7. This glitch is more evident in the PC version of the game than in the Xbox or *Anniversary* editions.

8. The fade-out error may be conceptualized in two ways, either as a fade-out that is not triggered, or as an instruction for musical silence that is triggered too early/in the wrong position. Based on the music programming (see later), it is far more likely that the problem is caused by the ending fragment of the cue, which contains a recorded "fade out", not playing.

9. On musical histories in games, see Cook, 2014.

10. "*Qavvālī* . . . is the musical assembly held by Sufis throughout the year . . . The term *qavvālī* denotes the Sufi song itself, and only by implication the occasion of its performance . . . *Qavvālī* normally combines group and solo singing and is accompanied by drum, harmonium and hand-clapping . . . [The *Qavvālī*] formal scheme combines metric group refrains and rhythmically free solo improvisations, including rapid melismatic passages" (Qureshi et al., 2014)

11. Websites can be notoriously volatile with content changing and evaporating without warning, though projects like the Internet Archive (https://archive. org/web/) have helped to preserve some websites. *Music4games.net*, one of the premier game music criticism sites, ceased to function in 2009, but much of the content (including valuable composer interviews) was saved by the Internet Archive project.

12. "It's amazingly hard to explain how or why the music does such a good job of setting the mood for each and every scene that you are presented with, but it does, and does it very well" (Ahearn, 2001).

13. The music "comes on at the right time" ("E Nomini Patri", 2002).

14. "[I]t can hit with a bang to let you know there's something significant coming up" (Boulding, 2001); "In times of action it really gets you pumped up and ready to kick some ass" (Peters, c. 2001); "The soundtrack is epic, kicking up just at the right times to help create a sense of tension" (Riach, 2001).

## References

Ahearn, N. (2001) "Halo." *xboxweb.com*. http://www.xboxweb.com/reviews/xbox/halo. html (accessed December 28, 2014).

Boulding, A. (2001) "Halo Review." *ign.com*. http://uk.ign.com/articles/2001/11/10/ halo-review?page=1; http://uk.ign.com/articles/2001/11/10/halo-review?page=2 (accessed December 28, 2014).

Bungie (2005) "Halo 2: One Year Later." *bungie.net*. http://halo.bungie.net/news/content. aspx?type=topnews&cid=7139 (accessed January 11, 2015).

Cheng, W. (2014) *Soundplay: Video Games and the Musical Imagination*. New York: Oxford University Press.

Collins, K. (2008) *Game Sound: An Introduction to the History, Theory, and Practice of Video Game Music and Sound Design*. Cambridge, MA: MIT Press.

Cook, K. (2014) "Music, History, and Progress in Sid Meier's *Civilization IV*." In *Music in Video Games: Studying Play*, edited by K. J. Donnelly, W. Gibbons and N. Lerner, pp. 166–82. New York: Routledge.

Cooke, D. (1969) "The Bruckner Problem Simplified. 1: Sorting Out the Confusion." *The Musical Times* 110/1511: 20–22.

Donnelly, K., W. Gibbons and N. Lerner (eds) (2014) *Music in Video Games: Studying Play*. London and New York: Routledge.

"E Nomini Patri" [Anon.] (2002) "Staff Review of Halo." *xboxaddict.com*. http://xboxaddict. com/staff_review/2058.html (accessed December 26, 2014).

Fielder, J. (2001) "Halo: Combat Evolved Review." *gamespot.com*. http://www.gamespot. com/reviews/halo-review/1900-2823816/ (accessed December 28, 2014).

Huntley, J. and R. Manvell (1957) *The Technique of Film Music*. London: Focal Press.

Johnson, P. C., M. O'Donnell and J. Weinland (2008) "Audio Post-Mortem: *Halo 3*." *Game Developers Conference 2008*. http://halo.bungie.net/images/Inside/publications/ presentations/halo3audio.zip (accessed September 2, 2014).

Kramer, L. (1990) *Music as Cultural Practice, 1800–1900*. Berkeley: University of California Press.

Lipson, P. (2011) Liner notes. *Halo: Anniversary*. SE-3014-2 Microsoft.

Moormann, P. (ed.) (2013) *Music and Game: Perspectives on a Popular Alliance*. Wiesbaden: Springer VS.

O'Donnell, M. (2002a) "Producing Audio for Halo." *Game Developers Conference*, San Jose, March 21–23. http://halo.bungie.org/misc/gdc.2002.music (accessed January 11, 2015).

O'Donnell, M. (2002b) Liner notes. *Halo: Original Soundtrack*. SE-2000-2 Microsoft.

O'Donnell, M. (c. 2007) "Martin O'Donnell Interview – The Halo 3 Soundtrack." https:// www.youtube.com/watch?v=0snVL36OypI (accessed February 25, 2016).

O'Donnell, M. and J. Weinland (2004) "A DirectSound Case Study for *Halo*." In *DirectX 9 Audio Exposed: Interactive Audio Development*, edited by T. M. Fay, S. Selfon and T. J. Fay, pp. 417–32. Plano, TX: Wordware.

Peters, E. (c. 2001) "Halo: Combat Evolved." *xboxexclusive.com*. http://www.xboxexclusive. com/reviews/Halo/ (accessed December 28, 2014).

Qureshi, R. et al. (2014), "India, §VI: Religious musics 2. Muslim (ii) Qavvālī." *Grove Music Online*. http://www.oxfordmusiconline.com/subscriber/article/grove/music/43272pg13#S43272.6.2.2 (accessed December 28, 2014).

Riach, S. (2001) "Halo." *game-over.net*. http://www.game-over.net/reviews.php?id=3&page=xboxreviews (accessed December 28, 2014).

Vgchartz (2015) "Halo: Combat Evolved [PC]." *vgchartz.com*. http://www.vgchartz.com/game/12371/halo-combat-evolved/ (accessed January 11, 2015).

Waugh, E. (2005) "GDC 2005 Report: Audio Production for *Halo 2*." *gamasutra.com*, March 14. https://web.archive.org/web/20090223205745/http://www.gamasutra.com/gdc2005/features/20050310/postcard-waugh.htm (accessed January 11, 2015).

## Websites

Global Chant Database: http://globalchant.org/search.php (accessed January 11, 2015).

The Internet Archive: https://archive.org/web/ (accessed January 11, 2015).

# 3 Analysing Game Musical Immersion
## The ALI Model

*Isabella van Elferen*[1]

## Immersion

In her pioneering analyses of cyberspace narratives, Janet Murray describes immersion as being "submerged" in the "enchanted place" of cyberspace, which can be experienced as "more real than reality" (Murray, 1997: 98, 99, 97). These general characteristics of immersion were described in more concrete terms by Laura Ermi and Frans Mäyrä, who define the deep engagement in the virtual reality, the gameplay and mood of a game, as "becoming physically or virtually a part of the experience itself" (Ermi and Mäyrä, 2005: 4). Charting the ways in which such engagement in gaming is established, they developed the now well-known SCI model, which identifies what to them are the three key factors in game immersion: sensory, challenge-based, and imaginative immersion.

Ermi and Mäyrä's SCI model was the first multi-dimensional analysis of video game immersion, and as such it provided an important modification of earlier, more generalizing theories of virtual engagement. In his 2011 monograph *In-Game*, Gordon Calleja further refines the components of what he calls "player involvement", the "blending of a variety of experiential phenomena afforded by involving gameplay" (Calleja, 2011: 3). The experiential phenomena that comprise gameplay immersion, in his analysis, are more specified than those in the SCI model: he distinguishes kinaesthetic, spatial, shared, narrative, affective and ludic game involvement (Calleja, 2011: 43–44).

It seems self-evident that sound and music would play an important role in these models, but surprisingly little attention has been played to the sonic component of player involvement. A number of quantitative inventories do provide ample proof of the significance of game soundtracks for immersion (Jørgensen, 2008; Lipscomb and Zehnder, 2005; Nacke and Grimshaw, 2010). Empirical data, however, often raise as many questions as they answer: while they offer proof that sound and music are important for game involvement, they offer no insight in the questions of how musical player involvement is brought about and which factors play a role in it. An interpretation of these data and theorization of game musical immersion would be of prime importance for a further understanding of player involvement.

In theoretical surveys of gaming immersion, the exact role of sound in the process of immersion has only been hinted at in terms that are as general as they are divergent. Ermi and Mäyrä place the sonic aspects of a game in the sensory realm of gaming immersion, claiming that "powerful sounds easily overpower the sensory information coming from the real world" (Ermi and Mäyrä, 2005: 7). Game soundtracks, however, achieve much more than a mere blocking off of environmental sound. In music games such as *Rock Band* (2007), for instance, music itself is the gameplay, and is thus rather part of what Ermi and Mäyrä would call challenge-based immersion. Moreover, the compositional style of game soundtracks is carefully chosen to match plots and graphic designs: immersion in fantasy games such as *Assassin's Creed* (2007) or *World of Warcraft* (2004), for example, is supported by epic soundtracks in the style of film composers such as Howard Shore and John Williams. This aspect of game music contributes to the player's imagination of the fantasy world of the game, and would therefore much rather fit the "imaginative immersion" in Ermi and Mäyrä's model. In her initial discussion of game audio and immersion, Karen Collins refers to this component of the SCI model and argues that game sound, like film sound, can function as metaphoric representation of the virtual reality of a video game. She adds that this imaginative immersion is caused by the "physical effect" as well as the "affect" of the sound, but does not qualify these broad concepts further (Collins, 2008: 133–36). In similarly vague terms, Calleja, the sophistication of his model of player involvement notwithstanding, only mentions game soundtracks in passing, considering audio-visual design part of the "affective" setting of games (Calleja, 2011: 140). Collins's more recent work focuses not so much on the affective, but rather on the physical aspects of sonic game immersion, arguing that 3D game sound design creates a sonic "envelopment" enhancing players' experience of "presence" in a game (Collins, 2013: 54).

These quantitative and qualitative studies of sonic game immersion, thus, have yielded many useful insights, but simultaneously also illustrate the existing lack of academic consensus with regards to musical immersion, and urge a more systematic theorization of this aspect of gaming. It is my aim in this chapter to outline an analytical model for game musical immersion. Expanding on Calleja's definition of video game immersion, my working definition of sonic player involvement will be "a blending of different *music-specific* phenomena afforded by involving *sound play*". Which music-specific experiential phenomena afford musical player involvement, and how are they made operative in sound play?

## A-L-I

Integrating the sensory, challenge-based, imaginative and emotional aspects of game musical immersion outlined above, I propose an analytical model consisting of musical affect, musical literacy and musical interaction. The convergence of these three key components of musical game involvement is graphically represented in Figure 3.1.

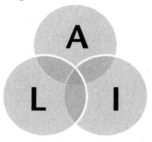

*Figure 3.1* The ALI model: musical affect, musical literacy and musical interaction converge in game music

The ALI model enables investigations of the separate areas of musical game involvement, including those outlined by earlier research, but also offers room for their integration: player involvement is likely to be most intense where the three areas of the framework overlap. Offering a systematic overview, the model can provide the existing quantitative data regarding musical immersion with a theoretical reflection.

**Affect** can be defined as the personal investment in a given situation through memory, emotion and identification. Affect has been an increasing focus of research in arts and humanities since the "affective turn" in critical theory, which had its roots in Brian Massumi's 2002 monograph *Parables for the Virtual*. Massumi describes affect as a performative dimension of intensity, an emergent "expression event" that is caused by sensual perception, anchored in embodied subjectivity and engenders a "participation in the virtual" (Massumi, 2002: 26–27, 35). Melissa Gregg and Greg Seigworth elaborate on Massumi's definition of affect, focusing on the embodied aspects of such emotional virtuality. They discuss it as liminal, changeable and multi-faceted, rendering subjectivity "webbed" through the corporeal phenomenology of affective response:

> Affect is integral to a body's perpetual becoming (always becoming otherwise, however subtly, than what it already is), pulled beyond its seeming surface-boundedness by way of its relation to, indeed its

composition through, the forces of encounter. With affect, a body is as
much outside itself as in itself – webbed in its relations – until ultimately
such firm distinctions cease to matter. (Gregg and Seigworth, 2010: 3)

Affect is a vital and inevitable aspect of any musical experience: listening to
music cannot but stir emotions, connotations or identifications. Music's affective
performativity takes place at levels that tend to surpass conscious perception:
whenever we hear music – even inattentively – our affects will be stirred and
subtly bent along the vectors of musical connotation. When music accompanies
films, these connotations provide unconsciously perceived commentaries to
visual or interactive events, and video game music has often been compared to
film music in this respect (e.g. Collins, 2008: 127–28; Whalen, 2007). Empirical
research has shown that music provides vital emotional connections to video
gaming: without sound, players express a lack of involvement even in dramatic
gameplay developments such as fighting and death (Jørgensen, 2008: 171–74).

As affect itself is a "webbed" agency (Gregg and Seigworth, 2010), it does
not only guide the interactive processes of musical experience in a game, but
also, in and of itself, establishes a form of virtuality drawing gamers out of
the here and now. Massumi argues that the time and the place of affect are
necessarily virtual, and therefore always potentially present but not always
stable: even if its momentum is not fully actual (which it arguably never can
be), affect itself is always virtually, and therefore indeterminably, present
(Massumi, 2002: 30–34). He describes it as

> *cross-temporal*, implying a participation of "temporal contours" in
> each other, singly or in the looping of refrains. This cross-temporality
> constitutes the movement of experience into the future (and into the
> past, as memory). (Massumi, 2002: 34)

The "affective" immersion in video game music noted by Collins and Calleja,
thus, can be analysed as caused by the emotional connotations of its soundtrack
and leading to a cross-temporal affective virtuality.

Musical affect is a determining factor in the attribution of personal and
collective meanings to music. Because musical meanings – like the emotions
with which they are entwined – are far from fixed, objective or universal,
affective musical immersion would seem to be highly subjective and therefore
unpredictable. Such unpredictability, however, is undesirable. Game audio needs
to evoke predictable emotions so that it can help assess gameplay situations:
dangerous situations, for instance, have to be immediately identifiable as such,
and should therefore be sonically announced by recognizably frightening music.
To ensure its relative predictability, game musical affect is guided by the ALI
component of literacy.

Martina Roepke has defined media **literacy** as "habituated practices of media engagement shaped by cultural practices and discourses" (Roepke, 2011). These habituated practices may concern any kind of medium – from film and television to video games and music – and include not only the traditional literacy skills such as "the ability to access, analyze, evaluate and communicate messages in a variety of forms" (Aufderheide, 1993) but also, and increasingly, a set of social and sensory practices. Having engaged with and interpreted movies or TV commercials or any other type of medium, their audiences have developed a certain expectation curve with regards to their form, style and possible socio-cultural meanings. Building on these notions of media literacy, José Zagal has described the "ludoliteracy" of interactive gaming, which entails the heterogeneous skills of hardware competence such as handling a console, knowledge of generic gameplay such as picking up food or ammunition, and interpreting the virtual game world's relation to the actual day-to-day world (Zagal, 2010).

Musical media literacy is the fluency in hearing and interpreting film, television or advertising music through the fact of our frequent exposure to them and, subsequently, our ability to interpret their communications. We know, for instance, to expect catastrophes when a horror film protagonist's descent into a dark cellar is accompanied by low, dissonant cello motifs; we also know that slow-motion camera shots accompanied by rock music in commercials are to be interpreted as "cool"; and we understand that we should not expect real-life romantic tableaus to involve string orchestras. As these examples illustrate, media literacy is an important designator of genre: the concurrence of well-known tropes and conventions helps audiences interpret the type of film, television show or video game with which they are presented – not many horror film viewers will interpret the aforementioned cello motifs as an indication that the protagonist is to be identified as a classical musician with a penchant for the nineteenth century.

Combining the audio-visual literacies of film and television music with ludoliteracy, game soundtrack design appeals to a specific game musical literacy. Through intertextual references to audio-visual idioms from other media, game soundtracks deploy player literacy for their immersive effect: it is because gamers recognize certain composing styles that they are able to interpret gaming events and feel involved in gameplay, game worlds and game plots. Boss fights, for instance, are often accompanied by the high-tempo, brass-heavy, dissonant orchestral scores with syncopated percussion that players recognize from exciting scenes in heroic action movies: the player recognizes the idiom and its action connotations, which helps her realize that she should spring into action. The closing cutscene after a boss fight, conversely, tends to be scored with slowly cadencing, string-orientated music, reminiscent of the end scenes in such films: thus communicating to the player that the fight is now over. The recognizability of the boss fight example illustrates that game composing does not only depend on non-game musical literacies, but has also developed its own, game-specific literacy. Tim Summers has demonstrated that consistent game musical genres have emerged from existing – often cinematic – musical idioms. Continuous player interaction and game-specific developments have increasingly detached these idioms from their non-game roots, leading to independent game musical genres – in this case survival horror, strategy and fight game music (Summers, 2011).

The importance of audio-visual literacy for game musical immersion is evident, for instance, in fantasy role-playing games (RPGs) such as *World of Warcraft*. As mentioned above, immersion in these games is supported by an "epic" composing style that relies heavily on existing compositional idioms from epic and fantasy films. Previous assessments of such scoring choices as "imaginative immersion" (e.g. Collins) do not quite suffice to explain their effectiveness: player imagination is not stirred in any random fashion, but in explicit reference to an already-existing audio-visual literacy. When fantasy RPG composers choose an epic musical idiom they can rely on players recognizing, interpreting and reacting to their music, and thereby may ensure immersion in the game (Kizzire, 2014). It is for this reason that even if the soundtrack to a *Lord of the Rings* game does not quote directly from Howard Shore's film score, employing the epic scoring conventions evident therein is enough to create immersive game music: airy female voices indicating the fantasy world's idyllic peace; heavy drums, brass and choir indicating the threat of evil powers; the consonant, cadencing relief of heroic rescue. Different from cinema audiences, however, gamers are not watching movie characters going through these adventures. Because of gaming interactivity they are their own epic heroes, who fight Sauron's evil together with Boromir, Gandalf and Frodo: it is their own interactive heroism that is underlined by such sweeping music.

Game music is not often very original or complicated, and this has a clear reason. Literacy in game music's interpretation should be easy to acquire: because of music's crucial role in gaming interaction, the sonic cues that the player gets must be immediately recognizable and interpretable. Game musical literacy's contribution to immersion, thus, must be characterized by an almost clichéd audio-visual intertextuality.

Musical **interaction** is interaction with and through music. It may take place in music-making, composing and DJ-ing; in dance and sports; in music-driven games such as singing games and musical chairs; and in music games like karaoke and "Name that tune/TV theme/". Musical interaction in video games establishes a direct connection between player actions and the game soundtrack, and can take a range of different concrete shapes. Interactive musical performativity is most evident in music games such as *Rock Band* and *DJ Hero* (2009), games in which the player's goal is to play music by way of haptic interfaces shaped like musical instruments. Other types of musical interaction in video games include the interaction with musical content in *Brütal Legend* (2009), a game in which the player engages with the repertoire of metal music as well as the subcultural capital pertaining to that genre; interactively creating music in *Wii Music* (2008), in which the player can play an instrument "by proxy" through the kinetic metaphor of game interface movement; and music-driven interactive gameplay in games such as *Patapon* (2007), in which the player is to play the Nintendo DS like a drum to move gameplay forward by the sound of an army of squeaky voices scanning "pata-pata-pata-pon!". Recently an arguably even more direct type of musical interaction has emerged in so-called adaptive audio toys, in which players create ambient soundscapes by interacting with touchscreen interfaces. As they often lack competition elements or a straightforward goal these games have come to be referred to as toys rather than as games. *Remembering* (2013), for instance, is described by its designers as "a poetic exploration driven by sound" in which players interact with their own musical instincts and memories. Instead of goal-oriented gameplay, *Remembering* provides an "empty mysterious place filled with sounds that invite you to use your own imagination".[2] Such games, in effect, make every player a composer.

The games mentioned so far all revolve around explicitly musical forms of interaction, but similar types of interaction can also be observed in non-music games. A number of video games feature diegetic music as a distinguishing part of gameplay. In the *Grand Theft Auto* games, for instance, players can choose from many radio stations to accompany their death drive; *Grand Theft Auto V* (2013) features more than 130 stations of licensed "real world" music. This music is partly responsible for the game's popularity. Choosing a station and setting a playlist is a form of direct musical interaction comparable to that in *Rock Band*. It is also a play with subcultural connotations like in *Brütal Legend*, and even a form of musical memory play comparable to *Remembering*, as the player's musical memories, connotations and identifications provide important guidance for the development and (perceived) mood of the gameplay. Similar, but possibly even more interesting, is non-diegetic game audio, in which game musical interaction takes the shape of the player's influencing of a pre-composed game soundtrack by way of her movement through the game. In order to achieve this type of interactivity, game music is adaptive in its design, with themes and motifs looping in nonlinear patterns so as to match the nonlinear gameplay progress (cf. Collins, 2008: 125–30, 139–65). The epic music for the *Assassin's Creed* games, for instance, not only creates the right mood for the game – employing game musical literacy and affect

– it also guides the player through gameplay by way of musical navigation clues such as leitmotifs, stingers and stereo effects, just like the more explicit "pata-pata-pata-pons" do: moving through this game, in effect, is a form of interactively producing game sound (cf. Reale, 2014). Providing 3D cues for navigation through surround sound, this latter type of non-diegetic game musical interaction functions as a "musical GPS", an interactive navigation system helping players find their way through the game space (Van Elferen, 2011: 32–34).

Game music enhances and demands game interaction, as a game needs to be played for its soundtrack to be heard. Like improvised music, game music's very presence requires interaction: the sound of game music is dependent upon the way in which a player moves through the various stages of the game. Playing games, thus, quite simply, equals interacting with music. Musical interaction is an important contributor to gaming immersion because of this direct connection between player actions and game soundtrack. The flow of game musical interaction, in turn, can lead to highly personal affective investments: the magic circle of music does not only include harmony and rhythm, but also memory and emotion. In terms of the ALI model, this is where game musical affect and game musical interaction overlap.

In order to illustrate how game musical immersion can be analysed with the help of the ALI model, the second half of this chapter compares the workings of the musical affect, literacy and interaction in *Dead Space 2* (2011) and *Amnesia: The Dark Descent* (2010). Both are considered horror games, but they show remarkable differences in their approach to the genre: *Dead Space* is a classic example of survival horror in which the avatar fights his way through monster-infested surroundings, while *Amnesia* is a psychological horror game in which the avatar wanders alone through the dark with no clear gameplay directions. As a result, immersion in *Dead Space* is immersion in the horror survival and fights, while immersion in *Amnesia* is rather an immersion in the terror of unknown danger (Van Elferen, 2015). Both games feature critically acclaimed soundtracks, which are said to contribute to their immersive effects (KM, 2011; Elchlepp, c. 2011). An ALI analysis of both games' sound design can help highlight the immersive differences between these two subgenres of horror.

## *Dead Space 2*: The Convergence of ALI Factors in Survival Horror

In survival horror games such as the *Resident Evil* (1996–2012), *Dead Rising* (2006–2010) and *Left 4 Dead* (2008–2009) series, players usually have the task of fighting their way through post-apocalyptic environments that can somehow only be rescued through a monster genocide. The gameplay consists of a series of shoot-outs, to which end the player avatar has the choice of a generous array of weaponry. Unlike many other shooting games, this weaponry is sometimes hard to find and, because the inventory devices tend to be limited in capacity, hard to store. The "survival" elements of difficult shooting and weapon storage situations notwithstanding, the main avatars in survival horror games invite a winner-oriented form of scripted player identification through the avatar's relentless fighting spirit and the programmed path to victory.

Survival horror game *Dead Space 2* is set in the year 2508. Avatar Isaac Clarke embarks upon the task of saving the starship USG Ishimura from the grotesque Necromorph zombies that have taken over all human life on the ship. His versatile navigation capacities are performances of his RIG (Resource Integration Gear) spacesuit, a wearable technology that enables real-time health management, holographic information regarding ammunition and inventory, and sports the helpful "stasis" and "kinesis" fight modules. The gameplay moves from smaller to larger shoot-outs and from bosses to end bosses: in all these situations, Clarke remains calm and in control, showing himself the uncontested master of dead space as well as outerspace.

The sound design of *Dead Space 2* blends orchestral and digital timbres. Both on diegetic and on non-diegetic levels, this mixture of timbres juxtaposes the nature of the gameplay characters. While the enemies are the result of evil sentient technology, which is represented sonically by the "machinic" timbres of white noise and digital distortion, the human heroes are connoted as the epitome of all that is good, brave and natural, which is represented musically by the "natural" timbre of a full orchestra. Emphasizing this distinction between "machinic" and "human" sounds, the digital part of the horror soundscape consists of atonal, nonlinear drones lacking such properties as harmony, melody or rhythm (Donnelly, 2005, 44–51, 99ff.; Summers, 2011). These "inhuman" sounds contrast sharply with the pleasant euphony of tonal melody and harmony dominating the orchestral sections (see also Sweeney, in this volume).

Game musical affect is especially powerful in survival horror games, as these games are designed to move players' emotions (Ekman and Lankoski, 2009). The gameplay of survival horror games is often dark, so that the auditory prevails over the visual, which lends itself easily to frightening effects. Don Veca, audio director for *Dead Space*, acknowledges the affective importance of game music. He stresses that in order to maximize the emotional effects of the soundtrack, his team strived to have all sound and music contribute to the "dark and eerie vibe" of the game (Napolitano, 2008). Throughout the game, the orchestral and digital timbres, the crescendos and fortissimos, the screaming dissonances and quiet cadences are used to guide players emotionally into and out of the battles that Isaac Clarke must go through.

Survival horror games show a relatively high dependence on players' musical literacy. The cinematic horror genre has become crammed with recognizable audio-visual conventions stemming from horror traditions at least as old as the Hammer movies, whose soundtracks have been described as "a musical reference bank for . . . horror-film composers" (Hannan, 2009: 71). The *Scream* films (1996–2011), which play with exactly these traditions, are the most obvious example of the ways in which these tropes have developed into clichés that make it very easy for the viewer to interpret events on screen. Horror video games add a specific game musical literacy to the idiom of the genre. Dan Pinchbeck has argued that horror games are often designed according to certain, rather predictable, ludic schemata or frames (Pinchbeck, 2009: 82–84). The deployment of these schemata in game design facilitates successful gameplay, as players can proceed through the game guided by their own audio-visual and ludic horror literacy. A particularly effective aspect of horror literacy occurs in survival horror leitmotifs. Using the technique that Michel Chion has described as *acousmêtre*, the occurrence of acoustic characters that are "neither inside nor outside the image" (Chion, 1994: 129), the zombies and monsters of survival horror announce their presence before they appear within the player avatar's sight. The acousmêtric signalling of danger is familiar from cinematic horror idioms, in which monster leitmotifs have acquired great fame precisely because of their independence from screen visibility (the *Jaws* [1975] and *The Grudge* [2004] leitmotifs are paramount examples).

In the third chapter of *Dead Space 2*, the ambient soundscape of white noise and wind is completed by worn-out horror film clichés such as disembodied laughter, ephemeral childsong, ghostly music boxes, and the sounds of half-broken arcade game consoles. Like in horror film soundtracks, these sounds have been distorted by digital phasing and an overlay of (reversed) echo. Recognizing these well-known tropes, the player is helped in her assessment of the situation, which is musically branded as eerie, haunted and potentially threatening. Game musical literacy, in short, guarantees the clarity of stable signification, which is often crucial for player movement through gameplay: it guides game musical interaction.

The ALI component of game musical interaction is very explicitly present in *Dead Space*. Through the combination of adaptive audio and 3D sound reproduction, its soundtrack has a clear GPS (global positioning system) function: sound tells players that a new situation is coming up even before they can see it; it tells them from which direction it will be coming, and whether that situation is dangerous, neutral or pleasant. Such navigational use of adaptive audio becomes most evident in fight scenes. When approaching a group of Necromorphs, the player hears monstrous grunts and the onset of metallic drones. This explicit musical guidance is of great value for heroism-oriented survival horror gameplay. Upon hearing the leitmotifs of threat, the avatar can run in their direction and kill off the source of that danger. Upon coming closer, the monstrous sound increases in volume while the texture of the non-diegetic music is intensified by added violin glissandos and brass stingers when Necromorphs become visible. During the fight the screeching, the sloshing, the splutter of exploding Necromorphs are combined with ever louder shooting and exploding sounds: these diegetic noises are overlaid by roaring brass motives, rapid woodwind movement, sharp dissonances, digital distortion and pounding syncopated timpani. As the end of the fight approaches both diegetic and non-diegetic sounds further increase in speed and volume until the last monster is dead – after which there is silence, and the player knows that there are no more monsters lurking behind any corner.

The three ALI components in *Dead Space*'s sound design show important overlaps. As Rebecca Roberts remarks, music in survival horror games is never mere background music, but it is always used in such a way that the frightening sounds emerging from out of the dark have clear interactive functions (Roberts, 2014: 138); these affects and interactions depend on players' audio-visual horror literacy. The concurrence and interdependence of the three components become evident in the "fear emitter" software that the *Dead Space* sound design team implemented in the gameplay. The fear emitters are adaptive audio software attached to a game object such as a Necromorph: when the avatar approaches the Necromorph, the audio software influences the ambient soundtrack so that the sonic build-up of the fighting scene starts (Paul, 2013: 75–77). Don Veca describes the fear emitters as the outcome of their attempts to achieve a maximum immersive effect in interactive situations. The aim was to make the game soundtrack as frightening as a horror film soundtrack, but to have it emulate the cinematic fear factor by expanding the linearity of film music with the interactivity of video games. Veca's description of the design process illustrates the importance of all three ALI factors for game musical immersion:

> One of the first questions that we asked ourselves was, "How can we make the music 'build up to the boo' like they do in linear horror movies?" That is, a key dramatic technique in classic horror movies is the gradual build-up of tension through music, but often with ambience and sound effects as well, and we needed a way to simulate this in an interactive video game context. This is pretty straight-forward for linear media where the composer/sound designer knows exactly what is going to happen, when and how long, exactly, the build-up should take, and exactly when to play the big "boo!" stinger. This is not the case, however, for interactive media; the video game player is

the one that determines how the scene plays out. It occurred to me that the "reason" the music swells in horror movies is because things are getting "scarier"; that is, the amount of "fear" that the movie is attempting to evoke is always increasing or decreasing throughout the entire production. It's the composer/sound designer's job to support and emphasize this emotional flow with the appropriate audio. So it occurred to me that we already have the ability to emit point-source or global sound and light in our game, for instance, and all we needed was a way to emit fear. This was the birth of the game "fear emitter," which is simply a first-class game object that designers can place in the world or attach to other objects, most notably, the enemy alien creatures. Fear emitters are simply a "sphere of influence". However, with this one tool, we can affect a myriad of audio sources, such as music, streamed ambience, adaptive ambience, reverb control, general mixing parameters, or whatever. (Napolitano, 2008)

Veca discusses the intended effect of the fear emitters as a result of the convergence of emotion, a well-known musical idiom, and adaptive audio. These three key aspects of game musical immersion are represented in the ALI model as affect, literacy and interaction, and the immersive effects of *Dead Space* sound design can be analysed as the concurrence of all three components. The closer the player comes to a Necromorph, the more intense the sonic horror of the game: the sounds of the well-known horror film conventions are explicitly intended to evoke fear, and the fact that the player's active navigation influences the extent of sonic horror suggests that she has influence on the process. The *Dead Space* team has succeeded in making all three components of game musical player involvement converge in order to achieve maximum immersion: predictable horror film conventions are employed to evoke player *literacy*; this literacy makes the soundtrack more *affectively* powerful; both facilitate the *interactivity* of the game.

## *Amnesia*: Under- vs. Overtriggered ALI Factors in Psychological Horror

Psychological horror games such as the *Silent Hill* series (1999–2012), *Call of Cthulhu: Dark Corners of the Earth* (2005) and *Slender: The Eight Pages* (2012) feature psychologically unreliable main characters whose past trauma affects their perception of the world as well as their sanity. While set in surroundings that are visually darker and emotionally bleaker than those of survival horror games, game avatars have access to very few (if any) weapons, many of which are hard to find and have limited effects on enemies. Enhancing the helplessness embedded in gameplay, psychological horror games often adopt a first-person rather than third-person view, so that the distance between avatar and player is psychologically minimal: looking through the avatar's eyes, the player has a close experience of the avatar's loss of control.

The most significant gameplay innovation introduced in psychological horror games intensifies this effect. Each of these games contains sections in which the flow of gameplay is interrupted by "sanity effects" (first popularized by *Eternal Darkness* [2002]). In these disturbing sequences, the avatar's perception is severely undermined by way of visual and sonic hallucinations. Visual sanity effects may include oblique camera angles, increased darkness, apparent warping of spatial proportions, blurred vision, and the occurrence of paranormal events. Auditory sanity effects may involve sudden crescendos, pounding drums, glissandos, (reverse) echo, disembodied whispers, and the avatar's own loud panting and heartbeat. Sanity loss is undesirable for gameplay reasons as it can lead to death, just like the loss of avatar health can in other games. These insanity sequences add yet another destabilizing factor to the already opaque character of psychological horror gameplay.

*Amnesia: The Dark Descent* is set in 1839, in a deserted castle haunted by the late Baron Alexander and his monstrous servants. The game avatar is Daniel, an archaeologist who suffers from amnesia and sanity disturbances that can kill him. There is no clear game goal other than those suggested by Alexander's irregularly present acousmêtric voice, which gives the avatar instructions. The gamer can only figure out what to do, how to do it and what the dangers are by simply stumbling around in the darkness: all she can rely on are the ears, eyes and memory of the avatar, but these are explicitly unreliable. There is a little torch to light the path, but even that small amount of light can attract the monsters. Looking at the monsters causes sanity loss, as do too much darkness and too much stress, and there are no weapons.

Mikko Tarmia's sound design for *Amnesia* complements the game's first-person view with what could be described as "first-person hearing". As Daniel walks through the castle the player mostly hears diegetic sounds: the avatar's footsteps, his panting upon seeing distressing things, creaking doors, and an occasional disembodied "Help me!" crying through the dark. The non-diegetic music accompanying these sections is very modest in design: slowly moving minor chords and clusters are looped in complementary layers, with single violin glissandos mixed into the background of the soundscape. Interface sound is restricted to a brief chromatic bassoon motif when doors are opened. Though unobtrusive, these parts of the soundtrack are carefully designed for their emotional effect, as the dark timbres of woodwinds and screeching violins as well as the gloomy harmonic effects of minor keys and chromatics blend seamlessly with the understated terror of the diegetic soundtrack.

In the insanity sequences, silent understatement abruptly flips into sonic hyperbole. Without any warning Daniel's vision blurs and the player perceives an indistinguishable accumulation of sounds. When Daniel is about to collapse all these melt into piercing white noise on a high F sharp.

The procedures of musical player involvement in *Amnesia* deviate significantly from those in *Dead Space*. The workings of the ALI components are manipulated in two different ways: while regular gameplay is too silent to provide the player with information about the game's plot and play, the insanity sequences are too loud and too full of information to be of any interpretive value.

## Regular Gameplay Sections

The larger part of *Amnesia*'s gameplay is characterized by the absence of any gaming events. There are no major changes in game space, no fights, no puzzles, and no real meetings except that with the spectral Alexander: the player merely wanders through the darkness. The soundtrack to these sections stands out by similar forms of absence.

On the level of affect, the regular sections of gameplay are characterized by emotional understatement. The only prominent sounds are the diegetic noises of the avatar's hurried footsteps and panicked breathing, which are mixed into the foreground of the soundscape. Because the distance between Daniel's and the player's experience is minimized by the first-person perception of sight and sound, the effect is that of hearing through the ears of a very frightened person. The non-diegetic music appears at a low volume in the background of the soundscape, and the minor chords, slow tempo, and dissonances subtly enhance the tense atmosphere of these unpleasantly quiet sections. The contrast in volume between the noises made by Daniel and the non-diegetic background music is so big that the castle almost appears to be completely silent. The avatar's frightened whimpers reverberate through the empty halls of the castle, and this suggestion of such utter silence – as *Silent Hill* amply illustrates (Whalen, 2007) – is meant to evoke uneasy feelings. If musical affect in *Dead Space* is achieved through the foregrounded use of the conventions of "fearful sound design", the regular gameplay in *Amnesia* rather takes the opposite route, using a limited number of musical means that suggest fear but never make it as explicit as survival horror soundtracks do. There is a difference in the ways in which that fear is conveyed to the player in both games. In *Dead Space*, frightening events and noises are typically presented as a part of the outside world, with radio static originating from machines and monstrous grunts appearing from locatable directions. In *Amnesia*, however, frightening noises seem to emanate from the avatar himself as much as from his surroundings: the player's auditory perception is guided towards Daniel's frightened panting and scurrying, and the non-diegetic silence and looped music only very quietly affirm the emotions expressed in the diegesis. By sonically leading the player into Daniel's psychology, the game involves the player in the avatar's deep-seated fears.

In terms of literacy, the absence of gaming rules and goals further adds to the game's disturbing character. All the usual gaming conventions are negated, so that the player has no idea what may happen next: not-knowing can be very frightening, especially in circumstances where all audio-visual parameters are set to the affect of fear. The thwarting of gaming expectations means that players can make no use of the gaming literacy they have acquired by playing other horror games; while survival horror follows pleasantly predictable patterns, psychological horror's only pattern is the disturbing fact that nothing much happens. The same negation of player literacy is operative sonically. The minimal design of the soundscape in *Amnesia*'s regular gameplay very much does *not* communicate any genre conventions or game goals, with the slowly looping drones merely providing musical question marks. There is no music for the bad guys, no easily recognizable leitmotifs warning for imminent danger, nothing to even suggest any obvious genre except the vague reminiscence of horror and Gothic narratives: the uncanny silence, for instance, is a metaphor often occurring in novels, films and television as a forbearer of terror. Lacking the game sound clichés that dominate survival horror composing, these parts of the psychological horror soundtrack also lack the interpretative clues that such clichés offer the player. The result of this negation of game sound design conventions, therefore, is a simultaneous negation of game sound signification. Players of *Amnesia* are very much left in the dark as they do not get inter-pretative clues, so that the interpretation of the game is significantly more difficult than in games that follow clear genre conventions.

The dimension of interaction is as minimal as those of affect and literacy in regular psychological horror gameplay: the avatar just wanders almost aimlessly through endless dark spaces. The soundtrack does not provide gameplay indications like it does in other genres. There is no real sonic differentiation between different spaces, there are no indications that danger is approaching, no warnings that running or fighting are in order. The principle of sonic interaction is inversed by the musical motionlessness of the slow nonlinear loops overlaying a constant suggestion of silence: rather than triggering direct actions, like the fast motifs of survival horror do, this silence-in-sound almost inhibits any action. The absence of sound and of the possibility of sonic interaction is used here as a way to disorientate the player. Such undoing of the sonic GPS is the rule in the regular gameplay sections of *Amnesia*. As a result, interaction in this genre is made very unclear: what do players interact with, and can they even know it when they are?

Compared to *Dead Space*'s survival horror soundtrack, the regular gameplay parts of *Amnesia*'s psychological horror soundtrack continuously under-trigger each of the three ALI components. Musical affect is achieved with subtle means only, player literacy is thwarted, player interaction is stifled, so that players cannot know what to feel, understand, or do. Affect, literacy and interaction are faded dimensions of gameplay here, immersing the player in apprehensive anxiety only. The blending of "inside" and "outside" sounds in these sections leads to a curious form of meta-diegetic game music which has the potential to cross not only the border between diegesis and non-diegesis, but also that between these two and the real-life environment of the player. The game's first-person viewing and hearing offer a bridge between Daniel's and the player's perception: with all audio-visual input geared towards fear, the traumas haunting Daniel are sonically woven into the player's own fear of not-knowing. Thus, while the game narrates the avatar's psychological desta-bilization, it simultaneously plays upon the player's. Through the understated yet carefully performative sound design of these sections, both avatar and player are sonically led to the simple conclusion that there is nothing to be afraid of or to run from – yet.

## Insanity Sequences

Starting up at unexpected moments, *Amnesia*'s insanity sequences take very little time to build up into complete audio-visual chaos in which there is no way to tell the difference between reality, hallucination or memory. These sequences are overfilled with sounds – drums, organ chords, heartbeats, disembodied growls and cries, glissandos, stingers, panting and heartbeat, thunder claps, echoes – and it is impossible to distinguish those that emerge from the castle from those that originate in Daniel's overwrought mind. In *Amnesia*, musical insanity is a cacophony of sonic terror effects. Contrasting the quiet regular sections in every possible way, the immersive factors charted in the ALI model are all triggered in the insanity sections. But superlatively so.

Once again, the conveyance of affect diverges sharply from survival horror conventions. It is clear to the *Dead Space* player that the presence of Necromorphs causes unpleasant sounds, and that Isaac Clarke can put an end both to the threat and the horrific screeches and leitmotifs; the maddening sonic chaos of *Amnesia*'s insanity sections, on the contrary, partially represents unidentified external danger and partially emerges as hallucination inside Daniel's mind, and there is no way to stop it besides passively waiting until the cacophonic threat subsides. Because of the first-person hearing governing the gameplay, the accumulated emotions are tied directly to the player's own musical perception, where the soundtrack piles memory upon disturbing memory, emotion upon distressed emotion. Every single aspect of this soundscape connotes fear, but in the jungle of sounds it is impossible to tell what to be afraid of exactly. The result is panicked bewilderment: the unknown is the worst terror imaginable, precisely because its source lies beyond imagination. Just like Daniel's, the player's own mind proves unreliable here, and the effect of this over-connoted sonic fearscape is a direct transmittal of the avatar's psychological destabilization onto the player's own.

The affective performativity of the insanity sections is made operative by player literacy. None of the individual sounds in these sections is in any way original to the game: every one of them represents a cinematic cliché. The organ and the thunder are well-known Gothic tropes, the pounding drums and stingers are horror movie references, the heartbeat and fleeting vocal lines are psychological thriller formulas (Van Elferen, 2012). The player is well-versed in all of these idioms, each of which has evolved into platitudes through over-use in film and game composing. All these film clichés communicate unequivocal messages of threat, danger and disaster, but their cacophonic accumulation makes it unclear which meaning applies to what, where and how. Because of the unusual accumulation of so many musical cues indicating such a diversity of horror genres, over-signification blurs the message they transmit. It is clear the player moves in terror here, but as the soundtrack tells her that there could be ghosts *and* killers *and* monsters *and* madness all at once, it is impossible to know which kind of danger she is in and how to act upon it. In these sections, musical literacy is a trap instead of a guideline.

The indistinguishable mix of sonic cues does not offer any indication for interaction. The GPS function of survival horror soundtracks is obtrusively malfunctioning in the insanity sections. While the silent gameplay sections lack any sonic cues so that the player is left in an interactive vacuum, these noisy sequences provide rather too many aural cues. With so much sound coming from all around the avatar as well as from inside his own mind, the player effectively has no gameplay information at all. There is no indication of the location of the danger; no clue about the direction in which to move; the duration of the danger is unknown as there are no helpful crescendos or adaptive build-ups; and there are no means by which the avatar (or player) can get out of this situation. The monsters do appear to have a leitmotif of sorts – a sustained drone of white noise wavering in unsettling dissonance between G' and G sharp – but it sounds when they are already present, and so it does not serve as a helpful announcement of danger. Once the leitmotif is there, it is literally already too late, and the player, like the avatar, cannot but surrender to the threat, hide in darkness, and wait anxiously. Rather than a gameplay cue, this leitmotif functions as the sonic equivalent of a lingering, passive-making threat. The sonic GPS has been replaced by an evil ghost-in-the-machine.

Because this brimful soundscape of insanity moves and changes so quickly, the over-triggered ALI components spill over their own limits in a frantic expenditure of horrific hyper-affect, hyper-literacy and hyper-interactivity. If that was not confusing enough, it is unclear whether any part of this insane soundscape is audible within the diegesis or merely a non-diegetic musical commentary. As the sanity sections portray Daniel's hallucinations, it is very possible that all of these sounds occur in his head only: these sounds could be neither diegetic nor non-diegetic, but a meta-diegetic reflection of the avatar's mindset. The interpretation of game events therefore is ultimately left to the player's confused and scared imagination. Like the sound design of the silent sections, that of the insanity sections engenders a shift from game diegesis to extra-diegesis. In reversed parallel to the fading of sonic communication in the silent sections, however, here an overload of sonic communication leads to screaming oblivion, a sonic white-out. How can anyone make sense of a game that gives almost no audio-visual input one moment and an overload of audio-visual input the next? How does one interpret game information that meta-diegetically reflects an insane mind?

## Towards a Theory of Game Musical Immersion

At the beginning of this chapter, game musical immersion was defined as "a blending of different music-specific phenomena afforded by involving sound play". The ALI model identifies the music-specific phenomena as musical affect, musical literacy and musical interaction. The analysis of the ways in which these three dimensions converge in game sound design enables ludomusicologists to chart the mechanics of game musical immersion. It discloses the connections between the existing analyses of single aspects of game music and provides empirical data regarding musical involvement with a theoretical reflection. Each of the components of the model depends on and overlaps with the others, as the assessments of *Dead Space 2* and *Amnesia: The Dark Descent* in this chapter illustrate. The ALI analysis of these two games demonstrates that the process of musical player involvement may develop along significantly different routes in different game genres: the divergent deployment of musical affect, literacy and interaction in these games' soundtracks leads to marked distinctions between survival and psychological horror game immersion.

Naturally these aspects of musical immersion require far more research, reflection and theorization than these preliminary observations can account for: a range of different game genres could test the model's components in various contexts; further empirical research could focus on player perception of the three dimensions; and, building on such explorations, the definition of game musical player involvement itself could be further refined. Perhaps, with the help of such exciting future ludomusicological projects, the ALI model may mark the beginnings of a road towards a theory of game musical immersion.

## Notes

1. Isabella van Elferen is Professor of Music and School Director of Research at Kingston University London. She publishes on film, TV and video game music, musical critical theory, Gothic, horror, SF and fantasy, and baroque sacred music. Her most recent book is the award-winning *Gothic Music: The Sounds of the Uncanny* (University of Wales Press, 2012).
2. These quotations are taken from the game's official website http://www.rememberingthegame.com/ (accessed April 23, 2016).

## References

Aufderheide, P. (1993) *Aspen Media Literacy Conference Report*. Aspen: Aspen Institute.

Calleja, G. (2011) *In-Game: From Immersion to Incorporation*. Cambridge, MA: MIT Press.

Chion, M. (1994) *Audio-Vision Sound on Screen*. Trans. C. Gorbman. New York: Columbia University Press.

Collins, K. (2008) *Game Sound: An Introduction to the History, Theory, and Practice of Video Game Music and Sound Design*. Cambridge, MA: MIT Press.

Collins, K. (2013) *Playing with Sound: A Theory of Interacting with Sound and Music in Video Games*. Cambridge, MA: MIT Press.

Donnelly, K. J. (2005) *The Spectre of Sound: Music in Film and Television*. London: British Film Institute.

Ekman, I. and P. Lankoski (2009) "Hair-Raising Entertainment: Emotions, Sound, and Structure in *Silent Hill 2* and *Fatal Frame*." In *Horror Video Games: Essays on the Fusion of Fear and Play*, edited by B. Perron, pp. 181–99. Jefferson: McFarland.

Elchlepp, S. (c. 2011) "Dead Space 2 Original Videogame Soundtrack." *Game Music Online*. http://www.vgmonline.net/reviews/simonelchlepp/deadspace2.shtml (accessed October 31, 2014).

Ermi, L. and F. Mäyrä (2005) "Fundamental Components of the Gameplay Experience: Analysing Immersion." In *Changing Views: Worlds in Play. Selected Papers of the 2005 Digital Games Research Association's Second International Conference*, edited by S. de Castell and J. Jenson. Vancouver. http://www.digra.org/wp-content/uploads/digital-library/06276.41516.pdf (accessed October 30, 2014).

Gregg, M. and G. Seigworth (eds) (2010) *The Affect Theory Reader*. Durham: Duke University Press.

Hannan, M. (2009) "Sound and Music in Hammer's Vampire Films." In *Terror Tracks: Music, Sound and Horror Cinema*, edited by P. Hayward, pp. 60–74. London: Equinox.

Jørgensen, K. (2008) "Left in the Dark: Playing Computer Games with the Sound Turned Off." In *From Pac-Man to Pop Music: Interactive Audio in Games and New Media*, edited by K. Collins, pp. 163–76. Aldershot: Ashgate.

Kizzire, J. (2014) "'The Place I'll Return to Someday': Music Nostalgia in *Final Fantasy IX*." In *Music in Videogames: Studying Play*, edited by K. J. Donnelly, W. Gibbons and N. Lerner, pp. 183–98. New York: Routledge.

KM (2011) "Amnesia: The Dark Descent Soundtrack." *TIG Tunes*. http://tigtunes.com/2011/10/amnesia-dark-descent-soundtrack/ (accessed October 31, 2014).

Lipscomb, S. D. and S. M. Zehnder (2005) "Immersion in the Virtual Environment: The Effect of a Musical Score on the Video Gaming Experience." *Journal of Physiological Anthropology and Applied Human Science* 23 (2005): 337–43.

Massumi, B. (2002) *Parables for the Virtual: Movement, Affect, Sensation*. Durham: Duke University Press.

Murray, J. H. (1997) *Hamlet on the Holodeck: The Future of Narrative in Cyberspace*. Cambridge, MA: MIT Press.

Nacke, L. and M. Grimshaw (2010) "Player-game Interaction through Affective Sound." In *Game Sound Technology and Player Interaction: Concepts and Developments*, edited by M. Grimshaw, pp. 264–85. Hershey, PA: IGI Global.

Napolitano, J. (2008) "Dead Space Sound Design: In Space No One can Hear Interns Scream. They are Dead (interview)." *Original Sound Version*. http://www.originalsoundversion.com/dead-space-sound-design-in-space-no-one-can-hear-interns-scream-they-are-dead-interview/ (accessed October 28, 2014).

Paul, L. J. (2013) "Droppin' Science: Video Game Audio Breakdown." In *Music and Game: Perspectives on a Popular Alliance*, edited by P. Moormann, pp. 63–80. Wiesbaden: Springer.

Pinchbeck, D. (2009) "Shock, Horror: First-Person Gaming, Horror, and the Art of Ludic Manipulation." In *Horror Video Games: Essays on the Fusion of Fear and Play*, edited by B. Perron, pp. 79–94. Jefferson: McFarland.

Reale, S. B. (2014) "Transcribing Musical Worlds; or, Is *L.A. Noire* a Music Game?" In *Music in Videogames: Studying Play*, edited by K. J. Donnelly, W. Gibbons and N. Lerner, pp. 78–103. New York: Routledge.

Roberts, R. (2014) "Fear of the Unknown: Music and Sound Design in Psychological Horror Games." In *Music in Videogames: Studying Play*, edited by K. J. Donnelly, W. Gibbons and N. Lerner, pp. 138–50. New York: Routledge.

Roepke, M. (2011) "Changing Literacies: A Research Platform at Utrecht University." https://mmroepke.wordpress.com/publications/ (accessed March 1, 2016).

Summers, T. (2011) "Playing the Tune: Video Game Music, Gamers, and Genre." *ACT: Zeitschrift für Musik & Performance 2*. http://www.act.uni-bayreuth.de/en/archiv/2011-02/04_Summers_Playing_the_Tune/index.html (accessed March 1, 2016).

Van Elferen, I. (2011) "¡Un Forastero! Virtuality and Diegesis in Videogame Music." *Music and the Moving Image* 4/2 (2011): 30–39.

Van Elferen, I. (2012) *Gothic Music: The Sound of the Uncanny*. Cardiff: University of Wales Press.

Van Elferen, I. (2015) "Sonic Descents: Musical Dark Play in Survival and Psychological Horror." In *The Dark Side of Game Play*, edited by J. Linderoth, pp. 226–41. New York: Routledge.

Whalen, Z. (2007) "Film Music vs. Video-Game Music: The Case of *Silent Hill*." In *Music, Sound and Multimedia: From the Live to the Virtual*, edited by J. Sexton, pp. 68–81. Edinburgh: Edinburgh University Press.

Zagal, J. P. (2010) *Ludoliteracy: Defining, Understanding, and Supporting Games Education*. Halifax: Etc Press.

## Games

*Amnesia: The Dark Descent*. Frictional Games. Frictional Games. 2010.

*Dead Space 2*. Visceral Games. Electronic Arts. 2011.

*Remembering*. Monobanda. 2014. http://www.rememberingthegame.com/ (accessed April 23, 2016).

# 4 Modularity in Video Game Music

*Elizabeth Medina-Gray*[1]

One of the most critical – and critically challenging – aspects of video game music is that it is fundamentally *dynamic*. As Karen Collins describes the term, dynamic audio is "changeable"; it "reacts both to changes in the gameplay environment and/or in response to the player" (Collins, 2008: 139). Game music becomes dynamic, for example, when the player moves her character to a new in-game location and the music changes in response, when the player achieves a goal and a special piece of music sounds, and so on. Different games incorporate dynamic music to different degrees, but the soundtrack during one playthrough of a game will nearly always sound different and proceed differently from that of any other playthrough, depending on the timing and identity of the player's actions.

More specifically, *modularity* provides a fundamental basis for the dynamic music in video games. Real-time soundtracks usually arise from a collection of distinct musical modules stored in a game's code – each module being anywhere from a fraction of a second to several minutes in length – that become triggered and modified during gameplay. Indeed, most aspects of digital media are fundamentally modular; in this media, small discrete objects – or chunks of data – combine to form larger entities, and this is true of a game's images and events as well as its music and other audio (Manovich, 2001: 30).

Although video games are unique in many ways as culturally-situated multimedia objects, they are not alone in their use of modularity to create multiple and flexible sounding results. Several authors – Jesper Kaae (2008), Karen Collins (2008) and Axel Berndt (2009) – have compared this aspect of game music (without using the term "modular") to that of other compositions, including dice music of the eighteenth century and certain music of the twentieth-century avant-garde. Such comparisons have thus far been cursory, however, and primarily aimed at deriving inspiration for composition rather than an analytical study of game music.[2] In the current chapter, I refine and expand on these earlier comparisons by defining a broad category of modular music and situating game music within that category, thereby establishing a framework in which to examine and discuss this music and its dynamic qualities. This chapter draws especially on discussions of modularity in twentieth-century art music, including indeterminate, open form, and aleatoric music. This focus on twentieth-century art music, first, casts several significant and unique aspects of game music in helpful relief. Second, modular art music of the twentieth century has received more scholarly attention to date than have other types of modular music, and existing approaches to this music may inform new approaches to the study of music in video games. To be clear, I am not arguing for a direct historical connection between the twentieth-century avant-garde and video games (although I am also not ruling out this possibility, especially since individual game composers might draw from these earlier procedures). Most generally, different practical and aesthetic goals have led composers to use musical modularity at different times and for different reasons. At the end of the chapter, I suggest some broad directions through which we might productively analyse video game music while accounting for its modular and dynamic qualities.

## A Concept of Modularity

In 1962, Umberto Eco wrote about a long-emerging trend in art, in which authors, artists and composers created works that were "open". In such open works, the consumer was encouraged to freely interpret the artwork in a multiplicity of ways through a "theoretical, mental collaboration" (1989: 12) with the artistic material. Not only could such open works produce multiple interpretations in the mind of the consumer, but a special category of open works could produce a multiplicity of final forms before they even reached the consumer for interpretation. Eco described this category of open works as "works in movement": works that consisted of "unplanned or physically incomplete structural units", and where the artist left the final arrangement of the work's components to another participant, releasing the work from the artist's control while it was still, in a sense, "unfinished" (ibid.). Alexander Calder's mobiles, with elements that shift and rotate into various visual arrangements, are examples of such "works in movement", as is Karlheinz Stockhausen's *Klavierstück XI*, in which the pianist chooses the order in which to play discrete segments of music in the notated score.

More recently, James Saunders has formulated a subset of those artworks that Eco called "works in movement" into a more rigidly defined concept of *musical modularity* (2008). Saunders focuses especially on modular music – his article provides the theory and justification for his own modular composition – but he explores modular art more broadly as well, and he draws heavily from sources that treat modularity in the industrialized production of physical objects (e.g., a computer, or a bookshelf).

From Saunders, we see that the most basic and essential components of any modular system are "a number of standardized units and a procedure for fitting them together" (2008: 153). In other words, musical modularity requires, first of all, a collection of *modules* and a set of *rules* that dictate how the modules may combine.[3] In video games, the modules are often distinct containers of musical data – digital files – and the rules are programmed into the game in the form of triggers and other if-then conditions. For example, one rule in a game might state: if the player enters room X, then trigger music module Y. Another rule might specify that an ongoing module Z should get louder or softer depending on the player's distance from a particular in-game location. In pieces like *Klavierstück XI*, by contrast, the modules are visually separate segments of notated music, and the rules are the performance instructions printed with the score. Ultimately, in all modular music, the modules and rules must go through a process of *assembly* to yield the final *sounding music* (e.g. the real-time gameplay soundtrack or the concert performance).

*Figure 4.1* The modular musical process

Overall, modular music follows the three-part process shown in Figure 4.1: this music starts with (1) modules and rules, passes through (2) assembly, and results in (3) sounding music. To adapt Michael Nitsche's terms for video game spaces, the modular process therefore corresponds to a move from a more abstract, *rule-based space* (on the left-hand side of the diagram) to a *mediated space* (on the right-hand side) that the player or audience may more directly perceive.[4]

Critical to this modular process – as with any musical process – are the participants (human and/or mechanical) involved in each step. *Creators* establish the modules and rules, *assemblers* determine which modules will sound and when, and *producers* make audible the sounding music. A single participant might take part in more than one of these steps, and multiple participants might collaborate to execute a single step in the process. The role of the creator (composer, designer and/or author) of modular music bears similarities to traditional (non-modular) authorship, albeit with the added involvement of other participants in the assembly step. In this respect, Eco has emphasized that works in movement remain necessarily within a "world intended by the author" (1989: 19). Janet Murray provides a more nuanced view of authorship in digital interactive narratives that applies readily to modular music (as well as video games overall):

> Authorship in electronic media is procedural. Procedural authorship means writing the rules by which the texts appear as well as writing the texts themselves . . . The interactor [i.e. assembler] is not the author of the digital narrative, although the interactor can experience one of the most exciting aspects of artistic creation – the thrill of exerting power over enticing and plastic materials. This is not authorship but agency. (Murray, 1997: 152-53)

The involvement of assemblers – distinct from creators – is a critical aspect of modularity, and assemblers may have a great deal of influence over the results of a given modular system. Assemblers work, however, within a system's established design (i.e. its rules), and so authorship belongs overall to the system's creators.

Another critical aspect of modularity is the two distinct ways in which chance enters into these systems: first in the separation between the music's creators and its assemblers, and second in the actual assembly step. The first type of chance, *indeterminacy*, results from the fact that composers and designers establish the modules and rules, but they then cannot accurately see past this first step, since this music's assembly is out of its creators' hands. From a composer's point of view, the creation of modules and rules hinges on choice, but the rest of the modular process may occur in multiple possible ways – it is indeterminate – and so falls into the realm of chance.[5] Because composers create the rules as well as the modules, however, they are able to variously limit or increase indeterminacy, so that the resulting musical system falls somewhere along a continuum between creator control and non-control. At one extreme, complete control means that the composer knows exactly how the music will sound – that is, in only one possible way, and neither actually dynamic nor indeterminate. At the other end of the continuum, extreme non-control means that the creators leave as much of the music as possible up to the assemblers, even including the contents of the modules themselves. In general, most modular systems fall somewhere in the middle of this continuum, and may tend either towards creator control or non-control, depending on the given system's rules.[6]

Indeterminacy is not to be confused, however, with the second type of chance that sometimes plays a role in modular music: chance in assembly. Chance is here an impartial force – a special randomizing rule – that assembles modules, and it is distinct from choice, which involves decisions made by a thinking agent. We will explore chance and choice in assembly further as we treat various types of modular music.

## Modular Music and the Avant-Garde

With its shared modular process and diverse aesthetic and practical goals, indeterminate art music of the twentieth century provides a revealing backdrop for a study of modularity in video game music. Such "open" pieces had an early precedent in Henry Cowell's *Mosaic Quartet* (1935), with its five movements that could be performed in any order, but they began to appear in greater numbers in the 1950s with works by Pierre Boulez, Karlheinz Stockhausen, Morton Feldman, Earle Brown and others. It was this broad group of compositions – in which modularity surfaced as one possible method within wider contemporary ideas of indeterminacy and mobility in art and literature – that led to Eco's theories about "works in movement", and, in the twenty-first century, to Saunders's approach to modularity. The composers who used modularity in the twentieth century did so in service of diverse goals. I do not, therefore, mean to suggest that all of these composers belonged to a single artistic movement.[7] Individual composers took divergent positions on how, why and to what extent they would incorporate indeterminacy in their music, and they often disagreed with one another on the appropriate use of such procedures. Many of the composers who used modularity in the 1950s, moreover, continued to move in different directions and to explore other compositional techniques over the course of their careers.

Three composers in particular – Pierre Boulez, Earle Brown and John Cage – exemplify the wide diversity of goals and processes that led some composers to employ modularity in the mid-twentieth century. Each of these three composers used the general modular process in different ways, and an examination of some of each composer's work in turn illuminates several possibilities for modularity.

In his *Third Piano Sonata* (1956–1957), Boulez composed sets of modules and rules for each of five large movements (called "formants"), and placed the performer in charge of this music's assembly. The score for "Paranthèse", for example – one sub-section of the formant "Trope" – consists of several modules in a fixed order; certain of these modules are set off by parentheses, and the performer must choose which (if any) of these parenthetical modules to include while playing through the score from beginning to end. Throughout the *Third Piano Sonata*, the performer thus assembles the music using choice rather than chance.

Boulez used modularity in his *Third Piano Sonata* because he wanted to explore ways in which a single piece of music might incorporate multiple structural realizations, becoming "a kind of labyrinth with a number of paths" (Boulez, 1991: 29). At the same time, however, Boulez was concerned with limiting the role of indeterminacy in his work. He created detailed and restrictive rules

– with only a few options from which the performer might choose at a given time – in order to maintain a high degree of creator control throughout. Boulez did this because he saw indeterminacy as a threat to the very status of music as creative work. As Boulez put it, "there could not possibly be total indeterminacy, for such a phenomenon is contrary – absurdly so – to all organizing thought and to all style" (1963: 35).[8]

Although Boulez allowed the performer to make decisions about the final form of the piece, Boulez's main focus was *not* on the performer as an active participant in the music; rather, the performer's agency was more accurately a side effect of Boulez's conception of the work (Granat, 2002: 29). In the *Third Piano Sonata*, the performer thus fills the critical role of the assembler, but his or her influence is second to the composer and remains restricted overall.[9]

Earle Brown's modular music also casts the performer – or in some pieces, the conductor – as the assembler. Unlike Boulez, however, Brown wrote indeterminate music in order to grant a significant portion of the creative power to this participant, thus tending more towards creator non-control.[10] In his words, Brown was interested in creating what he saw as a "truly collaborative, creative synergy" between the composer and performer, as well as the audience, and the score (1999: 41).

Brown granted power to the performer through modularity, but also through another source of indeterminacy: ambiguous musical notation. Some of Brown's pieces combine both of these procedures. The score for *Twentyfive Pages* (1953), for example, consists of 25 sheets of musical notes on uncleffed staves. Each page is a module, and the performer (or performers, at up to 25 pianos) can choose to play the 25 pages in any order. Moreover, the musical material *within* each of these modules is indeterminate: Although the pitches are notated on staves, the performer may read the page either right-side-up or upside-down, and may apply either treble or bass clefs to each staff. Also, while Brown has provided durations for the notes relative to each other – using a system he has called "time notation" – the performer may play the piece at any tempo; Brown (1975) has suggested that each two-staff system take between 5 and 15 seconds to perform, but even these very broad limits are "not compulsory". Together, these procedures in *Twentyfive Pages* yield indeterminacy through what Saunders calls the "physical material" – the notated modules – and an "interpretive layer" – open musical qualities such as tempo and pitch, which modify the physical material (2008: 166). This distinction between "physical" and "interpretive" layers applies similarly to the modular music in video games, since these modules (fixed in the game's code) can sometimes be modified (e.g. speeded up, faded out, pitch-bent) during gameplay according to programmed parameters and rules.

John Cage is well-known as a proponent of indeterminacy and chance in music, and known also for pushing the boundaries of composition with experiments in sound and silence. Many of Cage's indeterminate pieces do not use modularity, relying instead on various graphic and verbal methods to give the performer wide-ranging interpretive influence over the sounding music. Cage did, however, employ a modular process in some of his early chance pieces, but in a different way from his contemporaries, and again for different reasons.

In *Music of Changes* (1951), for example, Cage first composed a large collection of musical modules and arranged them on a chart. He then established a system of rules whereby he would toss coins and consult the *I Ching* – that is, utilizing chance – in order to identify a position on this chart and therefore a module to add to the notated score. By repeating this process, he gradually assembled the modules into a performable score.[11] Unlike Boulez's and Brown's modular systems, which yield many different sounding results upon multiple performances, Cage's system therefore resulted in only one performable realization out of the many that might have been.

This procedure was a way for Cage to excise his own decisions from the composition as much as possible, thereby abdicating the composer's traditional position of control. In an address in 1957, Cage stated that "those involved with the composition of experimental music find ways and means to remove themselves from the activities of the sounds they make" (1973: 10). Cage expressed similar views regarding *Music of Changes* in an article published in 1952: "It is thus possible to make a musical composition the continuity of which is free of individual taste and memory (psychology) and also of the literature and 'traditions' of the art" (1973: 59). The high degree of non-rational randomization in the organization of *Music of Changes* and other similar pieces was thus one of Cage's main aesthetic goals.

Boulez, Brown and Cage diverged in their uses of modularity and indeterminacy, and they also often disagreed – sometimes vehemently – with the validity of one another's compositional approaches. Boulez, especially, took pains to distance himself from the other composers' freer use of indeterminacy, writing in his position-taking article, "Alea", that in such instances, "the composer flees from his own responsibility, shying away from the choice inherent in all creative work" (1991: 36).[12] Cage and Brown, in turn, defended their positions against those (not only Boulez) who maligned the validity of their compositions.[13]

Despite Boulez's, Brown's and Cage's – and other composers' – differing positions on indeterminacy, a few features of modularity in twentieth-century art music are basically consistent. First, modularity is here one means by which a composer may incorporate indeterminacy into this music, and second, the creator's uncertainty regarding the music's final form becomes a positive component of the musical process. Another feature is the distinction between the composer's abstract collections of modules and rules as "the work" or "the piece", and the actually-sounding realizations of the music as "versions" or "instances" of that work.[14] This may be the case even in Cage's chance compositions, although the production of a single performable score might initially suggest otherwise.[15] In short, rather than the modules and rules serving as a pre-compositional system, a means to an end, modularity here becomes absorbed into the concept of the composition itself.[16]

Overall, twentieth-century art music composers have utilized modularity in order to access a wide variety of aesthetic and conceptual goals. Composers such as Boulez have exerted high degrees of control over indeterminacy through restrictive rules, whereas other composers – for example, Brown and Cage – have taken positions that tend more towards non-control. These instances of modularity also demonstrate diverse means of assembly: chance (through coin tossing) in Cage's *Music of Changes*, and choice (on the part of the performer, who is both the assembler and the producer of the sounding music) for Boulez's *Third Piano Sonata* and Brown's *Twentyfive Pages*.

## Modular Music and Video Games

The music in video games shares its general modular process with the art music treated above. Like this earlier modular music, video game music variously involves chance and choice for its creators and assemblers, utilizes Saunders's physical and interpretive layers, and may occupy nearly any position on the indeterminacy continuum, from heavy creator control (strict rules and very limited modular combinations) to relative non-control. Moreover, as in previous types of modular music, indeterminacy is an overall positive aspect of game music, since it allows this music to be dynamic along with gameplay.[17]

Video game music differs, however, in several critical ways from its avant-garde predecessors, and these differences make game music at once unique and a particularly puzzling object of study. First, game music involves the intended receiver of the audio output in the modular process's assembly step.[18] The player's actions often determine which modules sound and when, and so the player becomes both audience (receiver) and participant (assembler) of the sounding music.[19] In addition to the player, the computer – the entity that runs the game in real-time – also takes part in this music's assembly. Indeed, it is the computer that actually executes the modular rules, with input from the player's actions. (The computer is also the producer of the sounding music.) In video games, chance – similar to tosses of dice or coins – enters into modular assembly in the form of occasional randomizing algorithms on the part of the computer; they are programmed into the game. In Nintendo's *The Legend of Zelda: Ocarina of Time* (1998) (hereafter "*Ocarina of Time*"), for example, the score for the Hyrule Field area of the game world consists of several possible modules, and computer randomization determines the order in which those modules play (Collins, 2008: 158).[20] While chance enters modular assembly through the computer, choice in the assembly step is the purview of the player. Since the computer is a non-thinking mechanical agent, I avoid ascribing choice to this participant. Even in instances that might seem like choice – for example, a computer-controlled character's artificial intelligence – the computer is instead simply engaged in the execution of the game's rules, often including some randomizing procedures, namely, chance.

The player's choice-based involvement in the modular process highlights another critical difference between modular assembly in video games and in many other types of modular music, hinging on the fact that game music is part of a larger multimedia object. In most modular avant-garde pieces that involve choice in assembly – Boulez's *Third Piano Sonata*, for example – performers choose how to assemble the modules with the sounding music foremost in mind. This assembly, in other words, involves *musical choice*. This is the case in certain instances of player-assembled game music as well; for example, in *Ocarina of Time*, the player chooses which individual notes to play on a virtual ocarina – and in what order – to yield particular melodies. Many other choices that affect game music's assembly, however, may bear no conscious musical reference at all, and are often directed towards non-musical elements of the game. The player may choose, for example, to move her character into another area of the game world because she wants to progress through the game's events, not because she wants to stop the current musical module and start another, although this may nonetheless happen as a direct result of her actions. This latter instance of assembly thus involves *non-musical choice*.

Non-musical choice – more than musical choice – is the most common way in which the player's actions affect game soundtracks, but the player has additional inlets into modular assembly as well. If the player tries to perform an action and fails, this no longer falls entirely under the umbrella of deliberate choice, but it may also affect the music. For example, when the player misses a note in a skill-based music game such as Harmonix's *Guitar Hero* (2005), that note/module is then absent in the ongoing song. This situation bears some relationship to chance in that the player's actions are not entirely under his or her own control, but it more accurately engages a separate assembling force: error. This may be error due to skill or even miscommunication, if, for example, the game console's controller's battery dies and the player is no longer able to convey his or her choices to the computer.[21]

Figure 4.2 expands the earlier diagram of the modular process (Figure 4.1) to include the various forces available during assembly. This new diagram is especially relevant to video games, but many of these forces apply to other modular music as well. While *rule execution* is implicit in every assembly step, it is included here to account for situations in which the computer assembles modules without reference to player input, such as in response to an in-game change from day to night. Just as a single assembly step may involve more than one participant (computer and/or player(s)), it may also involve multiple (cooperative) assembling forces.

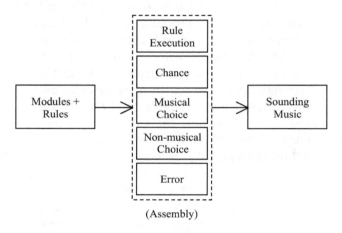

(Assembly)

*Figure 4.2* Assembling forces in video games and other modular music

Not only does the player help to assemble a game's modular music, but this music affects the player and gameplay in turn, especially through its relation to other real-time aspects of the game (visuals, actions, etc.). In particular, game music often facilitates *usability*, enhancing the player's ability to interact with the game (as a user system) by providing information and feedback to the player.[22] A particular musical module might alert the player to a dangerous situation in the game world, for example, while another module might confirm and reinforce the successful execution of a particular action. By interacting with the game, the player helps to assemble the game's soundtrack, then this music influences the player's actions, which yield more music, and so on. The player's role as assembler is, in other words, entwined with the game's fundamental interactivity.

Another critical consideration for modular game music is an aesthetic one. In certain avant-garde music – in the music of John Cage, for example – all sounds and sequences of sounds are equally valid.[23] The situation with video game music, however, is very different. Not only does this music refer frequently to popular and value-laden concepts of tonality, functional harmony, and consonance and dissonance, but it also matters how modules sound together during gameplay. In particular, and especially with advances in technology over the past 15 or so years, game music aesthetics tend to privilege *smoothness* – a quality in which distinct modules fit well together – as multiple modules combine. Composer Aaron Marks, for example, provides the following basic rule for composing dynamic music for games: "Any change in the soundtrack must blend with any other music cue at the time" (2009: 234). More specifically, Marks cautions the prospective game composer to think carefully about the sonic result as one module fades into another module during gameplay:

> What will your music sound like as these two cues crossfade? This type of situation has the potential to sound like fingernails across a chalkboard as the two cues overlap. If you know ahead of time, perhaps it's possible to use the same key for each piece – something to tie them together successfully. (2009: 249)

In another guide for prospective composers, G. W. Childs provides a similar warning regarding this music and meter:

> [Y]ou don't want a sideways crossfade to happen out of tempo, do you? It would be highly audible to the listener, as well as to you. There's nothing more agonizing than hearing a beat out of step. It reflects poorly on the game and on the composer! (Childs IV, 2007: 152)

This aesthetic of smoothness in video game music is closely related to similar aesthetics in other popular types of dynamic and modular media of the twentieth and twenty-first centuries. Accompanists for silent film, for example, were concerned with creating smooth transitions from one musical segment to the next, and smoothness continues to be a concern in music accompanying live stage performances (including theatre and circus).[24] Smoothness is also an important aesthetic consideration for DJs mixing live electronic dance music (EDM), especially regarding rhythm and meter ("beat-matching") but also in other musical aspects as well (e.g. pitch) (Butler, 2006: 242–43; Hadley, 1993; Bakker and Bakker, 2006: 79). Amid this smoothness aesthetic, however, musical *disjunction* – a lack of smoothness – often serves important functions in video games; disjunction might support a change in the game's environment, for example, or enhance usability through clarified feedback.[25] Similarly, in other popular musical multimedia – even non-dynamic media such as film – the continuity and cohesiveness that comes with smoothness is generally desirable except in certain special situations where disjunction is more appropriate (usually because of some dramatic consideration) (Prendergast, 1992: 11–12). Overall, whether smooth or disjunct, the way that modules sound together in the resulting music is important for games.

Modularity provides a practical means through which game music can achieve its necessary dynamic quality: the sounding music is able to gain a degree of flexibility suitable to each individualized gameplay situation that would not be possible with more fixed, traditionally linear music. A practical benefit also comes from the economy of building an expansive soundtrack from relatively small, repeatable modules.[26]

Finally, modularity in game music raises intriguing questions about what constitutes "the work". On the one hand, all the musical modules in a game, together with other game components, produce a single overarching concept of *the game* as a multimedia object – a flexible object that every player will play differently, but a singular object nonetheless – and the modules become *the game's music*. In this respect, the status of video game music is closely related to that of twentieth-century indeterminate music: the actual realization of the game's music during a particular play session is transient (as is the play session); it is an instance of the composition, not the composition itself. On the other hand, the opposite is also true: a game produces a real-time soundtrack that matches an individualized instance of gameplay and contributes to the player's experience of the game, similar in some ways to a singular film score. With such an experiential, end-oriented view, the sounding music becomes the composition, and the modules and rules are merely the components necessary to yield the final musical product.

Video game music offers additional complications as well, in that these modules commonly become independent pieces of music in themselves, outside of a gameplay context. Game music modules appear as individual tracks on purchasable albums, fans listen to these tracks in isolation from the game, and orchestras perform this music in concerts. This situation is notably different from twentieth-century indeterminate art music, in which individual modules have no valid status outside of the larger work. This situation is similar, however, to the common treatment of individual songs or numbers in opera and musical theatre, as well as in some film soundtracks. So while musical modules perform critical roles within the game and as components of the game's larger soundtrack, they may also thrive outside of the game context in a way that is more commonly found in more structurally fixed forms of multimedia.

All of these various views of video game music may be possible precisely because of the interactivity of the medium. The player can become aware of particular modules and their modular rules through repeated actions within a single playthrough (or multiple playthroughs) of a game. By visiting (and re-visiting) a particular in-game location, for example, the player might become familiar with a looping module that accompanies gameplay in that environment. Once the player is able to recognize that module, the player may hear it both in the context of the current ongoing soundtrack and as a self-contained musical object. It is possible, in other words, that through repetition, some aspects of the abstract modular system itself – in addition to its real-time realization – may become relevant to the player's experience.

## Analytical Approaches to Modular Music

While musical modularity provides intriguing practical and aesthetic possibilities, it also poses distinct challenges for analysis. How should an analyst approach music whose final content and arrangement is – until the assembly step – unfixed and unknown? Scholars have begun to address this question with regard to some twentieth-century art music, and this work provides a backdrop for new analytical approaches. Although video game music differs from avant-garde music in many significant ways (as the above discussion shows), the shared modular process allows for approaches in one realm to at least suggest some important focal points in the other.

Authors who analyse modular art music often specifically stress that the approach to this music must be different from traditional approaches, and that it should take the special indeterminate aspects of this music into consideration.[27] Pamela Quist, in her dissertation exploring Brown's modular work, outlines two types of analytical problems in this music: "(1) analysis in a microscopic sense of a particular moment", which is to say, analysis interior to an individual module (similar, therefore, to small-scale analytical challenges in non-modular music), "and the more difficult (2) analysis or description of the macroscopic, explaining the interrelationship of the materials used with the overall shaping of the piece" (1984: xii). Such a balanced attention to individual modules as well as larger-scale relationships among those modules provides a suitably broad analytical framework for any modular music. With respect to the second, macroscopic aspect of this broad framework, two main analytical approaches arise: On the one hand, the analyst might focus on the modules and rules in their abstract rule-based space – that is, at the left-hand side of the diagram in Figures 4.1 and 4.2. These components of the music are open to possibilities of eventual assembly, but are not yet definitively arranged. On the other hand, the analyst might treat the music after the assembly step, in its more concrete mediated space, and as it actually sounds in real time (at the diagram's right-hand side).

Several authors have advocated for analyses that focus on the first option, sometimes to the exclusion of the second. James Pritchett promotes this view most strongly in his approach to Cage's chance works, asserting that: "The compositional system, not its random product, is of musicological interest, and should become the focus of our attention" (1988: 8).[28] This approach is useful because of its broad scope and its ability to treat all the music's components, possibly even from the creator's perspective. For video game music, this approach allows for a global view of this music as part of *the game* as a whole. No matter how the game might eventually be played, all of its components already exist, and can be examined in terms of their broad rule-based relations. Such a global view provides important context for this music's possibilities, but it limits musical analysis to certain broad observations such as key, meter, motive, and the modules' abstract associations with the game world (associations between a particular module and a place or event, for example).

Dora Hanninen argues for the second analytical option, however, in her treatment of Morton Feldman's modular piano piece, *Intermission 6* (1953). Hanninen examines several recorded performances of this piece in order to explore the ways in which the same module *sounds* different depending on which other modules it succeeds and/or precedes in the piece's realization. For Hanninen, the sounding music is critical: "The sound-objects' salient properties are a mystery, not to be found in the abstract space of the score, but only when embedded in the performance time of individual passages" (2004: 169). The ability to examine sounding music is especially appealing in the case of video games, since much of the power of this dynamic music hinges precisely on how the soundtrack unfolds in time, and on how the player hears the modules and their combinations – including the resulting smoothness and disjunction – in relation to the game's real-time events. It is at this stage in the modular process, in other words, that the music becomes most relevant to a particular game-playing experience. However, just as a single performance of an indeterminate work cannot accurately represent the entirety of the piece, a single playthrough cannot entirely represent a game. In other words, although a particular realization of the soundtrack is critically linked to an individual player's experience of the game, no one such experience takes theoretical precedence over all other players and all other instances of gameplay.[29] Moreover, since a player can begin to apprehend the music's modular structure through gameplay, analysis of even a single real-time soundtrack would miss an aspect of the player's experience if it didn't take the modular structure into account.

These beginning- and end-oriented analytical focuses each come with benefits and drawbacks. A single analytical approach, therefore, might potentially incorporate aspects of both views of the modular process.[30] With an eye to the rule-based as well as the mediated spaces of games and game music, we may productively balance the abstract with the concrete, and the composer with the player and the computer in these participants' chance- and choice-based roles. From these various perspectives, we can begin to address the special challenges of dynamic game music and modularity.

## Notes

1. Elizabeth Medina-Gray received her PhD in Music Theory from Yale University in 2014, where she completed her dissertation on the analysis of modular music in video games. Her research interests include music in video games and interactive multimedia, and twentieth-century tonal music.

2. Kaae emphasizes "lessons that might be learned" for future creation of game music (2008: 91), and Collins states that such historical precedents are "worth exploring as possibilities for game music" (2008: 155). David Bessell espouses the same thinking (relatively early in writings about game music), saying that "lessons might be learned" from procedures in indeterminate avant-garde compositions (2002: 142).

3. Saunders refers to such systems of rules as an "interface" (2008: 155). Since this term has another meaning in the context of video games, however, I will not adopt it here.

4. Michael Nitsche defines five spaces in which video games and gameplay operate: rule-based space, mediated space, fictional space, play space and social space (2008: 15). Rule-based space consists of the underlying code on which the game runs, while mediated space encompasses the game's actual audio-visual and tactile presentation to the player; the three other spaces correspond to the player's imagination, the physical/real space, and interactions between multiple players, respectively. Nitsche is mainly focused on the screen in his treatment of these spaces, but we can expand this framework to include audio and other components as well.

5. Forces external to the composer introduce indeterminacy in non-modular situations as well, of course. Performers of traditional concert music, for instance, produce different-sounding instances of a given piece with every performance, and listeners interpret a single performance in a multitude of ways. Modularity, however, expands the degree to which participants other than the composer may affect the sound and shape of the music while still adhering to the composer's instructions.

6. Systems that tend towards creator control often correspond to what Saunders has called a "closed" modular structure, where limited flexibility in assembly yields a finite number of possible results, as opposed to the infinite possibilities of "open" structures (2008: 156–58). Similarly, Robert Zierolf describes modular systems with a finite number of realizations as containing "statistically limited openness", the opposite of which is "ultimate" or "infinite openness" (1983: 103–104, 112). Unlike Saunders's and Zierolf's binary views of indeterminacy, the current conception of a continuum between creator control and non-control facilitates a more nuanced treatment of modular music and its various aesthetics and practices.

7. Michael Nyman provides a nuanced distinction between "avant-garde" and "experimental" music, separating Boulez and Stockhausen, for example, from John Cage, based on these composers' views of their music and musical traditions (1999: 1–31).

8. For more on Boulez's relationship to and control over indeterminacy in the *Third Piano Sonata*, see Trenkamp, 1976 and Walters, 2003.

9. For more on the choices that individual performers have made across the performance history of Boulez's *Third Piano Sonata* – with an eye to how these choices intersect with issues of composer control and service of the work – see O'Hagan, 1997: 1–42.

10. Pamala Quist attributes this desire to Brown's experience with improvisation and jazz (1984: 11). In pieces where the conductor is the assembler, Clemens Gresser argues that this participant becomes "an extension of the composer" (2007: 380).

11. Cage also used charts and chance to determine other qualities in this music, such as dynamics and tempo, and his system included a means by which modules in the chart could be swapped for new ones, again depending on chance. For a detailed examination of Cage's compositional process in *Music of Changes*, see Pritchett, 1988.

12. For more on Boulez's rejection specifically of Cage's use of chance, see Piencikowski 2002: 51–55. In an interview in 2006, Boulez clarified his perceived relationship with Brown's music in a more diplomatic manner: "Earle and I both evolved in mostly the same direction: the composer must always be present in his music and his guidelines must be precise. Our differences are mainly in how 'open' a work could be without giving up control as a composer" (2007: 339).

13. Brown, for example, in a letter in 1970, stated emphatically: "My 'open-form' work is not to *evade* compositional responsibility!!!" (quoted in Dubinets, 2007: 417).

14. See, for example, Saunders's language about his own modular work (2008: 172).

15. Pritchett describes the score in Cage's pieces in this way: "In chance composition it is a randomly derived product of a system designed by the composer; it is a *result* of his work rather than the work itself" (1988: 7, emphasis original).

16. Thomas de Lio connects this expanded concept of the musical work to wider contemporary trends in art: "Thus, recent concepts of structure have extended the traditional view of the fixed art object to include, as active ingredients in the very structure of the work itself, all the activities of either a perceptual or constructive nature invoked by the artist in the course of its creation" (1981: 528).

17. Although indeterminacy is important in game music, issues of composer control versus non-control arise. Composer Leonard Paul points to several negative aspects of game music indeterminacy from the composer's point of view, including one example of a game's design in which the composers "simply hoped" that the resulting soundtrack (assembled based on the player's actions) would be something they, the composers, wanted (2013: 78).

18. In making this distinction, I am assuming that art music is typically performed for someone else (an audience of people separate from the active performer), whereas video games are more typically played for the player him- or herself. This is not always the case, of course; a performer of art music may play the

music alone, and gameplay is sometimes performed for an audience other than just the active player(s).

19. Karen Collins puts it this way: "While [game players] are still, in a sense, the receiver of the end sound signal, they are also partly the transmitter of that signal, playing an active role in the triggering and timing of these audio events" (2008: 3).

20. *Ocarina of Time*'s composer Koji Kondo explains his use of randomization in this way: "I thought about what I could do to have different music playing whenever you listened to it, and eventually I created several eight-measure 'components' to play randomly" (Iwata, 2011).

21. There is also the question of how much choice a player actually has when playing a game, and how much of the player's actions result from the execution of ludic rules. For more on player choice and control, see Cheng, 2014.

22. For more on usability and game audio, see Jørgensen, 2009.

23. Cage has put it this way: "A 'mistake' is beside the point, for once anything happens it authentically is" (1973: 59).

24. For more on the smoothness aesthetic in silent film music, see Prendergast, 1992: 11–12; Altman, 2004: 261–63. For more on issues of smoothness in modular music accompanying live performance, see Paul, 2012.

25. For more on the effects of smoothness and disjunction in video game music, see Medina-Gray, 2014.

26. This lessens the amount of musical content both that a composer needs to write and that a game needs to store in its memory. Data storage constraints are much less severe in more recent video game systems than they were in earlier, less technologically advanced devices, but this is still an important consideration. For a detailed discussion of technological limitations in early video games, see Collins, 2008: 39–58.

27. Zierolf states this position most strongly: "The theorist must, in either case, dismiss all existing Western methodology" (1983: 147). Without adopting Zierolf's extreme position – since video game music can respond well at least in part to existing analytical methods regarding harmony, melody and other familiar components – new methodology and new viewpoints that account for the indeterminate aspects of modular music are undoubtedly important.

28. Similarly, Granat – in emphasizing the performer's relative lack of freedom in Boulez's *Third Piano Sonata* – argues that the analytical focus here should be not on "the performance of the work" but rather on "the work itself" (2002: 42). Zierolf also states: "I suppose a somewhat traditional analysis of any particular performance of an indeterminate piece might be interesting, but it would certainly not lead to a comprehensive theory of indeterminate form" (1983: 130).

29. Zach Whalen has criticized such a focus on an arbitrarily singular musical output of gameplay – especially when divorced from active gameplay as if from the point of view of a listener separate from the player – as closing off the "gameness" of the game (2007: 74). Steven Beverburg Reale has also highlighted the limited

relevance of transcribing and analysing a singular musical result from a game's indeterminate system (2014: 93).

30. I have attempted to do just this in my own analytical approach to this music. See Medina-Gray, 2014.

## References

Altman, R. (2004) *Silent Film Sound*. New York: Columbia University Press.
Bakker, J. I. and T. R. A. Bakker (2006) "The Club DJ: A Semiotic and Interactionist Analysis." *Symbolic Interaction* 29/1: 71–82.
Berndt, A. (2009) "Musical Nonlinearity in Interactive Narrative Environments." In *Proceedings of the International Computer Music Conference (ICMC)*, pp. 355–58. Ann Arbor, MI: University of Michigan.
Bessell, D. (2002) "What's That Funny Noise? An Examination of the Role of Music in *Cool Boarders 2, Alien Trilogy* and *Medievil 2*." In *ScreenPlay: Cinema/videogames/interfaces*, edited by G. King and T. Krzywinska, pp. 136–44. London: Wallflower Press.
Boulez, P. (1963) "Sonate, Que Me Veux-Tu?" Trans. D. Noakes and P. Jacobs. *Perspectives of New Music* 1/2: 32–44.
Boulez, P. (1991) "Alea." In *Stocktakings from an Apprenticeship*. Trans. S. Walsh, pp. 26–38. Oxford: Oxford University Press.
Boulez, P. (2007) ". . . 'Ouvert', Encore . . ." *Contemporary Music Review* 26, no. 3/4: 339–40.
Brown, E. (1975) *Twentyfive Pages: For 1 to 25 Pianos*. Toronto: Universal Edition.
Brown, E. (1999) "Transformations and Developments of a Radical Aesthetic." *Current Musicology* 67–68: 39–57.
Butler, M. J. (2006) *Unlocking the Groove: Rhythm, Meter, and Musical Design in Electronic Dance Music*. Bloomington: Indiana University Press.
Cage, J. (1973) *Silence: Lectures and Writings*. Middletown, CT: Wesleyan University Press.
Cheng, W. (2014) *Sound Play: Video Games and the Musical Imagination*. New York: Oxford University Press.
Childs, IV, G. W. (2007) *Creating Music and Sound for Games*. Boston: Thomson Course Technology PTR.
Collins, K. (2008) *Game Sound: An Introduction to the History, Theory, and Practice of Video Game Music and Sound Design*. Cambridge, MA: MIT Press.
De Lio, T. (1981) "Structural Pluralism: Some Observations on the Nature of Open Structures in the Music and Visual Arts of the Twentieth Century." *Musical Quarterly* 67/4: 527–43.
Dubinets, E. (2007) "Between Mobility and Stability: Earle Brown's Compositional Process." *Contemporary Music Review* 26, no. 3/4: 409–426.
Eco, U. (1989) *The Open Work*. Trans. A. Cancogni. Cambridge, MA: Harvard University Press.
Granat, Z. (2002) "Open Form and the 'Work-Concept': Notions of the Musical Work after Serialism." PhD dissertation, Boston University.
Gresser, C. (2007) "Earle Brown's 'Creative Ambiguity' and Ideas of Co-Creatorship in Selected Works." *Contemporary Music Review* 26, no. 3/4: 377–94.

Hadley, D. (1993) "'Ride the Rhythm': Two Approaches to DJ Practice." *Journal of Popular Music Studies* 5: 58–67.

Hanninen, D. A. (2004) "Associative Sets, Categories, and Music Analysis." *Journal of Music Theory* 48/2: 147–218.

Iwata, S. (2011) "Iwata Asks: The Legend of Zelda: Ocarina of Time 3D." *Iwata Asks.* http://iwataasks.nintendo.com/interviews/#/3ds/zelda-ocarina-of-time/0/1 (accessed December 14, 2014).

Jørgensen, K. (2009) *A Comprehensive Study of Sound in Computer Games: How Audio Affects Player Action.* Lewiston, NY: Edwin Mellen Press.

Kaae, J. (2008) "Theoretical Approaches to Composing Dynamic Music for Video Games." In *From Pac-Man to Pop Music: Interactive Audio in Games and New Media,* edited by K. Collins, pp. 75–92. Burlington, VT: Ashgate.

Manovich, L. (2001) *The Language of New Media.* Cambridge, MA: MIT Press.

Marks, A. (2009) *The Complete Guide to Game Audio: For Composers, Musicians, Sound Designers, Game Developers,* 2nd ed. New York: Focal Press.

Medina-Gray, E. (2014) "Modular Structure and Function in Early 21st-Century Video Game Music." PhD dissertation, Yale University.

Murray, J. (1997) *Hamlet on the Holodeck: The Future of Narrative in Cyberspace.* New York: The Free Press.

Nitsche, M. (2008) *Video Game Spaces: Image, Play, and Structure in 3D Game Worlds.* Cambridge, MA: MIT Press.

Nyman, M. (1999) *Experimental Music: Cage and Beyond,* 2nd ed. Cambridge: Cambridge University Press.

O'Hagan, P. (1997) "Pierre Boulez: 'Sonate, Que Me Veux-Tu?' An Investigation of the Manuscript Sources in Relation to the Third Sonata." PhD dissertation, University of Surrey.

Paul, L. A. H. (2012) "Sonic Vegas: Live Virtuality and the Cirque Du Soleil." PhD dissertation, Yale University.

Paul, L. J. (2013) "Droppin' Science: Video Game Audio Breakdown." In *Music and Game: Perspectives on a Popular Alliance,* edited by P. Moormann, pp. 63–80. Wiesbaden: Springer VS.

Piencikowski, R. (2002) ". . . Iacta Est." In *Correspondance et Documents,* edited by R. Piencikowski and J.-J. Nattiez, new edition, pp. 41–60. Mainz: Schott.

Prendergast, R. M. (1992) *Film Music: A Neglected Art. A Critical Study of Music in Films,* 2nd ed. New York: W. W. Norton & Company.

Pritchett, J. W. (1988) "The Development of Chance Techniques in the Music of John Cage, 1950–1956." PhD dissertation, New York University.

Quist, P. L. (1984) "Indeterminate Form in the Work of Earle Brown." DMA dissertation, Peabody Institute, The Johns Hopkins University.

Reale, S. B. (2014) "Transcribing Musical Worlds; or, Is *L.A. Noire* a Music Game?" In *Music in Videogames: Studying Play,* edited by K. J. Donnelly, W. Gibbons and N. Lerner, pp. 78–103. New York: Routledge.

Saunders, J. (2008) "Modular Music." *Perspectives of New Music* 46/1: 152–93.

Trenkamp, A. (1976) "The Concept of 'Alea' in Boulez's 'Constellation-Miroir'." *Music and Letters* 57/1: 1–10.

Walters, D. (2003) "Boulez and the Concept of Chance." *Ex Tempore: A Journal of Compositional and Theoretical Research in Music* 11/2: 1–25.

Whalen, Z. (2007) "Case Study: Film Music vs. Video-Game Music: The Case of Silent Hill." In *Music, Sound and Multimedia: From the Live to the Virtual*, edited by J. Sexton, pp. 68–81. Edinburgh: Edinburgh University Press.

Zierolf, R. (1983) "Indeterminacy in Musical Form." PhD dissertation, University of Cincinnati.

# 5 Suture and Peritexts
## Music Beyond Gameplay and Diegesis

*Michiel Kamp*[1]

When do we begin playing a video game? Or for that matter, when do we begin watching a film or reading a book? Chapter one, first sentence? The first establishing shot, or the musical interlude that precedes it in the dark of the cinema? The moment in a game when we see a familiar camera angle and interface elements (health bar, minimap, etc.) and we can start controlling our character or manipulating the playing field? For some of these media, it is harder to say where they begin than others. A book often has a clear demarcation of its text: its cover, chapter titles, white pages, and so on. Many modern films blur these boundaries, slowly fading in their diegeses through sound advances, introductory scenes that overlap with the title credits, and a musical score that "bathes" the audience with the first signs of a narrative, often before the first shots: the Christmas bells of *Home Alone* (1990), the needle dropping on vinyl in *High Fidelity* (2000), or the lone trumpet of *The Godfather* (1972). With video games, there is an additional movement from non-interactive introductory cutscenes (often imitating film's gradual introduction of its diegesis) to the point where controls are handed over to the player: gameplay. But even before these cutscenes there are title menus and start screens, and diegetic gameplay can be – and sometimes has to be – interrupted by pause menus, inventory screens, loading a new level, or the death of a player's avatar. In many games, the amount of material that surrounds diegetic gameplay seems much greater and more rigidly demarcated than in films, closer to a book's white pages, chapter headers and front matter.

In this chapter, I am interested in the role music plays in everything leading up to and surrounding those parts of the game that we actually play. I will begin by introducing Gérard Genette's concepts of paratext and particularly the "peritext" (1997), which will help categorize and contextualize those video game domains beyond gameplay and diegesis. One of the few elements of a game that can play a part in both peritextual and textual (that is, gameplay and diegesis) domains is the nondiegetic musical soundtrack. I want to offer an account of music as overarching a game in its totality, in the hopes of both broadening our understanding of the unique contribution of music to games, and of how game music relates to music in other audiovisual media. Apart from considering music's peritextual functions – particularly those identified by Philip Tagg (1979) for television music – I will also consider its "suturing" functions, a term borrowed from Claudia Gorbman's (1987) theory of film music. Following a discussion of peritexts and suture in relation to video games as well as a preliminary categorization of peritextual situations, I will present three case studies that exemplify music's role beyond gameplay and diegesis. The first, dealing with the event of an avatar's death in three platform games, is concerned primarily with music's suturing functions; the second, a discussion of *Max Payne*'s menu theme (2001), proposes how to interpret music in a peritext that can be turned to at any moment, occupying no "fixed" place in a game's overall structure; finally I will discuss how music, during something as incidental and unwanted as a loading screen, can achieve such an iconic status as that of *Battlefield 1942* (2002).

## Video Game Paratexts

Where do games begin and end, and where does game music begin and end? Isabella van Elferen suggests that music has the unique ability to "expand the magic circle, as far as musical associativity goes: almost infinitely" (2011: 35).[2] She gives the example of the *Guitar Hero* series (2005–), wherein our physical bodies and living room environment become subsumed into musical gameplay. We can translate this spatial extension of game-musical experience into the living room to a temporal extension: *when* does game music begin and end? It is too reductive to state that game music only begins to matter with gameplay – the moment when we start moving sticks and pushing buttons and plotting to overcome the challenges that a video game poses us. It might even be too reductive to state that music only begins to be significant when we boot up the game. Psychologically we could think of musical mood regulation as an entry into a competitive mindset, to "get into the mood" (cf. DeNora, 2000), or of "affiliating identifications" (Kassabian, 2001) we form with a licensed soundtrack, based on connotations with musical encounters outside the game.

Particularly for a narratological approach to games, which defines its objects of study as clearly demarcated texts, these vague boundaries pose methodological problems. One way to deal with this is to chart the textual boundaries themselves. This is exactly what Gérard Genette's *Paratexts: Thresholds of Interpretation* (1997) sets out to do. Genette meticulously categorizes what he calls the "paratextual" elements of books: "accompanying productions" that "surround and extend" a text, "precisely in order to present it" (p. 1). Literary paratexts include titles and prefaces, but also author interviews and promotional materials. A paratext acts as a zone or "threshold" of transition and "transaction", which is "at the service of a better reception for the text and a more pertinent reading of it (more pertinent, of course, in the eyes of the author and his allies)" (1997: 2). This suggests a double role of clarifying and guiding the audience's understanding of a text, which will form the basis of my investigations below. Genette also makes a broad distinction between "peritexts" and "epitexts". The former includes all those materials that surround and are attached to the text itself: a book's cover and index for instance; the latter includes those texts "not materially appended to the text within the same volume but circulating, as it were, freely, in a virtually limitless physical and social space" (1997: 344), such as advertisements and reviews.

While Genette focuses solely on physical books, others have adopted his terminology for other media. Jonathan Gray argues that "films and television programs often begin long before we actively seek them out" (2010: 47), with film trailers, posters and ad campaigns. These epitexts introduce new story worlds, create and perpetuate intertextuality through genre conventions, and celebrate their star actors.[3] So when a television series' intro starts, or the Universal logo or the Twentieth-Century Fox fanfare appears in the cinema – all peritexts themselves, accompanied by what Guido Heldt calls "extrafictional music" (2013: 26) – we have already been introduced to and immersed into the text that is about to unfold. Steven Jones warns against defining paratextuality as anything more striated than a "continuum of 'threshold' effects active in any textual or other expressive object with a life in the world" (2008: 25), citing blurbs on dust jackets as both belonging to a book's physical peritext and existing in the larger epitextual world of criticism. He goes further to suggest that distinctions between peritext and epitext "are clearer when it comes to codex books of the modern era than they are for more complex multi-media productions" (2008: 25, n. 11), echoing Peter Lunenfeld's earlier remarks that "the rigid demarcations between formerly discrete texts become fluid liminal zones" (2000: 15) in new media. Jones himself defines video game paratexts such as "packaging, game guides, collectible objects, [and] online stats" as "a collective and *potential* reality, a transmedia, multidimensional grid of possibilities surrounding any given game" (2008: 10). Mia Consalvo, on the other hand, suggests that "[p]aratexts are . . . anything but peripheral, and they grow more integral to the game industry and player community with every year" (2007: 182).

Game music, too, is subject to this paratextual fluidity. We can think of the licensed menu music in EA Sports games such as the *FIFA* and *Madden* series as crossing over from its peritextual domain into the game's epitext. Just as films with compiled scores work because of "histories forged outside the film scene" (Kassabian, 2001: 3), these games work because of the associations and encounters we have with their pop songs outside the game. Through these associations, the world of sports continues even off the pitch – in the menu screens and beyond – through music that we know and love, and now come to associate with the games and the sports they represent. By employing popular music in the game that is receiving radio play and attention regardless of the publisher's input, Electronic Arts can create epitexts where there are none, allowing their games to "begin long before we actively seek them out" (Gray, 2010: 47) without having to resort to (equally) expensive ad campaigns. It seems that there is truly nothing outside the paratext, to paraphrase Jacques Derrida (1997: 158).

## Between Gameplay and Diegesis: Peritextual Domains

In the rest of this chapter, my interests will primarily lie with peritextual music, but the fluid boundaries within which it exists are important to keep in mind. Having moved from outside text to epitext, and from epitext to peritext, leaves the question of the relation of peritext to text. What really *is* the game-text? Michael Hancock (2014) argues that "every feature a sandbox game adds, every mini-map icon, crafting system, and side quest" is a peritext that "contributes to the notion that the game is vast and therefore valuable". Robert Yang (2013) goes even further than that, suggesting that the colours and materials of certain wall panels in *Portal* are essentially paratextual, affording no direct interaction that will help the player progress through the game, comparing them to font types and colours in books. Both Hancock's and Yang's arguments point towards a particular problem with textuality in video games, addressed in detail by Jesper Juul in his book *Half-Real* (2005). As rule systems represented through fictional elements, one has to address what "reading" a video game entails. If reading is equivalent to *playing* a game, then the actual text only begins when we start to interact with the game in order to overcome its challenges and reach its goals (what I will call the moment of "gameplay"). That means that in the case of narrative games that feature diegetic story worlds (e.g. *Zelda* or the games I will discuss in more detail below), the text is more narrowly defined than in, for instance, narrative films. An introductory cutscene that starts out a level would not be part of the game-text, but part of its peritext.

The concepts of gameplay and diegesis complicate paratextuality in video games. Figure 5.1 represents an attempt to categorize these elements into four temporally distinct situations. This means that one cannot experience both text and peritext at the same time, which circumvents the problem of the co-occurrence of gameplay and non-gameplay elements (e.g. *Portal*'s wall panels) and diegetic and nondiegetic elements (e.g. music) – one finds oneself either in a text *or* in a peritext.[4] However, that still leaves the question of

|  | DIEGETIC | NONDIEGETIC |
|---|---|---|
| GAMEPLAY | Walking through corridors, conversing with characters, fighting enemies | Pausing and perusing one's inventory, dying and restarting a level |
| NON-GAMEPLAY | Watching cutscenes | Navigating game menus, waiting at loading screens, watching credits |

Figure 5.1: Textual and peritextual situations in video games

which situations are peritextual. Following Hancock and Yang, everything in the bottom row would be a peritext; following cinematic or literary logic, everything in the right column would be a peritext. It seems that only diegetic gameplay is indisputably textual, surrounded by liminal zones (cutscenes, death) and a clear peritextual boundary (menu screens and loading screens). In what I will argue next, I will turn towards our experience of *structure* as an essential determinant of text and peritext – the way we move between these zones from boundary to text and back when playing a game. In doing so I will create a space for music to play a central role in peritextuality.

## Suturing and Semiotic Functions

In *The Medium of the Video Game* (2001), Mark J. P. Wolf calls non-gameplay sequences (which include cutscenes, player death, menus, etc.) "interludes". He compares them to "breathers" or "slow" scenes in action films such as *Raiders of the Lost Ark* (1981):

> Just as slower scenes are often preceded by character's deaths in movies, there are typically breaks in the action between a player-character's "lives". These breaks are typically filled with short, animated death sequences ... [providing] a brief moment's rest while holding the player's attention and keeping the player involved in the game. (Wolf, 2001: 83-84)

Other examples of interludes come "after successfully completing a certain objective or before advancing to a new area or 'level' of a game. In CD-ROM games like *Tomb Raider* (1996), these pauses usually contain short animated scenes" (Wolf, 2001: 84), which are now generally called cutscenes. For Wolf, interludes can be interactive as well, but there is "often no time pressure" (ibid.). Examples of these are menus, and as Figure 5.1 suggests, these can be both gameplay related (in the case of inventory screens) and non-gameplay related (in the case of options menus).

Considering our experience of a game in terms of a temporal ebb and flow of periods of intensity and rest on the one hand, and moments of significance against periods of insignificance on the other hand, allows us to compare games to more linear phenomena such as films and music. Michel Chion (1994) invites us to look at audiovisual relations in terms of overlapping lines and points of synchronization. In film music, sudden stinger chords can draw attention to a visual event, and continuous music can cover up sudden visual changes. Claudia Gorbman (1987) calls this latter process musical "suture" (or "bonding"), a psychoanalytical concept that explains why the continuous wall-to-wall music of classic Hollywood films can bathe spectators in a pre-Oedipal "warm bath" (p. 62) to "glue them to the screen" (p. 58). Its flowing melodic lines and long harmonic progressions arch over "cracks" in the diegesis such as cuts and silences in the soundtrack, "smoothing" over them and suturing them together. Elizabeth Medina-Gray finds the same "aesthetic of smoothness" in video game music composition elsewhere in this volume, wherein separate modules or cues are supposed to blend into one another as seamlessly as possible. This smoothness or suture can extend to cover both gaps in the diegesis and gaps in the gameplay, but interruptions can also highlight and emphasize these gaps, as my case studies will show.

Gorbman finds a second, semiotic function of film music called "anchorage". She suggests that film music "throws a net around the floating visual signifier, assur[ing] the viewer of a safely channelled signified" (1987: 58). Video game music, too, often provides certainty about the nature of a situation to the player: low, dissonant quavers in *The Legend of Zelda: Ocarina of Time* (1998) render the threat that the game's protagonist Link encounters unambiguous. At the same time, this "danger state" music acts as a signal, calling players to act in certain ways (see Whalen, 2004). This signalling function of video game music is quite similar to the hailing or *reveille* functions of television music that Ronald Rodman (2010) and Philip Tagg (1979) identify, which "attract the attention of potential listeners to the fact that something (undefined) new is going to be presented" (Tagg quoted in Lerner, 2013: 332). If I am making tea in the kitchen and a slap bass riff from *Seinfeld* (1989) warns me that the commercials are over and the episode is about to continue, the semiotic process whereby the music functions is very similar to the dissonant quavers in *Zelda* that signal the intentions and presence of creatures in the game world. Neil Lerner (2013) finds this *reveille* function in the introductory fanfares of classic arcade games such as *Galaxian* (1979) and *Pac-Man* (1980). In noisy arcades, these short but distinctive musical cues could help attract the attention – and more importantly coins – of players (see also Collins, 2008: 7-8). We could say that this is also a structuring function of peritextual music: a *reveille* as an incipit for the gaming experience.

Semiotics and suturing can take different shapes in peritextual music. Suture does not work solely through diegesis-overlapping melodic and harmonic lines, and semiotics does not solely work through *reveilles* and other signals. Lerner, for instance, also notes the "preparatory function" of menu music that precedes gameplay, giving some indication of the "general mood found in the subsequent presentation" (Tagg quoted in Lerner, 2013: 332). This can be conceived of as both a semiotic and suturing function: either signalling a certain mood of the game, or inducing a certain mood in the player, immersing them in the game's gameplay and diegesis much like films' musical advances I mentioned in my introduction. Guido Heldt (2013) mentions the "transitional nature of title sequences" in films, whereby peritextual elements (such as credits and title lettering) are layered over textual elements as "part of a process that leads into the fiction" (p. 25). Production and distribution company logos and their extrafictional music has a "ritualistic" aspect to it, "delimiting a space for the fiction by pointing out its made-ness" (p. 26). Here, too, there is a double suturing (or rather non-suturing) semiotic role in creating structure: a clear demarcation of the outside world through extrafictional musical peritexts. When William Gibbons argues that "many developers use popular music as a way to mask the 'boring elements of a title'" (2011) such as the aforementioned licensed music that plays the menus of EA Sports titles, this too can be considered a kind of suture. Even though the music does not continue from match to menu, it takes over the level of excitement during a match, not just by virtue of its upbeat tempos, but also by virtue of its epitextual connotations. The rest of this chapter is devoted to a series of in-depth case studies that move from simple suture – music's relation to death in platform games – to more complex peritextual structures and functions wherein suture and semiotics are interwoven – the iconic status of menu music and loading screen music in *Max Payne* and *Battlefield 1942* respectively.

## Death and Diegesis in Platform Games

One consequence of the fact that games are part rules, part fiction, according to Juul, is that their diegesis does not have to be "consistent" or "coherent" in the same way as a (Hollywood) film is. The question "Why does Mario have three lives?" (2005: 123) does not require an explanation in the story of *Super Mario Bros.* (1985), because it makes sense in terms of its gameplay. (In Figure 5.1, I classify a player avatar's death in the game as a nondiegetic gameplay situation for this reason: while one is usually not interacting when one's avatar dies, as a fail state, death is a consequence of gameplay actions and part of the game's rules.) This means that *Mario*'s diegesis can be interrupted and reset whenever Mario dies, making for gaps that can be filled in by peritextual audio and visuals. It also means that music's behaviour in and around death plays an important part in structuring one's experience of a video game. In what follows, I compare three platform games that implement "death music" in different ways.

In an earlier study of *Super Mario Bros.* (henceforth *Mario*), I argued that its musical implementation and structure serve to highlight the experience of failure and repetition in the game (Kamp, 2014). For the central place in game music history and video game nostalgia that its soundtrack enjoys, *Mario* has a distinct lack of music in most of its nondiegetic, non-gameplay sections, and particularly the silence in its title menu stands out.[5] There is no musical introduction, no *reveille* or preparatory function to be heard; the music does not start playing until the player loads up the first level. *Mario*'s famous "Overworld theme" then starts with an introductory measure and loops until the player either successfully completes the level or enters a different area, picks up a power-up, or Mario dies. When falling into a pit or getting hit by an enemy, the game engine abruptly stops whichever theme is playing with a short dissonant sound and an equally short pause, followed by a "death sound", a four-bar $V^7$-I cadence. The black screen that introduces the level and reminds the player how many lives Mario has left comes up in silence, after which the level is reloaded and the Overworld theme starts from the beginning. When Mario dies without having any lives left, the game-over screen is shown, accompanied by a short game-over cadence that differs from the death sound through its use of a more "jazzy" IV-IIb-I progression. The fact that the only nondiegetic, non-gameplay music – in effect, the only musical peritext in *Mario* – plays over the game-over screen serves to emphasize the event of failure. But the musical structure goes further than that: through aligning the presence and absence of music and its introduction-loop-cadence form with Mario's "lifespan," the music makes the repetition of death and restart stand out to the player. The particular musical structure of *Mario* became a standard for subsequent games, with many platform games of the 8-bit and 16-bit console generations (i.e. the NES, Sega Genesis and SNES) adopting this introduction-loop-cadence structure.[6]

Recent years have seen a revival of the classic 2D platform genre to which *Mario* belongs, especially with the rise in popularity of cheaper downloadable games through online services such as Xbox Live Arcade and Steam. Many of these games have a certain self-awareness to them, such as *Super Meat Boy* (2010) and the puzzle platform game *Braid* (2008). Both games play with the conventions of *Mario* in particular, each in their own way. *Super Meat Boy*, as the title suggests, plays specifically with the difficulty of *Mario* and the event of death and restart. Even when compared with 1980s platformers, *Meat Boy* is extraordinarily difficult, requiring precise timing and control input from the player – but even then, dying over and over again is seemingly inevitable. Meat Boy's numerous deaths, represented as comical and gruesome at the same time through an overly squishy, meaty sound and blood splattering across the ground, are recorded by the game and played back (all at once) after the player completes a level. Although – unlike in *Mario* – death is presented so abruptly and violently to the player, the game "brushes over" the actual nondiegetic process of dying and restarting the level. There is no black screen, and most importantly, the music continues playing even when Meat Boy dies or completes a level.[7]

We can hear numerous similarities in *Super Meat Boy* to classic platform games, but no explicit adherence to any 8-bit or 16-bit era instrumentation. For instance, while featuring a relatively high fidelity sound, the menu music consists of an extremely short loop that foregrounds the technological restrictions of older games. Moreover, while I navigate the game's various menu screens, the music keeps changing between sharply contrasting cues with little in the way of transitions. This "crudeness" is further enhanced by the heavily distorted guitars, pronounced beats and (varying) high tempi. But when the player finally enters the game – diegetic gameplay – the music, while keeping its instrumentation and high tempo, features a longer loop that continues until the player exits to the menu screens or reaches a final "boss stage" after a number of levels.[8] The continuous quality of the music has a crudeness similar to that of the menu music, but rather than referring to older platform games that *did* have a musical structure aligned with avatar deaths, it serves to smooth over the cracks in the diegesis caused by Meat Boy's deaths and the player's failures. *Super Meat Boy*'s suturing soundtrack, in contrast to *Mario*'s, affords a more relaxing experience, with less pressure not to make mistakes: it allows a more trial-and-error-based approach to its obstacles, and the music structures the gameplay accordingly.

The music of *Braid* could not be more different from that of *Super Meat Boy* in both sound and structure. Where *Meat Boy*'s soundtrack consists of up-tempo electronic music with a heavy rock beat, distorted guitar sounds, and sometimes even an orchestral accompaniment to give it a sense of grandeur, *Braid*'s music is more intimate, folksy and pastoral. The instrumentation consists mainly of strings, harps and acoustic guitars that play simple mid-tempo melodies, often in 3/4 time.[9] There is less variation as well: the soundtrack consists of just eight cues (one of which, "Maenam", exclusively plays in the game's menus) that are repeated throughout the 37 levels. In broad terms, the musical structure is aligned with the start and end of each level, with soft transitions between the cues – unless the next level features the same cue, in which case the music continues playing. *Braid*'s references to *Mario* are more visual and narrative than auditory. The player's avatar, Tim, is on a quest to rescue a princess, and at the end of each set of stages he encounters a creature that tells him the princess is "in another castle", or a self-conscious variation thereof. Tim can jump on the heads of enemies to kill them, and when he dies, he falls off the stage like Mario. However, *Braid*'s unique gameplay mechanic revolves around the rewinding of time, and when Tim dies, the whole game stops abruptly, including the music. The level does not restart: instead the player is asked to rewind time and try another course of action. Whenever time is rewound, the music plays in reverse as well. This dramatically alters the player's perception of the music and the musical structure of the game. As the most prevalent and continuous sound in the game, the music draws attention to the variable flow of time while, conversely, interacting with the time mechanic draws attention to the music. The two combined give the suggestion that time in *Braid* is already written and set in stone, so that the player can move around on the timeline and mould it like a tape recording.

Like *Meat Boy*, *Braid* plays down the adverse effects of death, but in a different way. Where *Meat Boy* smooths over the gap in the diegesis that is so prevalent in *Mario*, in *Braid* there is no gap, the diegesis is just halted. And even though there is no death cadence, music does play a role in how we experience death. The music that accompanies the diegesis has very few "sharp edges" to its structure: there are soft transitions between the cues, and the cues themselves have no strong beats or sudden melodic or harmonic leaps. The only times when the music abruptly changes direction are when Tim dies and when the player intervenes in the diegesis by rewinding time. Death is accompanied by a dissonant sound similar to that of Mario's death, followed by abrupt silence. As in *Mario*, this aligns *Braid*'s music directly with Tim's lifespan and the diegesis. The flow of time, diegesis and gameplay become synonymous with the continuation of the music, and when the music is abruptly stopped due to Tim's death it will increase the severity of this event.

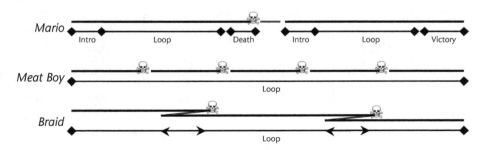

*Figure 5.2* A "timescape" of *Super Mario Bros.*, *Super Meat Boy* and *Braid*

The relation of music to death and diegesis in *Super Mario Bros.*, *Super Meat Boy* and *Braid* can be represented in a "timescape" (see Figure 5.2), where the top lines represent the diegesis (gaps for black screens or cuts, double lines for nondiegetic elements) and the bottom lines the presence of music. As an important obstacle in the player's path to complete a game's goals, the way death is represented affects how the player experiences the flow of gameplay. Musical suturing can de-emphasize the harshness of obstacles and fail states, just as its absence can highlight them.

### *Max Payne*'s Menu Music: *Reveille* or Respite?

The third-person shooter *Max Payne* presents itself as a cinematic experience, drawing on neo-noir and "heroic bloodshed" films.[10] Its gruff, down-on-his-luck male protagonist, Max, provides a cynical voiceover reminiscent of films such as *Double Indemnity* (1944) and *Sunset Blvd.* (1950). At the same time, its primary gameplay mechanic, "bullet time", has the player slowing the action down to a crawl at the press of a button, diving through the air and shooting two Beretta pistols in a manner reminiscent of John Woo's films. Its musical soundtrack cannot straightforwardly be traced back to these films, however, missing the jazz harmonies emblematic of film noir or the bittersweet piano ballads that contrast so sharply with the exaggerated violence of *The Killer* (1989). Instead, we need to look at noir beyond cinema, something the comic-book styled exposition sections of the game and the various references to television shows like *Twin Peaks* (1990-91) hint towards. The game's main theme, written by Kärtsy Hatakka and Kimmo Kajasto and first fully presented in its title menu, is more reminiscent of television title sequences than of film scores as well, due to its synth-heavy instrumentation and clearly demarcated structure. A *sforzando* low C on a piano sets up a slow-paced, triple metre accompaniment (further consisting of subdued synthesizer percussion, slowly moving airy synth-pad harmonies, and the twangy guitar from the intro video) for a C-minor piano melody. The melody starts from C4 and works its way up the octave to C5 and down again, only to land on a prominent leading tone B3 on the beat, having to circle around to end up back on C4. This structure allows the melody to revolve and repeat, building up by doubling at the octave, and later, after a B-section, bringing in more instruments (synth strings and a military snare drum). This ABA structure repeats and further intensifies over a span of over three minutes before quieting down, ending on the same low C that the cue began with.

To say that when starting up the game I am "greeted" by the menu screen and its theme, however, is wrong. The menu has no *reveille* function like that of television intros or arcade games, since it does not need to draw my attention in a busy arcade (Collins, 2008) or in the flow of television prime time (Williams, 1974); the game already announced itself to me through the epitexts that drew me to buy it: box art, (p)reviews in the gaming press, advertising posters, and so on. Moreover, the menu is preceded by a short video and a silent loading screen. The video consists of two parts: a montage of short gameplay clips (a kind of preview of things to come) and the game's title, developer and producer logos. The montage follows the conventions of many film trailers: short action shots fading in and out from black, cut to the beat of the music. The music consists of the back and forth interplay between a distorted C3 on an electric guitar and the sound of a heartbeat. The heartbeat slowly speeds up (the shots remaining in sync with the heartbeat), while the tempo of the music stays the same, creating an increase in tension leading up to the title card. After that there is silence, punctuated by metallic sounds accompanying the developers' logos echoing throughout the black screen. In spite of the audiovisual increase in tension, the steady pulse and unchanging pitch of the music in combination with the lack of diegetic gunfire sounds create a certain distance from the action, like an anempathetic slow-motion action scene from a John Woo film. Because of this distance, the developer logos that follow are not so much moments of rest as they are further ominous signs that pierce the silence and darkness. The loading screen that follows, on the other hand, is completely silent: there is not even the echo or faint noise of the video that preceded it. This silence seems to interrupt the preceding silence, creating a moment of tension that is released when the title menu appears, accompanied by another C, this time a low C2 on a piano that sets the tone and harmony for the menu music.

The consequences of this introduction sequence are that the appearance of the title menu feels not so much as a beginning as a coming to rest or a moment of respite – respite from action that has not even started yet. While to a certain extent the menu music *does* have the same preparatory function that Tagg's television intros and Lerner's arcade game title fanfares have, it later loses this function when doubling as the game's pause menu. The player can access this menu at all times during the game by pressing the Escape button, and, as Wolf would say, there is no time or gameplay pressure to perform actions when doing so.[11] The question is what this means for the way we experience the menu's music. *Max Payne*'s menu theme can be distinguished from preparatory fanfares in two ways: (1) by virtue of its musical structure, a longer, cyclical ABABA form consisting of two melodic statements versus a single, two-bar melodic statement that is not repeated; (2) through its place in the structure of the game, the menu functioning both as a title screen and a pause menu rather than purely an introduction to the game. As we have already seen, these two features, musical structure and game-(peri)textual structure, interact: both the place of the menu in the peritexts leading up to and interrupting gameplay, and the harmonic and rhythmic relations of its music to the game's introduction serve to create a moment of respite.

At the same time, the menu music is the first full statement of the game's main theme, repeating it over and over again. While the theme has a clearly distinguishable melody that can be heard at various other points throughout the game, for instance during one of the first cutscenes, it often underscores Max's omnipresent voiceover in a "softer", less intrusive synth string timbre. One of the few instances we hear the theme with the same piano-led instrumentation as in the menu is when Max finds his murdered wife at the conclusion of the game's prologue. There, the theme serves to underline a pivotal moment in the game's narrative. By virtue of its musical, timbral qualities then, *Max Payne*'s menu music occupies a prominent position in the game, much like a symphony's main theme or a pop song's chorus. This is further supported by the repetitive and circular ABABA structure of the cue. One also needs to consider the menu's peritextual place in the game's structure, however, as a non-time-pressured interlude. In this context, we never quite feel like we "arrive" at the theme as we would in a song or symphony. Although its cue is almost four minutes long, one would rarely spend that long in the game's menus. Even though the theme will overlap excursions into options menus to, for instance, change audio and video settings for the game, chances are that one exits the menu before even the first few bars of the melody are heard in full. Throughout a session of playing *Max Payne* (that is, between every time the player starts and exits the game), the game will "save" the progress of the menu theme when the player navigates the menu. This means that when playing, we hear snippets of the theme, not having to hear the opening bars each time we pause the game. Again, we experience the theme as already happening, as if we walk into a room – or rather, a lobby – where the music is playing. The game's title menu and its music become almost literally a threshold, a liminal space between the outside world and the game world that can be crossed at any moment, but has to be crossed nonetheless. Even though we might only hear snippets of the *Max Payne* theme when passing through the menus, its iconic status rings through in both its first appearance and its subsequent moments of respite.

## *Battlefield 1942*'s Loading Screen Music: Iconic Anticipation

In the previous section, I argued that menu music occupies a complicated place in a video game's structure. A menu can be accessed at any point in time by players wishing to turn away from the game for a moment of respite or to adjust their settings. The indeterminate amount of time one spends in menus makes for a very particular kind of engagement with the music: one that is more akin to entering a chill-out room in a club than following or partaking in any narrative or ludic chain of events. A loading screen, while equally incidental to gameplay and diegesis, plays a completely different role in a game's structure. If peritexts are "thresholds" (to adopt Genette's term), then there is no greater or more unwanted threshold than a game's loading screen. Whereas title screens and pause menus can be voluntarily navigated to and away from, loading screens are inescapable, a "necessary evil". In an ideal world full of infinitely fast gaming platforms there would be none, and our experience of them can only be described as one of waiting. If menus are chill-out rooms, loading screens are elevators.[12] This means that while loading screens occupy the same non-gameplay, nondiegetic space in Figure 5.1 as menu screens, their music functions quite differently.

*Battlefield 1942* is a first-person shooter set in World War II with a focus on online multiplayer matches. Its selling point and most original gameplay feature was the size of its levels and the amount of players they could accommodate: two teams of up to thirty-two players can take control of vehicles or fight on foot to capture control points and win a match. The (at the time unprecedented) size and scope of the game had the drawback of requiring exceptionally powerful PC hardware. It also meant that a large amount of data had to be loaded for each match, which made for uncommonly long loading screens.[13] The loading screens for *BF1942* are a static affair: a small loading bar against a pre-rendered background image depicting a WWII battle scene related to the level. The loading screen for the level "Battle of Britain", for instance, shows a flight of German bombers amidst exploding flak. The most prominent feature, one could therefore say, is the musical cue that plays. Every loading screen features the same cue: a rousing ultra-military theme composed by Joel Eriksson that builds upon a single repeated motif, whose distinctive rhythm has become synonymous with the identity of the *Battlefield* series of games.[14] The motif borrows its syncopated 6/8 rhythm from Brad Fiedel's famous five-note *Terminator* (1986) theme, adding a sixth note on the fifth beat to "straighten out" the original's off-putting syncopation. Additionally substituting *Terminator*'s eerie metallic synthesized sounds (Collins, 2004) for snare drums and brass, *Battlefield*'s theme is made to sound like classic films that celebrate WWII heroics, such as *The Dirty Dozen* (1967) and *Battle of Britain* (1969).

To fully understand this theme's peritextual function one needs to consider it within the game's structure as a whole – both its musical structure and the functions of its different peritexts. Where *Mario*'s music almost completely coincides with its diegeses and – save for the game-over cadence – there is nothing but silence in its menu screens and other peritexts, the soundtrack of

*Battlefield 1942* works almost exactly the other way around. Nondiegetic music can exclusively be found in the game's menus, loading screens and victory/defeat screens. Since diegetic gameplay is a game's central text, it would be wrong to argue that the music in *Battlefield* somehow "highlights" or "emphasizes" the game's menus for the sake of the gameplay. Instead, a loading screen's experience is one of anticipation: impatiently watching the progress bar fill up. This experience is projected onto the way we hear the music, and the music readily accepts this role of ad hoc progress bar. As a consequence, what Nicholas Cook calls the "enabling similarity" (1998: 70) between the structure of the musical cue – the gradual addition of instruments to the repeated motif and the slowly developing solo trumpet melody – and our own anticipation bestows upon the music a preparatory function. This also means that any movement in the cue that counteracts this anticipatory quality, particularly the sudden return from its darker B section to its A section, is heard as a kind of ludo-musical dissonance (paraphrasing Clint Hocking's term "ludonarrative dissonance", 2007): have we outstayed our welcome in the loading screen? Was the match supposed to have started already?

While the preparatory function of the loading screen music is a logical consequence of its place in the game's structure, the music has an iconic function as well. Much like *Max Payne*'s menu theme, it is experienced as the purest statement of game's "main theme". Its place in the game's structure however – loading screens as unwanted, necessary transitional spaces – raises the question why. Much like *Max Payne*, this is in part due to the game's musical structure, and in part to its (peri)textual structure. Like *Max Payne*, *Battlefield* starts with a pre-rendered introduction video that acts as a kind of "trailer" for the gameplay, showing action scenes of tanks, airplanes and submarines moving across warzones and getting ready for battle – all accompanied by the motif and melody from the loading screen. The subsequently heard music in the main menu has a similar structure to the loading screen music, with a shorter, more up-tempo, more chromatic motif, and a more fragmentary melody. It has an energy to its relative intensity that is released in the loading screen, creating a kind of ternary form in the game's peritexts in which the loading screen acts as a recapitulation of sorts: while we are anticipating gameplay, we have arrived at the game's main theme. So we can say that in a way, the game makes up for one of its most prevalent technical flaws – its long load times – by employing them in the game's musical structure.

## Conclusion

Peritextual music forms an important part of a game. As part of a threshold that has to be crossed in order to start playing, it can communicate the game's identity much like its box art or promotional material. Music also has the unique ability to overlap peritexts, diegeses and gameplay situations, and in doing so can structure players' experiences of a game. It can highlight certain parts, such as the death of an avatar in *Super Mario Bros.* or a particularly long loading screen in *Battlefield 1942*, and it can suture or smooth over other parts, such as the sudden interruption of the excitement of a *FIFA* match by pausing the game. At the same time, music's place in a game's (peri)textual structure determines how we understand it: music in the pause menu of *Max Payne* can sound like a moment of respite, its calm, continuous melody serving as a contrast to a frantic action scene; development in the structure of *Battlefield 1942*'s loading screen music is emphasized by our eagerness to start a match.

The main aim of this chapter has been to bring to scholarly attention a part of video game music that has heretofore been mostly neglected. My case studies have served as examples to show the variety in which music can work beyond gameplay and diegesis. In doing so, I myself have in turn neglected some important dimensions of musical peritexts: just as video game music has paratextual contexts, so does paratextual game music have historical and genre-related contexts. The reason *Max Payne*, *Super Meat Boy* or *Battlefield 1942*'s menu music sounds like it does is due in large part to the time and place they were conceived and released in. (A cursory look at the substantial musical differences between *Max Payne* and its most recent sequel *Max Payne 3* [2012] would serve as an example.) The current investigation should therefore not be seen as the final word on musical peritexts in video games, but a call for game music scholars to look beyond the thresholds of gameplay and diegesis.

## Notes

1. Michiel Kamp is Junior Assistant Professor of Music at Utrecht University, where he specializes in teaching music in film and digital media. Michiel completed his AHRC-funded PhD in Music at Cambridge University with his thesis, "Four Ways of Hearing Video Game Music", which focused on phenomenological approaches to listening. As well as presenting his research at international conferences, he has also written for journals including *Philosophy and Technology*. He has co-edited a special issue on video game music for *The Soundtrack*.

2. The magic circle is a term first introduced by Johan Huizinga (1955), denoting the imaginary (and sometimes real) boundary players draw between the real world and the game, which is governed by different rules. Since it was picked up by Katie Salen and Eric Zimmerman (2003), it has featured heavily in video game scholarship.

3. Genre is particularly important in film: "to say or to imply that a film is an action film, an eco-thriller, a sports biopic, or a romantic comedy is to summon entire systems of distribution, reviewer interest, and audience participation and reaction, ensuring interest, disinterest, and/or specific forms of attention from

given studios, theatres, audience members, and would-be censors" (Gray, 2010: 51). The establishment of a video game's genre through paratextual material is similarly important.

4. While one might object to this rigid categorization, I want to defend it by focusing on the player's actions in each situation: during gameplay, one is concerned with overcoming a game's obstacles to reach its goals; in diegetic situations, one is concerned with the game's story world. Any "fictional" elements, in Juul's terms (2005), are related to gameplay concerns.

5. Both contemporary NES titles (other US launch titles such as *Duck Hunt* [1985], *Ice Climber* [1985] and *Excitebike* [1985]) and *Super Mario Bros.*'s sequels (e.g. *Super Mario Bros. 2* [1987] and *3* [1990]) did have title menu music.

6. *Kirby's Adventure* (1993) and *Duck Tales* (1989) follow Mario's structure strictly for example, while *Kid Icarus* (1986) has a simpler loop-cadence, with introductory bars "embedded" in the loop. *Mega Man* (1987) and *Sonic the Hedgehog* (1991) on the other hand lack a death cadence. This suggests that the most important feature of the "*Mario* style" musical structure is its alignment with death and the restarting of a level.

7. As an even more obvious nod to *Super Mario Bros.*, Meat Boy can enter areas called "warp zones" that feature lower resolution graphics and music that sound like they have been created on an NES sound chip. In these warp zones, Meat Boy has limited lives, of which the player is reminded by a black screen whenever Meat Boy dies, similar to *Mario*. In this instance it is important to point out that unlike in *Mario*, the music continues playing.

8. A boss stage is common video game parlance for a special stage that closes off a sequence of levels in the game. It often features a single, unusually strong (and often large) "boss" enemy that requires special tactics to defeat. It is quite common for a boss stage to have its own music that is different from the music in the preceding levels, and more often than not this music features a relative increase in intensity, through use of a higher tempo and shorter melodic patterns, for instance.

9. Like both *Super Mario Bros.* and *Super Meat Boy*, *Braid* does have contrasting "boss stage" music that is faster in tempo with a darker quality to it.

10. "Heroic bloodshed" films are best represented by the Hong Kong cinema collaborations of John Woo and Chow Yun-fat; see Baker and Russell, 1994. One of *Max Payne*'s difficulty levels is even called "Hard Boiled", after one of Woo's films.

11. Nils Skare makes a distinction between pause menus that have one "'turn away' from the game" and that have the player "reflect *inside* the game" (2011), depending on whether the pause menu lets one issue commands that alter or affect one's progress throughout the game. For instance, *Mega Man 2* (1988) lets the player change their avatar's weapons, thus requiring them to reflect on their game progress; *Super Mario Bros. 3* (1988) only lets the player perform non-game related actions.

12. Some games present this quite literally: *Metroid* (1986) and more recently *Mass Effect* (2007) use elevators as diegetic non-gameplay transitions between areas in place of nondiegetic loading screens.
13. In his *GameSpot* review, Scott Osborne notes the "extremely long load times on anything other than a fast computer" (2002).
14. Subsequent instalments in the series have kept the rhythmic motif, but changed everything from instrumentation to its basic harmonies.

## References

Baker, R. and T. Russell (1994) *The Essential Guide to Hong Kong Movies.* London: Eastern Heroes Publications.

Chion, M. (1994) *Audio-Vision: Sound on Screen.* Trans. C. Gorbman. New York: Columbia University Press.

Collins, K. (2004) "'I'll be back': Recurrent Sonic Motifs in James Cameron's *Terminator* Films." In *Off the Planet: Music, Sound and Science Fiction Cinema*, edited by P. Hayward, pp. 165–75. London: John Libbey.

Collins, K. (2008) *Game Sound: An Introduction to the History, Theory, and Practice of Video Game Music and Sound Design.* Cambridge, MA: MIT Press.

Consalvo, M. (2007) *Cheating: Gaining Advantage in Video Games.* Cambridge, MA: MIT Press.

Cook, N. (1998) *Analysing Musical Multimedia.* Oxford: Clarendon Press.

DeNora, T. (2000) *Music in Everyday Life.* Cambridge: Cambridge University Press.

Derrida, J. (1997). *Of Grammatology.* Trans. G. C. Spivak. Baltimore: Johns Hopkins University Press.

Genette, G. (1997) *Paratexts: Thresholds of Interpretation.* Trans. J. E. Lewin. Cambridge: Cambridge University Press.

Gibbons, W. (2011) "Wrap Your Troubles in Dreams: Popular Music, Narrative, and Dystopia in *Bioshock*." *Game Studies* 11/3. http://gamestudies.org/1103/articles/gibbons (accessed February, 25 2016).

Gorbman, C. (1987) *Unheard Melodies: Narrative Film Music.* Bloomington, IN: Indiana University Press.

Gray, J. (2010) *Show Sold Separately: Promos, Spoilers, and Other Media Paratexts.* New York and London: New York University Press.

Hancock, M. (2014) "Epi(c)texts and *Ni No Kuni*." *What We're Playing: Reading Mia Consalvo's Cheating* (blog). http://www.firstpersonscholar.com/what-were-playing/ (accessed January 19, 2015).

Heldt, G. (2013) *Music and Levels of Narration in Film: Steps Across the Border.* Bristol: Intellect.

Hocking, C. (2007) "Ludonarrative Dissonance in *Bioshock*." *Click Nothing: Design from a Long Time Ago* (blog). http://clicknothing.typepad.com/click_nothing/2007/10/ludonarrative-d.html (accessed January 22, 2015).

Huizinga, J. (1955) *Homo Ludens: A Study of the Play-Element in Culture.* Boston, MA: Beacon Press.

Jones, S. (2008) *The Meaning of Video Games: Gaming and Textual Strategies.* New York: Routledge.

Juul, J. (2005) *Half-Real: Video Games Between Real Rules and Fictional Worlds*. Cambridge, MA: MIT Press.

Kamp, M. (2014) "Musical Ecologies in Video Games." *Philosophy & Technology* 27/2: 235–49.

Kassabian, A. (2001) *Hearing Film: Tracking Identifications in Contemporary Hollywood Film Music*. New York and London: Routledge.

Lerner, N. (2013) "The Origins of Musical Style in Video Games, 1977–1983." In *The Oxford Handbook of Film Music Studies*, edited by D. Neumeyer, pp. 319–51. New York: Oxford University Press.

Lunenfeld, P. (2000) "Unfinished Business." In *The Digital Dialectic: New Essays on New Media*, edited by P. Lunenfeld, pp. 6–23. Cambridge, MA: MIT Press.

Osborne, S. (2002) "*Battlefield 1942* Review." *GameSpot*. http://www.gamespot.com/reviews/battlefield-1942-review/1900-2880344/ (accessed January 22, 2015).

Rodman, R. (2010) *Tuning In: American Narrative Television Music*. New York: Oxford University Press.

Salen, K. and E. Zimmerman (2003) *Rules of Play: Game Design Fundamentals*. Cambridge, MA: MIT Press.

Skare, N. (2011) "How to Define a Genre: A Lacanian-Marxist Case Study of the *NES* Platform Game." *Eludamos. Journal for Computer Game Culture* 5/1. http://www.eludamos.org/index.php/eludamos/article/view/vol5no1-5/html5 (accessed February 3, 2015).

Tagg, P. (1979) *Kojak: 50 Seconds of Television Music. Toward the Analysis of Affect in Popular Music*. Göteborg: Musikvetenskapliga Institutionen.

Van Elferen, I. (2011) "¡Un Forastero! Virtuality and Diegesis in Videogame Music." *Music and the Moving Image* 4/2: 30–39.

Whalen, Z. (2004) "Play Along – An Approach to Videogame Music." *Game Studies* 4/1. http://www.gamestudies.org/0401/whalen/ (accessed February 25, 2016).

Williams, R. (1974) *Television: Technology and Cultural Form*. London: Fontana.

Wolf, M. J. P. (2001) *The Medium of the Video Game*. Austin, TX: University of Texas Press.

Yang, R. (2013) "The Unportalable: Games as Paratexts and Products." *Radiator Design Blog*. http://www.blog.radiator.debacle.us/2013/01/the-unportalable-games-as-paratexts-and.html (accessed January 22, 2015).

# 6 "It's a-me, Mario!"
## Playing with Video Game Music

*Melanie Fritsch*[1]

## Introduction

Video gaming, even in its earliest incarnations, can be seen as a form of "participatory culture" (Jenkins et al., 2009).[2] Besides exploring what can be done within the game during normal gameplay, players experiment with soft- and hardware components of a game, as well as content such as the game's artwork or even the narratives, in order to create something new themselves. The emergence of practices such as demos, remixes, mashup videos, fan-made movies, and – of course – the creation of mods,[3] self-made levels or entire games, is a vivid demonstration of the desire not just to play the games, but also to play *with* them.

The same holds true for video game music. Typing, for example, "Super Mario Bros music" or "Super Mario theme" into the YouTube search will deliver a huge number of videos containing tunes from this "Jump'n'Run" video game series. The *Super Mario* music, originally written by Japanese composer Koji Kondo for the NES game *Super Mario Bros.* in the mid-80s, has been rearranged and played by professional as well as amateur orchestras all over the world. One can find renditions of the "Overworld" theme or entire *Super Mario* suites sung a cappella or whistled, performed on regular instruments like pianos, guitars or flutes, or on other material such as bottles, rulers or Tesla coils (Collins, 2013: 106). People dance, free run or cosplay to it,[4] and it has been remixed for music games such as *Just Dance 3* (2011), *Just Dance Wii* (2011) or the *Dance Dance Revolution Mario Mix* (2005). Furthermore, people use the typical 8-bit NES sounds and/or visual style of the *Mario* video games in order to create tributes, crossover music videos or their own songs. With the *Automatic Mario* series, for example, even a distinct subgenre of remix videos has been established (Collins, 2013: 136–37).

But all these forms and practices do not come out of nowhere. It is not simply a single connection to the game itself since, as José Zagal puts it, "games exist in a broader cultural context, and it is important to use this cultural context in order to help understand a game and vice versa" (2010: 28). The same holds true for video game music. When people play with the sound and music, or create their own music videos using musical and other material from the games, they not only remix the music, but also mingle musical and other cultural practices. They use their knowledge of (and competences regarding) several contexts in order to create meaning themselves. During gameplay, the music is presented within the contextual frame of the game as one part of a multimodal structure of which the player has to make sense (see Fritsch, 2014). But what happens to this relationship when game and music are ripped apart and players start to play with the contents?

After a brief introduction to issues of musical meaning in video games, the concept of game literacy (Zagal, 2010; Zimmerman, 2009), and its application to the field of game music (Van Elferen, in this volume) will serve as my theoretical starting point. The main assumption of this chapter is that broadening the conceptualization of music to an understanding of it as a culturally induced and learned system regarding several cultural contexts, rather than something which is just contained in the notes, can not only help to obtain fresh insights into game music during gameplay performance, but can also be helpful when analysing game music cultural artefacts such as music videos and original songs created by players. Furthermore, it is assumed that in order to analyse such artefacts, one has to take the music, the respective game, and the overarching fan cultural discourse, into account. This assumption will be supported through the frame of the case study presented at the end of this chapter.

## Let's-a Go! – A Basic Framework of Game Musical Literacy

When reading about video game music (or game audio in general) one frequently encounters a range of typical statements: first, that music plays a decisive role in creating the feeling of immersion for players by helping them to become involved in the game's narrative and/or with the playable character (Liljedahl, 2010). Second, that game music "is a bridge on which the virtual visual world can travel out and become part of the real physical world" (p. 32). Besides drawing players into the game, music also embraces them in the physical world, expanding the game space outwards in front of the screen. And third, that game music is responsible for making the player feel by providing some kind of universal "emotional quality", thereby at least reinforcing or even entirely conveying the meaning of a scene or gameplay situation (p. 33).

However, as Isabella van Elferen points out, there is a substantial problem:

> In theoretical surveys of gaming immersion, the exact role of sound in
> the process of immersion has only been hinted at in terms that are as
> general as they are divergent ... Because musical meanings – like the

emotions with which they are entwined – are far from fixed, objective or universal, affective musical immersion would seem to be highly subjective and therefore unpredictable. (Van Elferen, 2016: 35)

This conclusion is supported by the work of Phillip Tagg, who ascertained in his cross-cultural research that "there are very few universally understood aspects of musical expression . . . All evaluative and affective musical symbols are culturally specific" (Tagg, 2002: 22). Similarly, Nicholas Cook states that, in general, "[p]ure music, it seems, is an aesthetician's (and music theorist's) fiction; the real thing unites itself promiscuously with any other media that are available" (1998: 92). As these examples imply, the issue of musical meaning in general has already been addressed in research, but not without controversy. Hoeberechts, Shantz and Katchabaw (2014) divide the major theoretical positions in two categories referring to film music as an example: The "referentialist" attributes "some or all of the emotions you feel to your knowledge of the plot of the movie or associations with cultural understanding of the film". The "absolutist" instead "would hold that the meaning of the piece is derived entirely from the music itself" (p. 421).[5] They further divide the second category in two subgroups, the "formalist" and the "expressionist". The "formalist holds that the meaning of a piece of music is primarily intellectual and is derived from perception of the structural relationships between elements in a composition" (p. 421). To the "expressionist", instead "musical meaning is primarily emotional" (p. 421). In both these subgroups in the "absolutist" branch of research, the focus is rather on music itself as a written phenomenon, more than on music as listened and experienced as sound by an audience. Even though it is, of course, reasonable to put the focus of analysis on the side of composers, and the meanings they intend to convey, considering how audiences (in the case of video games, the players) deal with the content they are presented with is a worthwhile endeavour.

One further problem needs to be addressed: splitting up a game's music (or the game's sound content more generally) and looking at the individual sonic segments can certainly help to provide insights into the musical cues or the overarching compositional idea. But when trying to address what happens during the act of play, or investigating player experience, this approach hits a brick wall because, as Inger Ekman writes,

Research on sound's ability to elicit emotions often seeks to establish the emotional reactions to the sound in isolation, and focuses on sound such as music, or emotional speech. In games, however, sound is typically present with other modalities (visual, haptic), as part of a narrative, and embedded in a functional framework of play. (Ekman, 2014: 196)

For these reasons, the "absolutist" perspective, which focuses exclusively on music, becomes critically revised in the discourses of interactive audio and ludomusicology. As both van Elferen and Ekman suggest, it is necessary to make "musical and game analysis compatible with one another" (Van Elferen, 2012: 2; see also Ekman, 2014: 196). For this to occur, the functions of music in games must be taken into account. In her chapter on emotional functions of game sound, Ekman works out a basic framework:

> The narrative fit of game sound reflects how helpful sound is to storytelling and helps bring out the emotions inherent in the story . . . The functional fit of game sound is not about story comprehension, but about how sound supports playing . . . Game sound is part of the feedback system that provides information on player action, constantly signaling which actions help the player to progress towards the goals of the game. (Ekman, 2014: 200)

These functions cannot strictly be isolated from one another in any case. To take up the *Mario* example: when Mario dies (in other words, the player made a mistake), this information is not just conveyed via graphic depiction, but also with the help of a "staccato pulse followed by a conciliatory musical cadence . . . The music is a descending figure, mimicking Mario's ejection from the playing field. The music is a coded message of failure reinforcing the consequence of having to replay the level one more time" (Whalen, 2004: 11). On the one hand, the form of this tune points to the narrative function of conveying the emotion of failure and regret. The descending figure fulfils the affordance of synchrony by mickey-mousing how dead Mario falls to the bottom of the screen (see Ekman, 2014: 201–202). At the same time, the tune is played consistently whenever Mario dies and thereby fulfils the affordance of functional fit by clearly communicating the player's failure and musically accompanying the events on screen (pp. 201–204). Building on the findings by Gerald Clore and Andrew Ortony, Ekman further demonstrates that the ensuing

> emotions are based on cognitive appraisal along two simultaneous processes . . . Bottom-up processing performs new situational evaluations (not necessarily consciously), assessing the stimuli in relation to a set of values and goals. The top-down system, on the other hand, works by reinstating prior emotional experiences based on association. (2014: 199)

In other words, in order to get to the emotional experience and/or grasp the meaning of the current gameplay situation, players first have to understand the function of this short tune. This may happen by decoding the narrative affective meaning "this is a sad tune, because you made a mistake and Mario died", the functional informative meaning "you lost and will have to start the level again", or both. In order to do so, players need a set of frameworks for evaluation. Such a framework can be built just by playing the game or the game series itself by which the connection "Mario dies – sad tune" is learned. But there is more to it.

A helpful approach can be found in van Elferen's proposition of game musical literacy:

> Combining the audio-visual literacies of film and television music with ludoliteracy, game soundtrack design appeals to a specific game musical literacy. Through intertextual references to audio-visual idioms from other media, game soundtracks deploy player literacy for their immersive effect: it is because gamers recognize certain composing styles that they are able to interpret gaming events and feel involved in gameplay, game worlds and game plots. (Van Elferen, 2016: 36)

Before taking a more detailed look at game musical literacy itself, the specific concept of games literacy to which van Elferen alludes needs to be introduced. Formulated by José Zagal, games literacy includes three fields of competence:

1. Having the ability to play games.
2. Having the ability to understand meanings with respect to games.
3. Having the ability to make games.
   (Zagal, 2010: 23)

Zagal subsequently focuses on the second field. He defines the ability to understand meaning with respect to games as the competence "to explain, discuss, describe, frame, situate, interpret and/or position" them concerning several contexts (2010: 24, bold in original):

1. in the **context of human culture** (games as a cultural artifacts [sic]),
2. in the **context of other games** (comparing games to other games, genres),
3. in the **context of the technological platform** on which they are executed,
4. by **deconstructing them and understanding their components**, how they interact, and how they facilitate certain experiences in players.

With this in mind, it becomes clear that players do not just have to learn how to handle a certain game (for example the specific control scheme), and understand the challenges the game poses and how to overcome them. They also must learn to understand and interpret what is presented to them with the help of their contextual knowledge in the fields listed by Zagal. These contexts refer to the game itself, to games in general, as well as to other cultural contexts.

Translated to the field of game music, this idea of literacy in connection with Ekman's findings implies that players develop game musical literacy:

1. within the context of a specific game or game series (narrative and functional fit),
2. within the functional context of gaming, for example to convey informative messages such as "the avatar's health is low" or "you successfully completed a task", and
3. within game external contexts, for example regarding the player's cultural background, the respective musical system, references to pop culture and other idioms.

So far, this framework has addressed the issue that musical meaning in video games does not just lie in the music itself and conveys only the "master's will", but it is part of a functional structure of which players have to make sense. The emerging musical meaning during play depends strongly on how music is presented and how game musically literate the particular player is. Vice versa, players can make sense of what they encounter during gameplay by using their game musical literacy.

## 1up – When Players Become Creators

In order to include the dimension of creative activity in the framework presented here, it needs to be developed further. Game designer and researcher Eric Zimmerman implies that the act of making meaning in video games not only depends on understanding, but also on creation, when he defines gaming literacy as "the ability to understand and **create** specific kinds of meaning" (2009: 25, emphasis added). From his point of view, players must be literate on three levels: systems, play and design. Being what he terms "systems literate" means

> understanding the world as dynamic sets of parts with complex, constantly changing interrelationships – seeing the structures that underlie our world, and comprehending how these structures function . . . Getting to know a system requires understanding it on several levels, from the fixed foundational structures of the system, to its emergent, unpredictable patterns of behavior. (Ibid.)

Due to the fact that video games are bound to a technical system and rely on their distinct formal system of rules he sees them as essentially systemic (p. 26). But it is on the level of play where things become interesting:

> Yet, play is far more than just play *within* a structure. Play can *play with* structures . . . A literacy based on play is a literacy of innovation and invention. Just as systems literacy is about engendering a systems-based

attitude, being literate in play means *being playful* – having a *ludic attitude* that sees the world's structures as opportunities for playful engagement. (p. 27, original emphases)

Here he further develops what Zagal briefly addressed as "having the ability to play": it means the competence to playfully explore and squeeze everything out of the system, be it planned by the designer, or be it emergent behaviour such as the creative use of bugs/glitches.[6] This refers to an issue that game developers know very well: whatever the technical system allows players to do, intended or unintended – at least some of them will do it. When people start to play a new game, they firstly build on their previous experiences of playing other games, be it within the same genre, or games in general. Secondly, they do not only learn the specific game controls, they also have to find successful strategies and playing styles for this particular game. In this way, players engage themselves in learning processes. Even though these learning processes are also somehow guided by the game (e.g. by tutorials) or channelled by the hardware, people also try out all sorts of possibilities to see what they can do by themselves. The process by which players have come to these aforementioned possibilities of uncommon play, and the way they use their findings in order to do something unexpected, could be described as "playful misbehaviour" or, in more positive words, being "literate in play". They have learned to recognize and exploit opportunities in the game system that let them explore the game in ways besides the primary expected mode of use. It is also for this reason that Zimmerman favours the term "gaming literacy":

> because of the mischievous double-meaning of "gaming", which can signify exploiting or taking clever advantage of something. Gaming a system means finding hidden shortcuts and cheats, and bending and modifying the rules in order to move through the system more efficiently – perhaps to misbehave, but perhaps to change that system for the better. (Zimmerman, 2009: 25)

However, this does not just hold true for games as technical or rule systems. In collaboration with Katie Salen, Zimmerman previously had defined the term "system" as "a set of parts that interrelate to form a complex whole. There are many ways to frame a game as a system: a mathematical system, a social system, a representational system, etc." (Salen and Zimmerman, 2004: 55). I propose that the contents of a game, such as the narrative, artwork, characters and music, as well as the respective emergent meaning(s), can also be framed either as parts of the overarching system or as distinct systems, which can be gamed by players by means of their play *with* them. Furthermore, this relates not just to playful misbehaviour during gameplay, but also to all of the emergent playful practices listed in the introduction.

As Henry Jenkins (2013) has demonstrated, this playing with structures is not only limited to video game culture, but it is a main ingredient of fan culture in general. Fans do not only watch and silently contemplate the contents they are presented with, but have instead developed a huge range of "gaming the systems" practices. One vivid example is the practice of fanfiction: fans write their own stories, thereby changing the narrative by recontextualizing the importance of, or relationships between, characters, adding content to bridge or exploit perceived gaps in the narrative, or even adding a totally new storyline. Other fans follow the same purpose, but use other artistic means of expression such as painting, drawing, writing songs, creating fan movies or music videos, and so on.

> [F]an-generated texts cannot simply be interpreted as the material traces of interpretive acts but need to be understood within their own terms as cultural artifacts. They are artistic objects which draw on the artistic traditions of the fan community as well as on the personal creativity and insights of individual consumer/artists ... A fan aesthetic centers on the selection, inflection, juxtaposition, and recirculation of ready-made images and discourses. (Jenkins, 2013: 223–24)

A recent and vivid demonstration of the complexity such a fandom can achieve is the *A Song of Ice and Fire* fantasy book series by George R. R. Martin. The original book series is already overflowing with characters, plotlines, historical, geographical and genealogical information about the book series' world, and the corresponding TV series *Game of Thrones* (2011) produced by HBO has further added to this universe. The discussions about the book and the TV series fill page after page of internet forums, thereby demonstrating how well people know the fictional universe's history, genealogies, plotlines and relationships, as well as information about the television production, such as casts for the next season and so on. The same holds true for fandoms such as *Star Trek*, *Star Wars*, the J. R. R. Tolkien universe, or comic book universes such as the Marvel or DC comics.

In short: in order to understand fan-made creations or even become creators themselves, fans need to become literate in the respective fandom as well as in the practices, discourses and aesthetics of the surrounding fan culture. Of course, a non-literate fan (such as someone whose only experience of the Tolkien universe is watching *The Hobbit* movies) may still create a fanfiction story or a music video based on the subject. But at the very moment the material is uploaded in a fanfiction forum or to YouTube without an "I am a beginner" disclaimer, the creator will run the risk of derision by the literate fan community who will point out every detail which in their eyes is deficient, or at worst, wrong.

Therefore, in order to become a creator within the context of fandom, video game culture, or – as in our case – video game music culture, it is also necessary to be competent regarding design, which Zimmerman had listed as the third component of gaming literacy. In his reasoning, he relies on his and Salen's definition of design as "the process by which a *designer* creates a *context* to be encountered by a *participant*, from which *meaning* emerges" (2004: 41, emphasis original). A designer might be one single person or a group, such as a professional design team, or in the case of folk or fan cultural games "the designer of the game can be considered culture at large" (ibid.). Even though Zimmerman and Salen relate this definition to games, it can nevertheless be applied to fan cultural artefacts as well. In order to design a well-made fan cultural artefact that adds to the respective fandom, it is necessary to be a literate designer in this sense.

Applied to the issue of video game music, we can broaden the focus as follows: game musical literacy not only enables players to understand musical meaning during play regarding all the contexts previously listed. It also enables them to understand creations made by other fans and create contexts themselves by playing with the music and its respective meaning within the frame of the game's universe – in other words, by gaming the game's music, understood as a system. Of course, they must also learn the respective technical skills,[7] but putting together a well-made game music cultural artefact, which will be understood and appreciated by other literate players, requires a designer who is literate in the fandom. Furthermore, that designer must be able to rip out parts of the overarching system (e.g. the narrative system) and create a new context that will be encountered, understood and accepted as authentic by literate fans.

## Case Study: *Super Mario Bros.: The 8-Bit Opera*

As Karen Collins shows in her recent book, *Playing with Sound* (2013), a range of participatory practices which build on game musical literacy has emerged around games and their music. She divides these practices into the following categories: performing music in games, performing to music in games, performing game music, creating music from the game, and interacting with the game as an instrument (2013: 89–120). It is the category "performing game music", which is of further interest here. Collins identifies "two common performative practices around music in games – covering songs and remixing game sound" (p. 105). Such practices are not exclusive to video games, but appear in fan cultures in general, as Jenkins has demonstrated (Jenkins, 2013:

250–76). A cover is a new recording of a given song from a video game. Some such cover versions are popular: Malukah's version of 'The Dragonborn Comes' from *Skyrim* (2011) has received over 10 million views since it was posted in December 2012,[8] while her a capella duet rendition of 'Baba Yetu' from *Civilization IV* (2005) with Peter Hollens received 1.2 million views within four months of posting.[9]

> Cover versions are similar to remixes, which maintain identifiable features from the original song but significantly change the original, particularly the structure of the song . . . Unlike a cover, a remix often uses the separate tracks or sounds as recorded by the original artist. (Collins, 2013: 107)

These two practices sometimes conflate into a third practice that "combines elements of remixing and cover versions by recording game songs and adding elements such as orchestration or lyrics" (p. 108). Collins relates this to the fan cultural practice of "filking". Filk songs are original songs written and sung by fans, which negotiate discourses, events, characters or other motifs taken from a fandom. Similar to fanfiction or fan videos they develop these motifs further, comment on them, or explore a character's personality by singing from his or her point of view. In other words: these songs play with the content of a fandom. It is also common to create parodies or add parodistic lyrics.

> Filkers borrow their subject matter from the contemporary mass media and their tunes from either folk music traditions or from the repertoire of showtunes and pop hits; the craft comes through the combination of these "poached" materials into a form that expresses the fans' interpretation of the primary text or fandom's identity as a social and cultural community. (Jenkins, 2013: 268)

The term filk does not accidentally sound similar to folk, because "[f]ilk shares many of the features musicologists have traditionally used to define folk music: oral circulation rather than fixed written texts, continuity within musical tradition, variation in performance, and selection by a community that determines which songs are preserved, which discarded" (pp. 268–69).

In the case of video games, it is often not just the narrative content such as characters, plotlines or background stories that creators of "game filk songs" (as Collins calls them, 2013: 110) use as material. Some songs also bespeak the community itself, such as "I'm Just a Noob", or pass on information for successful gameplay via the lyrics (Collins, 2013: 109–110). Whereas cover songs and remixes play a larger role and can get high numbers of hits on platforms such as YouTube, game filk songs are not similarly widespread (yet). One reason might be that "[m]any of these game filk songs are set to popular music that is not taken from video game soundtracks. In this way, the song is tied to the gaming world only through its lyrical content and risks bringing its own semiotic baggage from outside the game community" (p. 110). This bears the risk of importing unintended double meanings, or being dismissed by the community as not being the work of a skilful creator, because of the lack of display of musical craftsmanship.

With all this in mind, *Super Mario Bros.: The 8-Bit Opera* is an interesting case.[10] The video was created and posted on YouTube by the composers Jon and Al Kaplan in their channel named "legolambs".[11] In 2002, the brothers became famous with their Internet musical *Silence! The Musical*, which was a filk parody of the *Silence of the Lambs*. As their personal website informs us,

> What began as a set of songs eventually became a website with a cult following in 2003. Silence! was covered in magazines including *Entertainment Weekly* and *Maxim*, and aired on radio shows like XM's Opie and Anthony and Howard Stern's 100. In 2005, Jon and Al composed several new songs and expanded *Silence!* into a live musical. (JonandAl. com, accessed December 29, 2014)

Since that first success, the brothers "have continued to pursue their first love of writing unstageable theater works" (ibid.), including parodistic filk versions of *Conan the Barbarian* (1982), *Predator* (1987), *The Thing* (1982) and *Rocky IV* (1985), which have all gained six- or seven-digit viewing figures on YouTube. For that reason, they already have gained their credibility as skilful musicians and legitimate, literate filkers.

The *Super Mario Bros.: The 8-Bit Opera* video (hereafter *Mario Opera*) was posted on November 27, 2011, and reached 782,989 views by December 2014. Compared to other videos made by the brothers like, for example, *Conan the Barbarian: The Musical*, which had almost 3.5 million views since it was posted on June 25, 2010, the *Mario Opera* has not been one of the more popular projects. Nevertheless, when browsing YouTube, one can find several fan-made performances of the *Mario Opera*, including two elementary school choir live performances, one techno remix and one animated version.

The original video contains gameplay footage from *Super Mario Bros.*, accompanied by lyrics sung in an operatic style by Daniel Chaney and an unnamed female singer. Table 6.1 specifies the game level that is shown while each lyric of the song is sung. The video does not use the game's levels in the order they are encountered when playing *Super Mario Bros.*

*Table 6.1* Libretto from the *Mario Opera* with description of the accompanying gameplay footage

| Lyrics* | Video footage taken from |
| --- | --- |
| Opening | Loading screen |
| MARIO:<br>It's a-me, Mario!<br>It's a-me, Mario! | Overworld level 1-1 |
| So I'm off to find the princess,<br>magic mushroom make-a me tall,<br>Then I pick a pretty flower, it a give me fire-ball,<br>But the turtle he a-touch me and I'm back to being small,<br>And I got to be a-careful not to—(*Mario dies tune*) | "Lives remaining" screen |
| It's a-me[,] Mario!<br>It's a-me, Mario! | Overworld level 1-1 (restart) |
| I'm-a jumping on the Goomba<br>And I make him go a-squish, | Underworld and Overworld level 2-1 |
| Then I'm swimming under water with the pesky jelly fish. | Water level 2-2 |
| These a two-a Hammer Brothers, they a difficult to kill,<br>And the cannons, they a shoot the Bullet Bill! | Overworld level 5-2 |
| Now I run away from Lakitu,<br>He chase me in the cloud.<br>Try to go inside the tunnel but, a-no I'm not allowed. | Overworld level 4-1 |
| Climb-a da beanstalk,<br>take da coins and now I'm a really on a roll, | Cloud level in 2-1 |
| When I finish slide the flag a-down the pole! | End of level 2-2 |
| (BACKGROUND CHORUS JOINS)<br>I'm invincible, | Overworld level 1-1 |
| I'm invincible, | Overworld level 3-1 |
| Now I touch-a you | Overworld level 1-1 |
| and-a you die 'cause I'm | Overworld level 3-1 |
| invincible! | Overworld level 1-1 |
| All dee turtles and Goombas are | Overworld level 3-2 |
| toast, I'm like Pac-a-Man eating a ghost. | Overworld level 3-1 |
| I'm invincible, So invincible! | Overworld level 3-2 / 1-1 / 3-2** |

| Lyrics* | Video footage taken from |
|---|---|
| Now I jump up on the ceiling cause this level really tough,<br>I a-take the magic warp-a zone and skip a lot of stuff. | Underworld level 1-2 |
| I will find-a you a-princess | Overworld level 2-3 |
| and-a make-a you my wife,<br>Oh a-wait I got to chase the extra-life! | Underworld level 1-2 |
| It's a-me, | Overworld level 8-1 |
| Mario! | Overworld level 2-1 |
| It's a-me, Mario! Now | Overworld level and cellar 6-2 |
| I reach the final castle, | End of world 8-3 |
| It's-a the Bowser's evil lair.<br>Such a terrible a-hassle,<br>There's a-lava everywhere.<br>I defeat-a you-a Koopa King of level eight-a-four,<br>You a-jump, I run, and look, a-no more floor! | Castle level 8-4 |
| PRINCESS:<br>You came for me,<br>MARIO:<br>  (It's a me!)<br>You came for me,<br>  (Let's-a get outta here)<br>You came for me,<br>  (You is-a free now)<br>You came for me.<br>  (Thanks to Mario . . .)<br>And now that you've taken a rest,<br>It is time to begin your next quest.<br>CHORUS/MARIO:<br>It's a-me, Mario!<br>It's a-me! | Original ending scene |
| *NEXT TIME* | Text overlay |
| MARIO:<br>It's a-me, Mario!<br>It's a-me, Mario!<br>In the dreamy land of Sub-a-con, a magical a-place,<br>I a-pull a juicy vegetable and throw it in-a you face!<br>I'm-a gonna save the kingdom from the evil boss a-Wart,<br>He a-have an evil plan I must-a thwart!<br>(fade out) | Footage from *Super Mario Bros. 2* (SNES) |

\* The lyrics are provided under the original video at https://www.youtube.com/ watch?v=YpXPtAVdMIY (accessed December 29, 2014).

\*\* In this section the video switches too fast between the levels to assign the words to the pictures precisely.

The musical accompaniment uses timbres mimicking 8-bit NES sounds for melodic parts and percussion, together with a synthesized vocal chorus. The piece also includes a range of original game sound effects and musical fragments like, for example, Mario jumping, growing and shrinking, collecting coins, or the short motif heard when Mario dies. These game-sourced sounds are integrated into the music in such a way that they do not unfavourably interfere with the other musical material. Like the original *Super Mario* theme, the music begins with a short instrumental passage which is repeated when Mario is shown restarting the level after the "lives remaining" screen. Due to the 8-bit sounds, the style of the music strongly reminds viewers of the original game music, thereby reinforcing the retro feeling. The lyrics take up the – admittedly very rudimentary – narrative of the *Mario* game series: defeat Koopa King Bowser, save the abducted Princess.[12] In detail, the lyrics are a description of the *Super Mario* gameplay mechanics and dynamics, thereby explaining successful play (e.g. do not run into enemies, jump on enemies to kill them, catch the stars to become invulnerable) and giving useful hints such as the existence of bonus lives, warp zones, or the hidden beanstalks which lead to the cloud levels where the player can collect additional coins.

The pseudo-Italian accent adopted by the singer references that the character, Mario, is an Italian-American plumber. In *Super Mario Bros.*, the plumbing was just hinted at by the pipes and his dungarees.[13] Mario was first given the ability to speak in *Super Mario 64* (1995), since which time he has been voiced by Charles Martinet, uttering short Italian-tinged phrases such as "It's a-me, Mario!", "Let's a-go!" or "Mamma Mia!" Drew Paryzer gives a good impression on what these few words could mean for a fan at that time:

> I've been told that hearing your child speak words for the first time is a beautiful thing. Mind-opening. A milestone in their development and in your parental progress.
>
> I wouldn't know, from personal experience. But if it was anything like hearing Mario make his first utterances, I'll probably need tissues. (Paryzer, 2012)

Therefore, literate fans of the game series might be instantly thrilled when they hear the typical catchphrase "It's a-me, Mario!" at the beginning of the song, as a refrain. This again hints at similarly literate designers, who know the significance of this short phrase to fans.

The point where Mario dies in the song is also very well chosen. The video shows Mario falling down a gap in Level 1-1. Since this is the first level players encounter in the game, failing at this particular gap, as performed in the video, is certainly an experience with which many *Super Mario Bros.* players will empathize. For a beginner, it is not easy to assess correctly how far Mario can jump, and many players might have made the same mistake when they played the game the first time. Furthermore, taking footage just from the first *Super Mario Bros.* game (excluding the coda) instead of mixing it with footage from the many other *Mario* games, responds to the nostalgia many now-adult players (and "true" fans) feel. Also the line "I'm like Pac-a-Man eating a ghost" refers to the broader pop culture in which the *Mario* game series is deeply ingrained, alongside other "classic" games of the first and second generation, such as *Pac-Man* (1980). In an interview with *Wired* magazine regarding their *Scott Pilgrim* movie (2010), director Edgar Wright and actor Michael Cera describe their thoughts about the importance of *Mario* and other early Nintendo games as well as the nostalgic love players have for them:

> Wright: I remember seeing you get all misty-eyed any time *Super Mario Bros. 3* was mentioned.
>
> Cera: *Mario 3*. That one's deep in my DNA.
>
> Wright: Those Nintendo games are classics – and people still play them, which is a testament to them being pieces of art. You're so much younger than me, but *Mario* is a touchstone for both of us. (Miller, 2010)

The aforementioned choices can thus be interpreted as proof of a literate and skilful designer, because the makers of the video treat the feelings of the fans towards the games with respect, or even share their nostalgic love. To make music about the game in an operatic idiom (and not, for instance, a pop or folk song) can further be interpreted as another form of tribute to the game series as a classic: Similar to opera, the *Mario* games are part of shared cultural heritage.[14] Making an opera means equating gaming with other high cultural forms.[15] But this possible interpretation is again balanced with the humorous, spirited tone with which the song is furnished. In terms of the operatic style of the music, it is far from the dense orchestration and extended melodies of Wagner, and is instead reminiscent of the light-hearted tones of opera buffa, as user Sycamore's Assistant indicates by writing: "I like that it was a little Barber of Seville-esque." This Rossinian light-heartedness is typical of the mood associated with the *Mario* game series, as Charles Martinet explained in an interview, when asked what he likes about the characters he voices:

> [T]he part, that, you know, that I love the most to play is Mario, because it's a character full of life and joy and happiness and face these challenges,

you know, with a "wohoo! Let's a-go!", you know, enthusiasm and joy,
and of course he is in love with the princess and rescues her.[16]

This description of Mario's character is well-captured in the cheerful happy
tone of the song, which presents him as a light-hearted hero, who goes off to
win the noblewoman, thereby overcoming all difficulties such as his adversary,
the evil king.[17] He sings in a parlando style with an accent, and the entire song
culminates in an ensemble finale. Evidence for the well-made design of the
video is provided by the community's approval. The original video received
979 comments.[18] With very few exceptions, these comments are nothing less
than positive, and most are actively enthusiastic. Many are asking for a *Super
Mario Bros. 2* sequel, which is foreshadowed at the end of the video, but has
yet to appear. Some admire the craftsmanship and skilful design, such as user
MagicAccent who wrote "Now that's how you do musical quotes!" or user
SomeCallMeWeird, when he answers the user Art.Marioman574's question
"wtf am I watching?" just with a short "Art". One can find comments about
the compositional craft in which people point out their own competence as
creators and legitimate commentators: for example, user tommyopera asks
"Why no High C at 1:45 :) Perfect chord progression for it!!!!" and user Iliya
Moroumetz, who wrote "As a classically trained opera singer myself, I approve
of this video."[19] Others just show their deep affection towards the series and
express their appreciation of the song, such as user FanLouDavid, when he
writes, "Almost cried in the 'I'M INVINCIBLE' part," or user OsianLlew by
writing "The majesty of Mario is now realised. Thanks your for this slice of
awesome, legolambs!" Some users lament that the "jellyfish" mentioned in
the lyrics are actually squids and highlight this mislabelling as a mistake. But
such criticism is softened by other users, such as tilerh17, who wrote, "It's
called a blooper, but neither rhymes with squish anyway, so they had to use
jellyfish. C'mon man, allow for a little play :)".

One YouTuber took this last sentence literally, and, adopting a playful
approach to the *Mario Opera*, further processed the song into his own video
entitled *Mario Opera Animated*.[20] Instead of the *Super Mario Bros.* gameplay footage,
the opera is restaged with custom animated graphics from *Super Mario World*
(1990) drawing on the operatic theme. One reason for this choice of game
may be that it is easy to get the hacked graphics and other material from
*Super Mario World* with which to work (Table 6.2),[21] while another may be that
the Mario figure is more detailed in *Super Mario World* than *Super Mario Bros.*,
allowing for more expression in Mario's animation.

*Table 6.2* Libretto from the *Mario Opera* with description of the visual action in *Mario Opera Animated*

| Lyrics | Video |
| --- | --- |
| Opening | A red curtain raises, Mario appears in the middle of a stage, while the set decoration scrolls into the background from left to right. |
| MARIO:<br>It's a-me, Mario!<br>It's a-me, Mario! | Camera zooms on Mario showing his "operatic" lip and arm movements, while he "sings" towards the viewer. |
| So I'm off to find the princess,<br>magic mushroom make-a me tall,<br>Then I pick a pretty flower, it a give me fire-ball,<br>But the turtle he a-touch me and I'm back to being small,<br>And I got to be a-careful not to—*(Mario dies tune)* | Mario turns sideways, the background does not move.<br>The fireflower comes in from the right, "hanging" on a rope from the top.<br>Mario dies when jumping to the left, hitting a Goomba.<br>Mario re-enters the stage from the top, standing on a moving platform. |
| Opening | |
| It's a-me[,] Mario!<br>It's a-me, Mario! | Mario sings on the platform, |
| I'm-a jumping on the Goomba<br>And I make him go a-squish, | then jumps down, squishing three Goombas. |
| Then I'm swimming under water with the pesky jelly fish. | A set decoration showing a water level falls down from the top, a squid hovers through the air also "hanging" on a rope, Mario ducks and covers, and the water level decoration rises again. |
| These a two-a Hammer Brothers, they a difficult to kill,<br>And the cannons, they a shoot the Bullet Bill! | The characters mentioned in the lyrics shortly appear. The brick wall, from which the cannon is shot, is "taken out" by a rope. |
| Now I run away from Lakitu,<br>He chase me in the cloud.<br>Try to go inside the tunnel but, a-no I'm not allowed. | Lakitu shortly hovers through the air. A pipe falls down, Mario tries to enter it. |
| Climb-a da beanstalk,<br>take da coins and now I'm a really on a roll, | Two coins on "ropes" are let down, and Mario collects them. |

| Lyrics | Video |
|---|---|
| When I finish slide the flag a-down the pole! | A pole has appeared in the middle of the stage, Mario jumps on it and slides down it. |
| (BACKGROUND CHORUS JOINS)<br>I'm invincible,<br>I'm invincible,<br>Now I touch-a you and-a you die 'cause I'm invincible!<br>All dee turtles and Goombas are toast,<br>I'm like Pac-a-Man eating a ghost.<br>I'm invincible, So invincible! | A star comes in from the right, hits Mario and makes him sparkle. Close-up on Mario singing and gesturing properly to the music, as though he is raising his hands with the high notes. |
| Now I jump up on the ceiling 'cause this level really tough,<br>I a-take the magic warp-a zone and skip a lot of stuff. | Quick zoom out. At the left side the princess has appeared on a platform, singing along with the background choir. Mario does a wall jump towards her, while a set decoration picturing a warp zone falls down. Mario jumps on the middle pipe, ducks, and the decoration set raises again. |
| I will find-a you a-princess and-a make-a you my wife,<br>Oh a-wait I got to chase the extra-life! | A "Level Up" mushroom on a "rope" hovers through the air, Mario looks at it, and then catches it. The princess remains on her platform, gesturing properly while still singing along with the choir. |
| It's a-me, Mario!<br>It's a-me, Mario! | Alternating close-ups between Mario and the princess. |
| Now I reach the final castle,<br>It's-a the Bowser's evil lair.<br>Such a terrible a-hassle,<br>There's a-lava everywhere.<br>I defeat-a you-a Koopa King of level eight-a-four,<br>You a-jump, I run, and look, a-no more floor! | The castle falls down, Mario runs towards it. Scene change to the interior of the castle.<br>Mario runs towards Bowser, jumps over him, the floor disappears and Bowser falls. The platform with the princess floats towards Mario. He jumps to her side. |

| Lyrics | Video |
|---|---|
| PRINCESS:<br>You came for me,<br>MARIO:<br>  (It's a me!)<br>You came for me,<br>  (Let's-a get outta here)<br>You came for me,<br>  (You is-a free now)<br>You came for me.<br>  (Thanks to Mario . . .)<br>And now that you've taken a rest,<br>It is time to begin your next quest. | Close-up on booth. She sings to<br>him, while he faces the viewer. |
| CHORUS/PRINCESS/MARIO:<br>It's a-me, Mario!<br>It's a-me! | Both face the viewer. Zoom-out, the<br>curtain falls.<br>The foreshadowing to the second<br>Mario game is missing. |

The *Mario Opera Animated* video has only been viewed 4,200 times since it was posted in May 2012. Despite some criticism for animation errors and pixel artefacts, it has been acclaimed by the video's few commentators (six comments in total) for the effort. They also encourage the creator to make more. Nevertheless, it is a good example of how such content is further processed, thereby mixing several musical cultures – in this case, a game filk song with opera clichés transferred to the *Super Mario World* gameworld. Visual references to the opera theme are made regarding the staging and the "acting". The operatic frame is indicated by the red curtain, the stage walls at the sides of the screen that look like classical columns, the set decorations, and the props hanging on ropes. The animations of Mario and the Princess take up the clichéd images of opera singers: they raise their hands when singing high notes, stay relatively static, and underline important phrases with their hands, as Mario does during the lines "Now I touch-a you and-a you die 'cause I'm invincible!" Despite a few exceptions, the sound effects and short tunes from the original games are no longer synchronized with Mario's movements, and have simply become part of the "orchestration" and musical fabric. With its own playfulness regarding two different cultural contexts, the video overall underlines the playful approach of the original song, without destroying its basic humorous tone by taking itself too seriously.

## Conclusions

Since fan cultural practices and game development have been in a vivid communication since the earliest eras of video gaming, it was one of the aims of this chapter to include this same issue in the analysis of video game music and, in particular, game music cultural artefacts. With platforms such as YouTube and hard- and software for capturing and manipulating game content, it has become easier for many fans to get involved in the discourse of their preferred fandoms and become creators themselves.[22] In order to do so, they need game musical literacy, as defined above, to create a musical meaning themselves or, in other words, become skilled and legitimate designers in the eyes of their literate audience. Because video games do not exist in a separate universe, this literacy must be gained, which goes beyond the games and reaches into several cultural contexts. As we have seen, an extended concept of game musical literacy can be useful when analysing game music during gameplay, as well as stretching the focus of ludomusicology beyond the frame of the games themselves.

## Notes

1. Melanie Fritsch is a Berlin-based researcher. She worked as a research assistant at the University of Bayreuth between 2008 and 2013, and is currently finishing her PhD thesis "Performing Bytes: Musikperformances der Computerspielkultur". She is also a member of the AHRC research network "Guitar Heroes in Music Education? Music-based Video-games and their Potential for Musical and Performative Creativity".
2. Jenkins et al. define "participatory culture" as one:
   1. With relatively low barriers to artistic expression and civic engagement
   2. With strong support for creating and sharing one's creations with others
   3. With some type of informal mentorship whereby what is known by the most experienced is passed along to novices
   4. Where members believe that their contributions matter
   5. Where members feel some degree of social connection with one another (at the least they care what other people think about what they have created).

   Not every member must contribute, but all must believe they are free to contribute when ready and that what they contribute will be appropriately valued. (Jenkins et al., 2009: 5–6)
3. Mods are produced by altering the program code of a given game. This may lead to a completely new game or add new content to the original game. A famous example for this practice is the first-person shooter *Counter-Strike* (1999), which was initially developed as a mod of *Half-Life* (1998).
4. Cosplay (a coinage of costume and play) is a performance art with origins in Japan. Practitioners, the cosplayers, recreate costumes of characters from anime, manga, TV series, comic books, movies or computer games, and represent these characters on stage. Unlike live action roleplayers, cosplayers do not further develop these characters, but rather emphasize highly detailed costumes as well

as adopting character specific mannerisms and body language in order to be as similar to the chosen character as possible.

5. This distinction traces back to Meyer, 1956.

6. The website http://www.it-he.org/ gives a vivid demonstration of what this means: Some *Grand Theft Auto* players, for example, noticed that they do not die when jumping from high places such as a skyscraper while having a full healthbar. Combining the words "accuracy landing" or "proximity skydiving" with skyscrapers, blimps or helicopters in Vice City draws a perfect picture of what these people enthusiastically started to do, documenting their performances in YouTube videos. Other players found out that *Deus Ex* is by no means about multicorporate enterprises, hacking or epidemics. It is rather about farming immortal zombie seagulls who can fly under water. It is about not being lonely anymore in the single-player mode: just drug your contact, throw him over your shoulder and try to keep him alive as long as you can. See Kringiel, 2005.

7. Depending on the artefacts they want to create, this might be video editing, sound recording and mixing, hacking, composing etc.

8. The song appears in *Skyrim*, where it is sung in taverns by bards. The professionally trained musician Malukah had created a video, where she can be seen with her guitar in front of her microphone while singing. The song is presented in a professional mix, but makes very strong use of reverberation. Commentators praise her for her musical playing skills as well as for her soft voice and her looks. See https://www.youtube.com/watch?v=wr-buV4tYOA (accessed January 12, 2015).

9. The song, composed by Christopher Tin, serves as menu music in the game. For Malukah's and Peter Hollens's version in Peter Hollens's YouTube channel, see https://www.youtube.com/watch?v=17svtURunUk (accessed December 29, 2014). Malukah also uploaded the song to her channel, where it gained 750k views to the same date.

10. https://www.youtube.com/watch?v=YpXPtAVdMIY (accessed December 29, 2014).

11. https://www.youtube.com/channel/UCpad81d4S1iUjbNxNAO8Qsg (accessed December 29, 2014).

12. As commentator MG44ish noted: "The Super Mario story actuly sound [sic] like an opera". Quotations from comments retain the original typos, and other linguistic errors.

13. Mario's other rudimentary characteristics were steadily developed not just through the main game series (in which only spare information was given on him), but also through several game series adopting him as protagonist such as *Mario Kart*, *Mario Party*, TV shows such as *The Super Mario Bros. Super Show!* or the animated television series *Super Mario World*. In Japan, an anime series, as well as several comics and manga book series, were released. The Manga series *Super Mario-Kun* started in 1991, and counts 48 volumes at the time of writing. See http://www.mariowiki.com/Super_Mario-Kun (accessed December 29, 2014).

Furthermore, a rather mediocre live-action movie was made in 1993, featuring Bob Hoskins as Mario, John Leguizamo as Luigi and Dennis Hopper as King Koopa.

Mario fanfiction is extensive: the *Mario* division in the archive of FanFiction.net counts more than 7,000 stories about the game series and its characters. Fanfiction, fan-made videos, fan art and fan music all contribute to the development of the extensive repertoire of the Mario topos.

14. As the user PenguinSlime puts it: "Mario and Opera were made in Italian Heaven."

15. I allow myself to skip the tiresome "are games art?" and "high-brow/low-brow culture" debates here, because these are not the focus of this chapter. To make it short: Video games are a cultural form such as any other, and have to be taken as serious (or unserious) at the same level. For that reason, they are discussed here from that standpoint.

16. Transcribed by the author from https://www.youtube.com/watch?v=r4Eudb_Tqg8 (accessed December 29, 2014).

17. It could be interesting to think about Mario as a harlequinesque figure, who subverts the social order by loving a superior woman, jumps between the worlds, metamorphoses into different forms by eating mushrooms or other items, and always appears with the typical "Eccomi!"

18. The comments can all be found under the video: https://www.youtube.com/watch?v=YpXPtAVdMIY. Comment information correct as of December 29, 2014.

19. Some of these comments also sparked short debates.

    MoolahNasreddin: "Try another voice and remove this stupid 'echo effect' from it! I'm not a singer but I'm sure about delay and reverberation effects, had a lot of work using it."

    Enrique Dueñas: "You have no idea what are you talking about. Good day, sir."

    MoolahNasreddin: "+Enrique Dueñas Over seven years creating electronic music, some good releases . . . Sure I know a LOT about delays and reverberation effects :D

    It can be applied here . . . Something like 'Room' preset and about 4-7% of the voice's volume. Oh, and of course high frequencies must be cut off on the effect (or you'll get nasty 'shhh'-tails)."

    MoolahNasreddin: "+Enrique Dueñas P.S. I'm a Mario Bros. fan so it's not just a noise for me."

    Marcel Reinard: "+MoolahNasreddin Unfortunately, seems you don't know a lot about comedy though."

    Nick Vessel: "The effects add to the humor. Taking them away would make it less entertaining."

20. https://www.youtube.com/watch?v=h4cKr7zGQNg (accessed December 29, 2014).

21. See for example http://www.smwcentral.net (accessed December 29, 2014). Also the *Automatic Mario* videos are based on this game.

22. Some of today's professional video game composers such as Jesper Kyd or Chris Hülsbeck have their roots in such practices, including, in particular, demoscene music.

## References

Collins, K. (2013) *Playing with Sound: A Theory of Interacting with Sound and Music in Video Games*. Cambridge, MA: MIT Press.

Cook, N. (1998) *Analysing Musical Multimedia*. Oxford: Clarendon.

Ekman, I. (2014) "A Cognitive Approach to the Emotional Function of Game Sound." In *The Oxford Handbook of Interactive Audio*, edited by K. Collins, B. Kapralos and H. Tessler, pp. 196–212. New York: Oxford University Press.

Fritsch, M. (2014) "Worlds of Music. Strategies for Creating Music-Based Experiences in Video Games." In *The Oxford Handbook of Interactive Audio*, edited by K. Collins, B. Kapralos and H. Tessler, pp. 167–77. New York: Oxford University Press.

Hoeberechts, M., J. Shantz and M. Katchabaw (2014) "Delivering Interactive Experiences through the Emotional Adaptation of Automatically Composed Music." In *The Oxford Handbook of Interactive Audio*, edited by K. Collins, B. Kapralos and H. Tessler, pp. 419–42. New York: Oxford University Press.

Jenkins, H. (2013) *Textual Poachers: Television Fans and Participatory Culture*. Updated ed. New York: Routledge.

Jenkins, H., et al. (2009) *Confronting the Challenges on Participatory Culture: Media Education for the 21st Century*. Cambridge, MA: MIT Press.

Kringiel, D. (2005) "Spielen gegen jede Regel: Wahnsinn mit Methode." *Spiegel Online - Netzwelt*, September 30. http://www.spiegel.de/netzwelt/web/spielen-gegen-jede-regel-wahnsinn-mit-methode-a-377417.html (accessed December 29, 2014).

Liljedahl, M. (2010) "Sound for Fantasy and Freedom." In *Game Sound Technology and Player Interaction: Concepts and Developments*, edited by M. Grimshaw, pp. 22–43. Hershey: Idea Group Reference.

Meyer, L. (1956) *Emotion and Meaning in Music*. Chicago: University of Chicago Press.

Miller, N. (2010) "Director Edgar Wright, Actor Michael Cera Crack Wise about Scott Pilgrim." *Wired*, June 22. http://www.wired.com/2010/06/ff_cerawright/2/ (accessed 29 December 2014).

Paryzer, D. (2012) "Super Mario 64: A Love Letter." April 3. http://www.joystickdivision.com/2012/04/super_mario_64_a_love_letter.php (accessed December 29, 2014).

Salen, K. and E. Zimmerman (2004) *Rules of Play: Game Design Fundamentals*. Cambridge, MA: MIT Press.

Tagg, P. (2002) "'Universal' Music and the Case of Death." http://tagg.org/articles/deathmus.html (accessed December 29, 2014).

Van Elferen, I. (2012) "The ALI Model: Towards a Theory of Game Musical Immersion." Conference paper given at the RMA Study Day *Ludomusicology: Game Music Research. Approaches and Aesthetics*, Oxford, April 16.

Van Elferen, I. (2016) "Analyzing Game Musical Immersion: The ALI Model." In *Ludomusicology: Approaches to Video Game Music*, edited by M. Kamp, T. Summers and M. Sweeney, pp. 32–52. Sheffield: Equinox.

Whalen, Z. (2004) "Play Along – An Approach to Videogame Music." *Game Studies* 4/1. http://www.gamestudies.org/0401/whalen/

Zagal, J. (2010). *Ludoliteracy: Defining, Understanding, and Supporting Games Education*. Halifax: Etc Press.

Zimmerman, E. (2009) "Gaming Literacy: Game Design as a Model for Literacy in the Twenty-First Century." In *The Video Game Theory Reader 2*, edited by B. Perron und M. J. P. Wolf, pp. 23–31. New York: Routledge.

## Websites

http://www.jonandal.com/bio/ (accessed March 1, 2016).
http://www.it-he.org/ (accessed February 14, 2015).

# 7   Game and Play in Music Video Games

## Anahid Kassabian and Freya Jarman[1]

*June is a big month in my family: my dad, my son, and I all have a birthday within a week of each other, and it has become something of a tradition to throw a triple birthday party. Between this impending event and the fact that my son – on turning ten – seemed already to have more worldly possessions than is strictly decent, I was rather stumped as to what to get him. Starting by thinking about what he already enjoys, I reviewed a Wii game he owns called* Michael Jackson: The Experience, *a dance game where players hold their remotes and compete to replicate MJ's signature moves most accurately. The magic of Amazon's "Other customers bought . . ." recommendations system led me from this to a game called* Samba de Amigo, *and this was what he eventually unwrapped some few days later. The basic principle is familiar: hold the remote and nunchuck to simulate maracas, and move them in various rhythmic patterns to well-known popular music hits (in loosely Latin styles) and at specific angles to each other, to compete for accuracy against another player in "samba" choreographies. In turn, the simplicity of that principle made it quite ideal for the party that ensued. What I did not expect was quite how engaging the experience would be, and in particular quite how entertaining it would be even for those not participating. The gratuitous and psychedelic visuals combined with the music to generate a fun environment, and the refusal of the soundtrack to be impeded by player failure (as in the* Guitar Hero *series with false notes, for instance) helped the playing go on very late into the night, including "live" participation from non-players using the real maracas we also possess. The experience of playing this game, and of the relationship between playing the game and the illusion of playing samba music, remained very present to me while contemplating the issues Anahid and I raise in this chapter.* (Freya Jarman)

This article considers the various ways that music as a central activity is represented and negotiated in video games and smartphone apps – such as the differences between video games like *Samba de Amigo* (1999) and *Guitar*

*Hero* (2005) (where music is the vehicle for the gameplay) and others where music takes up a different role in relation to the game.[2] It does not consider sounds and music in games and apps and other virtual settings, which a steadily growing body of literature does,[3] but instead focuses on artifacts that might be labelled "music games" or "music apps" (although such terms are not unproblematic). But even with this limitation to a much smaller field of activity, we are still confronted with a host of definitional challenges, on which we will spend some time. The lack of immediate clarity around the objects about which we write here is not simply something that needs to be addressed at this early juncture in the argument, but it yields some of the means through which part of our argument emerges. That is, in saying that we write about "music games" and how they use and represent music, not only should we first explain what "music games" are, but in so doing we will simultaneously lay down the very foundations of our argument.[4]

The term "music game" is problematic on several counts, and it quite quickly offers up a knot of multiple conceptual strands, the first of which is the very notion of *game*. On the face of it, such a concept is quite self-evident; every one of us has played such a thing – chess, solitaire, "tag", "mummies and daddies". Yet to say that one has precisely *played* a *game* in turn throws up the question of the difference between *play* and *game*, and to parse those two concepts reveals that not everything we have played, or played with, is necessarily a game. If we were to consider briefly what it is that might hold together the examples listed two sentences ago as games, we could turn to Wittgenstein's suggestion that only "family resemblances" are at work (2009 [1953]: §66–§67),[5] and declare that there is at best only a limited connection; or, we could turn to Bernard Suits (2005), whose notion of a "lusory attitude" (p. 49) – a decision to engage in play – might be a common element. Importantly, though, all that is *play* is not *game*; rather, many definitions of the latter impose some criteria upon it, such that structure and order are defining features, and whether the underlying purpose itself is one of education or of entertainment. Definitions of *game* generally agree that there must be some goal, some quantifiable outcome, while play is, in most conceptions, more open. Such a differentiation is palpable in Roger Caillois's influential *Man, Play and Games* (1958), for instance, in which he distinguishes between *paidia* – "a primary power of improvisation and joy" (p. 27) – and *ludus* – a "disciplining" element that transforms *paidia* into a more structured play. Such categories do not map exactly onto *play* and *game*, but are certainly impulses that operate with variable levels of force in different video games, and whose variability lends important distinguishing characteristics to those games.

The relationship between "play" and "game" is quite complex, as it turns out, since each is in some sense a subset of the other. Games are composed of rules, contexts and gameplay, whereas play includes many types of activities, only some of which might be called games. "Play" is a very old word in English, which one might guess from the range of its uses. Etymologically, it comes to us through Old English from West Germanic (a language subgroup including German, Dutch, English, Yiddish, Frisian) (Harper, 2014). We use it to express activities (playing ball), behaviours (playing at something), skills (playing an instrument), and much, much more. Remove most of the examples and further refinements from the definition in *Oxford Dictionaries Online*, and we are still left with seven senses of the verb and another five for the noun:

verb

1. *[no object]* engage in activity for enjoyment and recreation rather than a serious or practical purpose: "the children were playing by a pool" . . .
*[with object]* engage in (a game or activity) for enjoyment: "I want to play Snakes and Ladders" . . .

- (**play at**) Engage in without proper seriousness or understanding: "it would be wrong to assume that he is simply playing at right-wing politics"
- (**play with**) Treat inconsiderately for one's own amusement: "she likes to play with people's emotions"
- (**play with**) Fiddle or tamper with: "has somebody been playing with these taps?" . . .

2. *[with object]* Take part in (a sport): "I play squash and badminton" . . .
3. *[no object, usually with negative]* Be cooperative: "he needs financial backing, but the building societies won't play"
4. *[with object]* Represent (a character) in a theatrical performance or a film: "early in her career she played Ophelia" . . .
5. *[with object]* Perform on (a musical instrument): "a man was playing a guitar" . . .
6. *[no object]* Move lightly and quickly, so as to appear and disappear; flicker: "little beams of light played over the sea" . . .
7. *[with object]* Allow (a fish) to exhaust itself pulling against a line before reeling it in: "no fisherman ever played a bonita more carefully or with greater wile"

noun

1. Activity engaged in for enjoyment and recreation, especially by children: "a child **at play** may use a stick as an aeroplane" . . .
2. The conducting of a sporting match: "rain wrecked the second day's play" . . .
3. *[count noun]* A dramatic work for the stage or to be broadcast: "the actors put on a new play"

4. The space in or through which a mechanism can or does move: "the steering rack was loose, and there was a little play"

5. Light and constantly changing movement: "the artist exploits the play of light across the surface"

(Oxford Dictionaries Online, 2015)

All of these definitions share some interest in space and motion. Casper Harteveld further observes some of the various negative connotations of the word "play", especially when used in relation to adults, as found in phrases such as "to play up to someone" or to be "a player" (2011: 75). It is no surprise, then, that play scholarship is similarly wide-ranging and difficult to pin down. For some, it starts with Plato's ideas about play and supervision from the fourth century BCE, discussed in *Laws* (1970); for others with Rousseau's *Émile* (1974 [1762]); and for others with Johan Huizinga's *Homo Ludens* (1980 [1944]). "Play" is often imagined as belonging to children, although recent scholarship has emphasized its importance both to adults and across species (Brown, 2009). Moreover, according to play scholars, there are many kinds of play (solitary, social, physical, object, fantasy, etc.), and "game" is just one form among many.[6] As Gwen Gordon puts it in her article "What is Play?", any definition of play will have to accommodate:

> the full range of forms conventionally understood as play, including both competitive and cooperative games, solo and social play, skill based and fate based games, introverted and extroverted play, intrinsically and extrinsically motivated play, as well as rule-based and rule-breaking play. (Gordon, 2009: 3)

Many, if not most, scholars disavow the possibility of coming up with a general definition of play at all (Myers, 2010; Grieshaber and McArdle, 2010).

However, attempts to define play often make reference to child development, including cognitive, psychological, social, motor skills areas and ethics (Gray, 2008); some explorations of play extend that focus on development to adults. Lumosity, a company based on research conducted at Stanford University, is one of a number of enterprises with websites promising the user greater mental health if one subscribes to the site and plays games that have been designed especially to develop and strengthen particular forms of mental acuity. As Luminosity's home page describes:

> Lumosity.com has been clinically proven to support brain health. Our users report profound results: faster name recall, greater attention to detail, better concentration, and quicker problem-solving skills ... Designed by neuroscientists, our web-based training program makes brains smarter, faster and more flexible. (Luminosity Brain Games, 2012)

These utilitarian senses of the purpose of play are underpinned elsewhere by approaches that focus more on the importance of freedom and leisure for future problem-solving and the like. Stuart Brown, in his talk on TED.com (2008), points out that rats that were deprived of play throughout their lives were far inferior in coping with problems with which they were presented than those who had engaged in play throughout their lives.

In fact, music games for animals are a growing area of research, however unlikely that may seem. There is a growing concern that zoo animals in particular suffer from boredom, and game designers are beginning to design games for animals based on games they already play. For example, Hanna Wirman, a video game designer at Hong Kong Polytechnic University, has designed a game for very young orangutans based on the poking game they play naturally. She designed a game plate with varying size holes, and sticks with sensors on the end. When the orangutans put sticks into the holes, sounds are emitted, creating what may well be the first music game for non-humans (Nuwer, 2014).[7]

One important pair of categories in play scholarship is structured vs unstructured play, and within this perspective, games clearly fall into the category of structured play.[8] Structured and unstructured play appear to have very different purposes and outcomes: while structured play often encourages team social skills, analysis, and a range of other abilities, unstructured play builds creativity, allows for the release of tension, establishes relationships within a group, and more.

However, in *The Trouble with Play*, Susan Grieshaber and Felicity McArdle take issue with many of these basic tenets about play. On the first page of their introduction, they say:

> We challenge these taken-for-granted understandings of play in early childhood education and argue that play in the early years is not always innocent and fun; that it is also political and involves morals and ethics. Further, there are other sides to play that are not so romantic, natural, or particularly educative, and play is not always the best way for young children to learn. (Grieshaber and McArdle, 2010: 1)

Grieshaber and McArdle's criticism is important for anyone looking to study play seriously and carefully. But the ideas they raise are also significant for questions of video gameplay in particular; questions of what games and gameplay do, socially and culturally, are not at all simple to unpack.

Furthermore, there is a definition of play that is rarely given much attention in the literature, namely its use as a transitive verb with a musical instrument as its object. Scholars thinking about the importance of playfulness might be forgiven if they set aside the opportunity to think about musicians playing instruments – after all, most representations of learning to play a musical instrument seem anything but playful.[9] (This, too, will become important when we begin to consider games below.) In this sense, play means to have acquired the capacity to be creative with sounds, in many (but by no means all) musical contexts after years of study, whether alone or with a teacher. Not for the first time does the question of the relationship between play and learning raise its oh-so-knotty head here. Does learning enable play? Does play enable learning? Certainly both are true, and not only of one's relationship with an instrument. (The rats discussed by Stuart Brown return to mind here.) No matter which way we turn, to children, adults, or other species, to games or unstructured or musical play, we keep finding this connection – between play and learning – cropping up. While the study of play is still very much a field in development, it is clear that an understanding of play will have to include its connection with learning in some form(s).

Another central component of play, according to many scholars from Huizinga onwards, is what is often referred to as the "magic circle" aspect of play, that is, all play includes an understanding that it is set apart from everyday life and ordinary activity. In *Homo Ludens* (1980 [1944]), Huizinga says "we might call it a free activity standing quite consciously outside 'ordinary' life as being 'not serious' but at the same time absorbing the player intensely and utterly" (p. 13). Similarly, Gwen Gordon says that "Most work on play characterizes it as a set of features that shift the frame of activity from one domain to another through the meta-message that 'this is play' (Bateson, 1972; Stewart, 1979)" (Gordon, 2009: 4). It is interesting to note that both of these definitions connect closely with how musicians describe their best experiences of music-making.

In Suits's work on games, one aspect of this "magic circle" is termed the "prelusory goal" (2005: 51), a goal understandable and achievable apart from the game, an idea that exists and can be manifested outside of the boundaries of the game. Thomas Hurka and John Tasioulas give the example here of golf, in which a player must make a ball land in a hole in the ground (2006: 219). This is the prelusory goal; the boundaries are the "constitutive rules", whose purpose is ultimately to define *how* the prelusory goal must be achieved, and in fact to forbid the most efficient means of achieving the goal. To continue with golf, Hurka and Tasioulas point out that one is not allowed simply to pick up the ball and place it in the hole (2006: 219). It is the combination of goal, rules and lusory attitude that, in Suits's understanding, make a game:

> To play a game is to achieve a specific state of affairs [prelusory goal], using only means permitted by the rules . . . where the rules prohibit the use of more efficient means [constitutive rules], and where rules are accepted just because they make possible such an activity [lusory goal]. (Suits, 2005: 54)

Or, in a tighter summary, "Playing a game is the voluntary attempt to overcome unnecessary obstacles" (p. 55).

In fact, definitions of *game* are more likely to agree on the importance of *goal* than that *play* is a necessary element. Even in Suits's identification of a lusory attitude, he is not saying that *play* occurs in *game*. Rather, the structuring and order necessary to define *game* are arguably contrary to the very notion of play as a free activity, as the very essence of freedom. His definitional framework seems workable enough but, within it, an argument can easily be made that such a thing as climbing a mountain is a game; it has a prelusory goal (standing at the top), constitutive rules (the climber must power the journey with his or her legs, and not drive, ride, or otherwise be transported to the top), and the necessary attitude could in theory be adopted. Instinctively, however, this activity – as enjoyable as it may be – does not seem like a *game* as such. Other attempts to define *game* make use of concepts of *conflict*, such that the goal implicitly involves winning or losing against other people (or a digital device – computer, console, phone, etc. – as an ostensibly active AI player), and *players*, in which said people (or digital devices) are typically figured as rational decision-makers. Under these conditions, mountaineering is no longer a game, but neither is something like *Snakes and Ladders*, since no decision-making can occur, as all players' progress is entirely subject to the roll of the dice. Moreover, under Suits's conditions, solitaire can be a game, but it cannot be under those definitions where conflict is a necessary precondition, for the pack of cards cannot be a "rational decision-maker". (And even if the medium through which one plays solitaire is a digital one, the digital device is not simulating a rational-decision-making pack of cards, and thus it remains a non-game.)

For the purposes of our argument, the blurry borders around the idea of *game* are precisely the sites at which we find some of the most significant points of interest regarding the more specific (and yet, actually, at least as troublesome) category of *music game*. The definition of a music game might at first glance seem simple, but turns out to be fairly complex: what makes a game a music game? Is controlling the production of sounds the entirety of the gameplay (e.g. *Sveerz* [2003], *Dhol-E* [2010]), a major part of the play (e.g. *Guitar Hero*), a consequence of gameplay (e.g. *Otocky* [1987], *Rez* [2001]), or is it just one part among many (*Legend of Zelda: Ocarina of Time* [1998])? We want to argue that those games in which controlling the production of music is all or much of the gameplay can reasonably be defined as a genre in their own right, that is, as music games, even if they cross other more traditional genre definitions in the gaming world. This is in contrast to other common, popular definitions of the genre, such as that given in the Wikipedia article "Music Video Games", which says: "A **music video game**, also commonly known as a

**music game**, is a video game where the gameplay is meaningfully and often almost entirely oriented around the player's interactions with a musical score or individual songs" (Wikipedia, 2015, emphasis original). This allows games like *Lumines* (2004) and *Rez* to be included in the Wikipedia entry, as in many gamers' conceptions of music games, whereas the fact that the point of those games is creating squares from falling blocks or shooting targets – and musical events are simply a consequence of that – means that we will not consider them music games.

Moreover, we argue that music games have a didactic function; we mean here not that they are educational projects, but rather that they "teach" or "improve" some kind of skill, be it memory, hand-eye-ear coordination, the liberty to shape and create patterns of sound, or an entry into (a) musical culture(s). That is not to say that the didactic function is a primary, or even necessarily intended, outcome of gameplay, but rather that the player necessarily learns something or acquires or improves a skill. In this way, they offer a path to the eventual mastery of some aspect of music-making, whether or not that aspect is traditionally recognized as music-making or not.

There are, from another perspective, two major types of music video games: games in which the player is right or wrong such as *Taiko: Drum Master* (2004), on the one hand, and on the other apps and other kinds of programs in which the player engages in "sandbox" play, such as in Mike Oldfield's *Tres Lunas* (2002) or Brian Eno and Peter Chilvers's iPhone app *Scape* (2012). Through a consideration of these various kinds of activities and their outcomes – intended or not – we will show that music is represented in virtual worlds as both disciplinary and liberatory, though usually not in the same virtual world. These competing visions of music are consistent with representations of music in popular culture more generally, where music is a hardship and a demanding taskmaster (see for instance *Shine* [Hicks, 1996]), but also a path to freedom, salvation and self-expression (see for instance *August Rush* [Sheridan, 2007] or *School of Rock* [Linklater, 2003]), often simultaneously.

Furthermore, we will focus heavily in this chapter on apps and games available on, and often designed specifically for, the smartphone, for several reasons. First, we believe that this is an important new sphere of cultural activity with its own sense of time (often small chunks, albeit chunks that easily add up into larger ones) and scale (the size of a smartphone screen being significantly smaller than that of a PC monitor or television screen), and a new economic position. Second, it is familiar to us, since we both have less time to play games than we would like, and smartphone games offer new possibilities to us (because, as mentioned above, the unit of play – for example, a level – is short enough to fit into a busy schedule). Finally, as the as-yet-least-studied gaming arena, we wanted to bring some attention to smartphone apps in general, and games and sandbox play apps in particular, as a fertile area for new scholarship.

## What is a Music Game?

In general, video game genres have settled into a recognizable set of terms based on various narrative features. There are first-person shooters (FPS), role playing (RPG) and massively multiplayer online role playing (MMORPG), real-time strategy (RTS), hack'n'slash, fighting, arcade, construction and management simulation, platformers/sidescrollers, and many more types of games. Each genre has conventions about what visual angles are available (first-person shooters, sidescrollers), about what kinds of problems one encounters (real-time strategy, construction and management simulation), and about numbers of players (one, two, many). Generally, genres are also defined by one or another narrative attribute: perspective, story type, obstacle type, setting, and so on.

In proposing to redefine the category of music games, we are not suggesting that the games we plan to discuss belong to that genre and not any of the existing ones. Rather, these games share a different set of commonalities, one based on senses rather than narrative organization. When medium gives definition to a genre, it works more in this sense. So, for instance, when we call a film a film, it has to do with:

- its sensory address, that it is auditory and visual,
- its original display on a very large screen that fills our field of vision,
- the experience of fixed seating in darkness, and
- the experience of light shining through transparent photographic images at a high enough frequency to trigger the perception of motion (caused by various neurological and optical phenomena, including, but not limited to, persistence of vision).

That it has unstably become the name for the narrative form – a c.1.5 hour linear narrative, usually centred on a main character – is interesting, but the extent to which terms such as "video", "DVD" and "Blu-Ray" are used suggests that the sensory specifics are quite important indeed. It is in this sense that we are calling a genre into being, and less in the sense of a narrative genre, such as romcom or thriller for films, and FPS or RPG for games.

Thus, music games and apps, as we define them, are those where the majority of gameplay or activity, and if applicable, winning and losing, are predicated on the ability to make good sound and/or musical choices. And yet such a statement is not as self-evident or simple as it might at first appear, and its complexities have to do with both the nature of games and the nature of music. There are to begin with a number of decisions to be made along the lines of what counts as a "musical choice". Is, for instance, a paramusical decision (one based on a world or information about, around, or next to music) such a thing, or must the medium in which the decision is made be one that involves music? That is to say, music quizzes – of which there are many available in DVD, console, and smartphone app formats – might be thought of as games *about* music, but not *music games* as such, mostly on the basis that no sound-production need necessarily be involved in the answering of the question. In other words, although the quiz is music-themed, nothing like a musical response or musical input from the player is required. We take music quizzes to be such games, and do not include them in the category of "music game". A sub-form of music quiz also exists, however, that might be considered more of a music game than the standard quiz format. The iPhone game *iHum Nation* (2009) – like a category of questions in the board game *Cranium* (1998) or in the television quiz programme *Never Mind the Buzzcocks* (1996+), and along the same lines as the whole of the radio/television show *Name That Tune* (1952–1998 in the US; 1983–1998 in the UK) – asks a player to hum a song named by the app for the other player to guess; if that second player identifies the song from the hum, they score points. In *Cranium*, the format is a team game, such that it is in the team's interests for one player to hum well, so that the teammates can guess the song, but it is difficult to see how this works effectively as a competitive one-on-one game as it is intended in *iHum Nation*, since it is in the humming player's best interests *not* to hum the song well, so that the guessing player – the opponent – is unable to guess correctly. It is also not clear what function the app has except as a generator of random song titles and a scoresheet.

Nonetheless, the principle is that of a quiz in which players are engaged in music-making, through the act of humming, and this engagement would, by our definition, fit the category of "music game". Also in this music or music-related quiz category are games in which players must identify a song from an extract played by the digital device on which the game is played. A typical format for this is an app such as *Music Quiz* (2003), in which the extracts and the multiple choice answers are selected randomly from the player's own smartphone tunes library. This, it seems to us, sits somewhere between the general knowledge music quiz and games like *iHum*; it involves musical sound in its gameplay, but its lack of musical engagement by the player(s) ultimately renders it not a music game for us.

Closer to the centre of the genre are the two related subcategories of simulator games and karaoke games. The former includes, famously, *Guitar Hero*, *DJ Hero* (2009) and *Rock Band* (2007), while the latter is exemplified by *SingStar* (2004) and also found in, for instance, *Karaoke Revolution Glee* (2010). In each type, players are rewarded with points and other benefits (unlocked characters, songs, outfits, and so on) for their achievements, where "achievement" is defined by "playing the song correctly". This is an admittedly loose way of terming what happens, but to be any more specific is to define the differences rather than the similarities between simulator games and karaoke games. It is that similarity that causes the games to be grouped together frequently in discourse around them, but there are important differences also. In *Guitar Hero* and other "Hero" type games, players typically wield a controller that resembles the instrument in question – a guitar, a record player, or a drum kit, for instance – and are required to press or hit parts of the equipment in time with visual stimuli on screen that (claim to) resemble the musical part being played by the player's instrument.[10] Accuracy of timing is essential to earn points. In karaoke games, a similar basic principle applies, but players are required to sing into a microphone while reading notes that are illustrated on-screen. The fundamental difference, then, and the reason we have subdivided these two types, is that karaoke games require the generation of music *by the player*, whereas the more general simulator games are exercises purely in hand-eye coordination in terms of timing.

The emphasis on timing appears to put them into closer proximity with rhythm games such as *Space Channel 5* (1999) or later incarnations. On one hand, other than drumming and using the keytar (as in *Rock Band*), there is a significant difference between the instrument being simulated (guitar, DJ decks, or the piano in one iPhone app) and the musicality of the input by the player. On the other hand, it could also be argued that a vast number of game types, particularly platform and FPS games, are also hand-eye coordination games where accurate timing is essential to success. Indeed, it would be perfectly possible, we would suggest, to read *Guitar Hero* and other such games as being, at heart, strikingly similar to most first-person shooters, as both game types require certain buttons to be pressed at specific times in relation to the location on screen of a visual event; once the note is "shot", it disappears, just like any one of the aliens in *DOOM* (1993). However, the very fact that music-simulator games announce themselves as such is crucial. The physical interface is often (certainly for console versions) a plastic simulation of the instrument itself, the on-screen world is narratively "about" playing music, and the player does not hear weapons firing but notes playing; failure to hit a note correctly results in the note being absent from the music being heard. This self-awareness of the simulator games *as* music games, and the attendant gesture towards simulation, then, distinguishes them not only from FPS, but also from a variety of closely related spin-off games, such as the *Tap Tap* series, created by Tapulous (2008). Here, a *Guitar Hero* visual format is used, with three lines of dots to tap on-screen, and music plays in the background – often, in fact, this is the justification for a new *Tap Tap*, and *Tap Tap Coldplay* (2009), *Justin Bieber Revenge* (2010) *and Linkin Park Revenge* (2011) are among the many that have been released. Importantly, though, the dot-tapping process – while it may be in time with the music – does not interact directly with the music, or claim to, and as such it is harder to characterize the *Tap Tap* games as music games.[11] Rhythm games like this seem not to have lost players' interest and to have maintained their popularity over the two decades plus of their existence.

An interesting hybrid of some of these principles – a focus on the vocal line and a gameplay where hand-eye coordination is central – is found in the iPhone game *Lyric Legend* (2011). Here, single words from song lyrics appear in bubbles at random places on the screen and the player must tap them in the right place and at the right time as the song is played. Such a game raises questions about the implicit conditions we have used so far for diagnosing "music games", for several reasons. There is no musical incentive for tapping correctly (whereas in simulator games the music depends on the player's accuracy), and therefore no direct control over the music by the player. This fact makes the game quite similar to the *Tap Tap* series on the surface of it, and yet there seems to be a more direct relation between the gameplay task and the music in *Lyric Legend* than in *Tap Tap* games; the dots in the latter bear only a spatial-temporal relation to the music, and a sonic-visual cue is given to the player, whereas in *Lyric Legend* the player must have a good level of familiarity with the lyrics, as by the time the word is heard, the optimum points-scoring moment for tapping has passed.[12] Moreover, it would be hard to imagine playing this game without being able to hear the track simultaneously with gameplay. (It is, however, quite possible to imagine playing a simulator or *Tap Tap* game without hearing the music.) Into this mix, however, comes another game created for smartphones by Tapulous: *Riddim Ribbon* (2010). The basic idea of the game is to keep a ball on a track by tilting the phone left and right (using the accelerometer to control the movement). While the ball is on the track, it will collect balls of various colours, which provide another element to the gameplay. Meanwhile, a song is playing to accompany the game (a song chosen by the player prior to commencing play), and certain events happen on the track (such as jumping a ramp) in time with key musical events. The sense in which this may be a music game, though, is that the point-scoring ball-collecting "right" track is one line on a wider track, and deviation from that "right" track changes the sound quality of the music; roll too far over to one side, and the sound becomes muffled and unclear. To this extent, then, the player does have control over the musical environment, as in simulator games, but unlike the *Tap Tap* games or *Lyric Legend*. Ultimately, though, the music is surplus to the core of the game, and it would be very possible indeed to play without the sound.

What has been established thus far, then, is that music games – like any other genre – have certain manifestations very close to the centre and others further from it. However, the ordering of games and game types – their position in relation to the centre – may not always be entirely obvious. Once we declare that a key factor is direct engagement with musical sound as a primary element of gameplay, it seems clear that *SingStar* is central and general knowledge music quizzes are not up for consideration; but how primary is "primary", and what constitutes "direct engagement" are two things that would affect the ordering of some of the other games mentioned above.

The "non-game" apps have another set of boundary problems. There are some obvious candidates for inclusion, such as the three apps from Brian Eno's Generative Music company, *Bloom* (2008), *Air* (2009) and *Trope* (2009); *Balls* (2009) from Iotic; *Bebot* (2009) from Normalware; *Pulsate* (2012) from Audiotool; and *NodeBeat* (2011), often compared to *Reactable* (2009), by AffinityBlue, and others. But then there are a whole range of music apps that may or may not be approached playfully, depending on the user. There are:

- instrument apps, such as *Ocarina* (2007) from Smule, which clearly seems at least partially playful in intent (the user can, for example, listen to what other players around the world are playing at any given moment);
- percussion apps, such as *Drum Beats* (2010), to provide a beat;
- soundscape apps like *Inception* (2010) that allow the user different levels of interaction and control with the way the filters treat and re-present the real-world audio environment back to the user;
- remix apps, ranging from specific artists (e.g. DJ Spooky's self-titled app, 2010) to more general ones (*DJ Mix Master*, 2012);
- record and live mix apps like *MadPad* (2011) from Smule, on which the user can record twelve sounds that can then be mixed together simply by tapping on the icon of the sound they want.

All of these apps can be used to make music with varying degrees of seriousness, but they also invite uninhibited, playful creativity. They invite a posture that encompasses many of the components of the various definitions of play – they are separated from routine activities, they encourage a kind of freedom with sound(s), and they present themselves as relaxation activities. While such playfulness is possible with apps more oriented towards professional musicians, and while many of the apps mentioned take care to be potentially appealing to musicians, we will bracket from consideration apps that present themselves as geared more towards professionals.

There is another group of apps that warrants mention here, and that is those that treat sound creatively but have some other primary purpose. So, for example, *Aqueous* (2009) is not a sound or music app as such, but its main components are sound samples and music loops. The app makes available a handful of visual backgrounds along with which one can choose a range of water sounds, a range of nature sounds, and a range of music loops. The water then appears over the chosen picture, and the user can "draw" patterns in it while listening to the sounds. In like kind, there are any number of apps to help one sleep that allow for a creative relationship to sound and music samples – since the central purpose of these is not music or music-making, they are again bracketed out of consideration.[13]

But to return to the central apps under consideration here, they share a number of important features that are worth mentioning. The first thing is that in a variety of ways, all of them multisensory, they enable the combining of sounds to make something that one might call music accessible and unintimidating. While notation and improvisation are both frightening to those not used to them, and instruments require years of practice, it is possible to make quite pleasant sounds with these apps within minutes of opening them for the first time. One drags a finger around an image in *Bebot*, or pushes balls in *Balls*, or taps the screen in *Bloom*, and suddenly quite acceptable sounds are coming out of one's smartphone or tablet. For at least some users, one of us included, these apps provide amusement and pleasure in ways that the pressure of competition and points present in games never could.

This returns us to the matter of game and play. Games are virtual worlds in which a telos is established in the form of a prelusory goal; one strives to achieve something and is measured accordingly. The apps, however, do not so much create virtual worlds as they do offer the tools to explore the audiovisual possibilities of the digital realm, in which one can make sounds and shapes and colours and patterns and rhythms *ad infinitum* for very low cost and with very little expertise whatsoever. This world of unstructured – or perhaps semi-structured (insofar as every app offers only a specific range of parameters) – play precludes any significant prelusory goal beyond perhaps "enjoyment" or "make pleasant sounds". It is inherently exploratory in nature, and it is consistently presented as such in the discourse around these apps.

It is in this difference that we see a very distinct split in the representation of music in these two kinds of virtual worlds. On the one hand, the games present music as a task to be achieved, a disciplinary activity in which the player should "play" again and again until the game (and thereby music) is mastered. This is very clear in the *Video Games Live* concerts, in which a pre-concert *Guitar Hero* competition leads to the winner playing a song with the live orchestra in the second half of the concert – on *Guitar Hero*, of course. On the other hand, the apps allow for dipping in and out, for the most casual of engagements as well as more intensive devotion, and for experimentation and creativity. These apps present the other side of music's two faces: the joyful, ecstatic, creative aspect of musical experience. While it is clear to any practising musician that the two are inextricably intertwined, and cannot be pulled apart, music in virtual worlds seems only to be able to appear – or perhaps sound? – as one or the other, but not both.

## Notes

1. Anahid Kassabian is a music and media scholar whose research focuses on listening in audiovisual contexts. She is the author of *Ubiquitous Listening* (University of California Press, 2013), *Hearing Film* (Routledge, 2001) and numerous journal articles and book chapters. She is the co-editor of *Ubiquitous Musics* (Ashgate, 2013) and *Keeping Score* (University Press of Virginia, 1997), past editor of both *Music, Sound, and the Moving Image* and *Journal of Popular Music Studies*, and past chair of the International Association for the Study of Popular Music.

   Freya Jarman is Senior Lecturer in Music at the University of Liverpool, and works primarily on cultures and ideologies of the voice, especially in relation to gender, sexuality and queer theory. She is the author of *Queer Voices* (Palgrave, 2011) as well as a number of articles and book chapters, editor of *Oh Boy! Masculinities and Popular Music* (Routledge, 2007), and co-editor of *Madonna's Drowned Worlds* (Ashgate, 2004).

2. This article was first invited for the *Oxford Handbook of Virtuality*, edited by Mark Grimshaw (2014). While it did not develop into an essay on virtuality, as we had at first intended, we are grateful that the invitation made us think about these games, which resulted in this article.

3. See the Ludomusicology Research Group bibliography for an excellent resource: http://www.ludomusicology.org/bibliography (accessed February 28, 2015).

4. For some discussions of music video games, see Pichlmair and Kayali, 2007; Smith, 2004 and Summers, 2012: chapter 5. This is just a small selection of the literature, which ranges from discussions of education and health to issues of game creation.

5. Wittgenstein used this idea of family resemblance to suggest that a group might be connected by multiple overlaps that did not necessarily mean every item has an overlap with every other one. This is an important shift from the notion that a single definition is the only way to think of things as connected to each other, and it became an important part of Wittgenstein's philosophy. Intriguingly, for our purposes here, one of the examples he leans on often is the "family" of games. See, for example, Biletzki and Matar, 2014.

6. There are many typologies of play in the literature, which are not pertinent here. Stuart Brown (2008; 2009), the National Institute for Play (2010) and Roger Caillois (2001) would be some places to start considering this literature. There is also a range of types of video gameplay that are frequently used by reviewers and gamers in casual conversation.

7. The main article (Nuwer, 2014) is about designing better interfaces for service dogs, and the orangutan project is in a sidebar. In addition, Nuwer also points

to a project that observes elephant audio interaction as a precursor to designing a game to help alleviate their boredom.

8. This distinction is particularly important in the early childhood education and psychology literature and less so in the literature that is more pertinent to our topic here. See, for example, Torkildsen, 2005: 89. It does, however, helpfully describe the distinction between games and apps that we will develop later in the chapter.

9. In this sense, it is interesting to note the difference between playing an instrument and playing with or playing around with one. The latter are clearly more relaxed, less expert, and probably more "playful".

10. For some examples that illustrate how playing a game can be the voluntary attempt to overcome unnecessary obstacles, see:

    *Guitar Hero* drum part – http://www.youtube.com/watch?v=ftKUnz6p5S4;

    *DJ Hero* – http://www.youtube.com/watch?v=dlgkl4K9nL4 (both accessed June 4, 2015).

11. The name "tap tap" presumably derives from the earlier *Dance Dance Revolution* games (1998–), involving a mat connected to a console, on which players would "dance" (press buttons with their feet). *Dance Dance Revolution* is in fact available with that name on the iPhone, but the necessary tapping interface – it would be hard to imagine a dance mat attached to a smartphone – makes it difficult to distinguish from handheld versions of *Guitar Hero*.

12. See http://www.youtube.com/watch?v=i9M-w3H_bZw for *Lyric Legend* gameplay (accessed June 4, 2015).

13. For a discussion of music and sound in apps to help one sleep, see Kassabian 2013.

## References

Bateson, G. (1972) *Steps to an Ecology of Mind*. Chicago: University of Chicago Press.

Biletzki, A. and A. Matar (2014) "Ludwig Wittgenstein." In *The Stanford Encyclopedia of Philosophy* (Spring 2014 edition), edited by E. Zalta. http://plato.stanford.edu/archives/spr2014/entries/wittgenstein/ (accessed February 28, 2015).

Brown, S. (2008) "Play is More than Just Fun." *TED.com*. http://www.ted.com/talks/stuart_brown_says_play_is_more_than_fun_it_s_vital.html (accessed July 30, 2013).

Brown, S. with C. Vaughan (2009) *Play: How it Shapes the Brain, Opens the Imagination, and Invigorates the Soul*. New York: Avery.

Caillois, R. (2001) *Man, Play and Games*. Trans. M. Barash. Urbana and Chicago: University of Illinois Press.

Gordon, G. (2009) "What is Play?: In Search of a Definition." In *From Children to Red Hatters: Diverse Images and Issues of Play*, edited by D. Kuschner, pp. 1–13. Lanham, MD: University Press of America.

Gray, P. (2008) "The Value of Age-Mixed Play." *Education Week* 27 (April 16): 26; 32.

Grieshaber, S. and F. McArdle (2010) *The Trouble with Play*. Maidenhead: McGraw-Hill and Open University Press.

Grimshaw, M. (ed.) (2014) *The Oxford Handbook to Virtuality*. New York: Oxford University Press.

Harper, D. (2014) "play (v.)." *Online Etymology Dictionary*. http://www.etymonline.com/index.php?term=play&allowed_in_frame=0 (accessed February 26, 2015).

Harteveld, C. (2011) *Triadic Game Design: Balancing Reality, Meaning and Play*. London: Springer.

Huizinga, J. (1980 [1944]) *Homo Ludens: A Study of the Play-Element in Culture*. London and Boston, MA: Routledge & Kegan Paul

Hurka, T. and J. Tasioulas (2006) "Games and The Good." *Proceedings of the Aristotelian Society*, Supplementary Volume 80: 217–35.

Kassabian, A. (2013) "Music for Sleeping." In *Sound, Music, Affect: Theorising Sonic Experience*, edited by I. Biddle and M. Thompson, pp. 165–82. New York and London: Bloomsbury.

Lumosity Brain Games (2012) *Luminosity.com* [main website]. http://www.lumosity.com/personal-training-plan (accessed May 5, 2012).

Myers, D. (2010) *Play Redux: The Form of Computer Games*. Ann Arbor, MI: University of Michigan Press.

National Institute for Play (2010) *NIFP Website*. http://www.nifplay.org/ (accessed February 28, 2015).

Nuwer, R. (2014) "Lassie Text Home: Pooches Get Technological." *New Scientist* 2997 (November 29). https://www.newscientist.com/article/mg22429970.500-lassie-text-home-pooches-get-technological (accessed February 29, 2016).

Oxford Dictionaries Online (2015) "Play." *Oxford Dictionaries Online*. http://www.oxford-dictionaries.com/definition/english/play (accessed February 26, 2015).

Pichlmair, M. and F. Kayali (2007) "Levels of Sound: On the Principles of Interactivity in Music Video Games Situated Play." In *Proceedings of DiGRA 2007 Conference, Digital Games Research Association*, pp. 424–30. Tokyo: University of Tokyo Press.

Plato (1970) *The Laws*. Trans. T. Saunders. Harmondsworth: Penguin Books.

Rousseau, J.-J. (1974 [1762]) *Émile*. Trans. B. Foxley. London: Dent.

Smith, J. (2004) "I Can See Tomorrow in Your Dance: A Study of *Dance Dance Revolution* and Music Video Games." *Journal of Popular Music Studies* 16/1: 58–84.

Stewart, S. (1979) *Nonsense: Aspects of Intertextuality in Folklore and Literature*. Baltimore and London: Johns Hopkins University Press.

Suits, B. (2005) *The Grasshopper: Games, Life, Utopia*. Peterborough, Ontario: Broadview Press.

Summers, T. (2012) "Video Game Music: History, Form and Genre." PhD thesis, Bristol University.

Torkildsen, G. (2005) *Leisure and Recreation Management*, 5th ed. London: Routledge.

Wikipedia [English Language] (2015) "Music Video Game." *Wikipedia.org*. http://en.wikipedia.org/wiki/Music_video_games (accessed February 28, 2013).

Wittgenstein, L. (2009 [1953]) *Philosophical Investigations*, 4th ed. Trans. and ed. G. E. M. Anscombe, P. M. S. Hacker and J. Schulte. Chichester: Wiley-Blackwell.

# 8 "Listening" Through Digital Interaction in Björk's *Biophilia*

## Samantha Blickhan[1]

When listeners open the iPad application containing Björk's 2011 album, *Biophilia* (One Little Indian/Well Hart, 2011), they are greeted with an audio file playing a long quotation, read by David Attenborough. The speech functions as a statement of artistic purpose for Björk, as well as an insight into the "restless curiosity" that is presented as an integral part of the project.[2] Björk has chosen to frame *Biophilia* in the realm of nature (hence the use of the famous naturalist's voice) and her categorical placement of music within the sense of sound results in a definition of music within this opening statement as "Sound, harnessed by human beings, delivered with generosity and emotion". The rest of the speech expresses Björk's desire to integrate music and technology by combining the sensory aspects of sound, sight, and touch – to "use technology to make visible much of nature's invisible world". Nowhere in the introductory statement is reference made to "games" or "playing" – instead, Björk uses words such as "learn", "create" and "explore" to describe the interactive elements of *Biophilia*. Yet, when using the individual resources (apps) for each song, the user makes choices that directly affect the resulting visual and auditory elements, a practice that can be considered game-like in its interactive quality.

Why, then, has *Biophilia* not been marketed as a musical video game? What weight does the concept of the word "game" carry that does not lend itself to musical interaction? On a surface level, the use of "game" might convey a light-heartedness or lack of seriousness that Björk does not intend to communicate to *Biophilia*'s listeners and users. Yet it is important to remember that the preferred verb used when describing an interaction with a game is "to play", a word widely used in regard to performing music without resulting in music being taken any less seriously than its context and genre dictate. This chapter will attempt to provide examples of ways in which *Biophilia*'s interactivity affects the listening process, as well as a discussion of the associated subtexts that the word "game" may bring to this process and whether this distinction itself has any effect on the project's cultural impact.

With *Biophilia*, Björk presents an enigmatic offering in terms of genre as well as the way in which listeners interact with the music and art she has created. Unlike most current pop releases, this album is not a purely auditory experience; each song is presented as an iPad application within a suite of ten songs (originally only available for iOS, but it has since become available for Android systems as well). This non-traditional approach is typical of Björk's artistic style; she has made a career out of releasing atypical pop records. Her unconventional melodies and widely varied electro-acoustic instrumental arrangements have allowed her to cross the divisive boundary between classical and pop music, a feat that is out of the ordinary for a musician nominated for a collective twelve Grammy awards and eighteen MTV Video Music Awards.[3] Yet, compared to her previous work, the songs on *Biophilia* are stripped down – gone are the driving bass beats of *Post* (1995) or the lush strings from tracks such as 'Jóga' (*Homogenic*, 1997). The album's focus is not on the human voice, either, as it was in the songs on *Medúlla* (2004), though several songs on *Biophilia* do feature a female choir. More than any previous Björk album, each track on *Biophilia* has a musical and a natural theme which complement one another, reflected both in the musical arrangement and the accompanying app.

In this respect it is ineffective to discuss the music of *Biophilia* as a separate entity from the app suite. As will be shown later in this chapter, critics of the album seem determined to review the album as if it were something autonomous from the apps. This is perhaps because critics of music are not accustomed to reviewing interactive mixed-media projects, and writing about the overall effect of the project as a whole can be a difficult task. It is less complex to pull *Biophilia* apart and only discuss the music or the app suite, but by separating them the reviewers are only critiquing part of the entire work. Björk's artistic intent cannot have effective results (be they positive or negative) unless people are willing to see the project as a combination of artistic media with a definite purpose. Björk has stated that there was a musicological intention behind *Biophilia*: the idea that she could use each song to pinpoint one musical element (such as tempo, form, counterpoint or arpeggio), and design an app to explain it using technological resources and an activity that combines multiple senses (Burton, 2011). By using the app, the listener is exposed to the building blocks of each song in a tangible, malleable form.

## Music, Technology, Nature

The main layout of *Biophilia* is designed in the form of a solar system, with each song represented by a planet. Björk worked with a team of app designers to create each of the apps, which can be downloaded individually, or as a "suite" containing all of the songs. Perhaps one cause of reviewers separating music and app suite is due to the availability of the album for purchase as audio-only, without any apps. Björk originally wanted to release the app suite before releasing the audio-only version, but her contacts at Apple discouraged this idea in order to avoid the project being seen as economically and techno-logically elitist (Burton, 2011). Yet this indicates that Björk's intended medium for the project was the interactive version and an artist's choice of medium must certainly have had an impact upon the composition of the music. Björk's concept of visualizing sound is incorporated into the very framework of the project. She chose a solar system as the visual layout, or "menu", of the app suite, effectively tying technology and nature together, since the only cultural engagement most humans have with space is typically mediated through science and technology. This can be taken in a very literal sense through the use of telescopes to allow the human eye to view space in greater detail, due to the physical and geographical limitations dividing human existence from outer space. In a similar vein, the *Biophilia* project functions as a telescope through which sound is visualized. In the app for the song 'Virus', the focus turns from an external view of space to an internal view of the cells inside a human body. However, in both settings the interactive possibilities existing between humans and technology remain a central theme.

If the app suite is Björk's preferred method of interaction with the musical elements of the album, the visual themes within the app suite are a major advantage in terms of artistic control and directed user interaction. Because of the variety of media types involved with *Biophilia*, there are more platforms on which Björk can present her conceptualization of the project. Nicola Dibben refers to this as a "curated experience" (2013: 688), bringing to mind a visit to a museum or gallery. Drawing attention to artistic control is not a criticism of Björk's motives; every artist has their own creative intention, and it will be realized and interpreted in diverse ways by different consumers. But she does have an advantage over most music albums. On its most basic level, a standard album of recorded music can only offer auditory stimulation. A listener may have different sensory reactions to the auditory stimulus of the music (emotional, memory-based, visual, physical), but that is a receptive response from the listener – the artist can only offer sound. Other stimuli can include album artwork, layout and liner notes, but users are not constantly viewing the art while listening to the album, and in the digital age packaging is becoming less essential to the musical album as a whole (though Björk does include an 18-page digital PDF booklet with the album-only download). A closer comparison might be the music video, which combines visual and aural stimuli, but lacks interactivity. *Biophilia* not only offers auditory stimulus, but visual, tactile and mental stimuli as well. Björk is able to design the extramusical elements (the visual and the mental stimuli) to fit within the scope of a scientific interaction with nature (space graphics, space-themed apps). The multisensory platform makes Björk's theme more potent; the user's constant exposure to a variety of stimuli ensures that the user will be less likely to attempt to multitask while engaging with the album, thus securing a greater percentage of the user's attention. There is no part of *Biophilia* that goes untouched by Björk's artistic concept.

## The Interactive Possibilities of *Biophilia*

When a user opens the *Biophilia* "Mother" app (*Biophilia*-speak for the home screen, which houses the individual apps for each song), an image of a solar system appears in the middle of the screen. The picture begins to zoom, as if the user were travelling towards the solar system, the image growing larger and larger until the user "reaches" their destination and the stars fill the iPad screen. Users can manipulate and rotate the solar system through 360° using the touch screen – even when no hand is touching the screen, the solar system has been animated to move ever so slightly back and forth, giving the eerie impression that it is alive, almost breathing. Small details like this are similar to common graphical effects used in many adventure games to support the reality of the game environment and draw the player in more fully to the story or scenario. This effect is adapted for use in Björk's hyper-stylized, non-realistic universe, but the result is a similar feeling of individual presence. Touching a star opens a new menu for that particular song, where the user can choose from a list of song-related options while listening to an audio clip of the album version of the song playing in the background. The options for each song include "play", "animation", "score", "lyrics" and "credits". Also available on the menu is a summary of the central idea of the song, with an option to "read musical analysis by nikki dibben" [sic], containing an analysis of each song written by Dr Nicola Dibben, who has published extensive research on the science and psychology of music, as well as on popular music, and whose previous publications include the 2009 monograph *Björk*.

The option "play" takes users to the actual app for each song, in which the user interaction most closely resembles play, both in the context of music and game. Not all of the apps could easily be classified as traditional "games", however. In *Biophilia* the distinction between a game and a learning tool is blurred, perhaps because the two are not mutually exclusive. When considering the general definition of a game, one might imagine a task that is pleasurable and diverting, but that also suggests the existence of a goal that, when reached, constitutes winning. Self-proclaimed "ludologist" Jesper Juul offers a broader definition, one that does not always assume a pleasurable experience for the user:

> A game is a rule-based system with a variable and quantifiable outcome, where different outcomes are assigned different values, the player exerts effort in order to influence the outcome, the player feels emotionally attached to the outcome, and the consequences of the activity are optional and negotiable. (Juul, 2005: 36)

Juul's definition, rather than discussing goals, focuses on the emotional investment of the player as the stimulus for effort. It implies emotional reward as an outcome for successful game play. The requirement of a "quantifiable outcome" excuses the *Biophilia* apps from consideration as games, as they do not seem to have any set goals that, if improperly followed, would result in game termination. It seems hardly possible to win or lose any of them, as many are based upon creation and musical manipulation, rather than reaching a finish line or rescuing a princess. The app for the song 'Moon', for example, is in all respects a sequencer – an illustrated spinal column expels fluid onto twin strings of pearls in a set rhythm, which "play" a particular note when the fluid touches them. According to Björk's U.S. record label, Nonesuch Records, "Fluid in the spine rises and falls with the moon above and tides below, and pearls play when fluid spills out from the spine and washes over them. In song mode the phase of the moon changes with the song structure" (Nonesuch Online Journal, 2011). The goal, if it can be said that one exists, is not to elicit a specific melody from the strings of pearls, but merely to explore and create new sounds. Juul's "quantifiable outcome" can exist as a variety of musical and visual results from exploration within the apps, with positive or negative emotional recompense depending on a user's interpretation of their own engagement.

Other apps include a new style of notation in the form of a font created specifically for *Biophilia*, "allowing you to see and hear music as you create it" ('Sacrifice'), and what possibly may be the most game-like app in the suite, 'Crystalline', where users fly through tunnels collecting different styles of crystals.[4] It is in the finer points of each app's guidelines of play where the individual elements of each song are highlighted. The notation in 'Sacrifice' is limited to the tones used in the recorded version of the song rather than providing access to a full chromatic scale; this is a practice Björk puts to use in several of the other *Biophilia* apps, allowing users to improvise on a set number of tones, all of which fit into the pre-existing harmonies and structure of each app's particular song. 'Crystalline', while seemingly in the style of a goal-oriented game (moving through tunnels, collecting crystals), is more of an experiment involving musical form: "The app allows you to find your own route through the song by changing the order in which sections are heard, and in doing so lets you learn about how the different sections function."[5] If a user is not initially familiar with the song, though, the change in structure is often too subtle to even notice that it is happening. It is difficult to interpret any functional information from the app relating to song form without first hearing the recorded version of the song multiple times before playing. The change in the player's understanding of the function of each app after exposure to the audio-only version of *Biophilia* suggests the possibility that the app and non-interactive versions should be used in tandem with each other. It is possible for a user who has not yet been exposed to the songs to play with the apps in an exploratory sense, but long-term exposure to the audio (whether solely within the app, or in combination with the audio-only version of the album) results in aural recognition during gameplay, and it is this recognition that facilitates the learning process in an app such as 'Crystalline'.

When attempting to classify any of the *Biophilia* apps as games, use of the word "app" can actually make the process of classification more difficult. An app can be defined as a downloadable application for a mobile device such as a phone or tablet. Most existing apps on the iOS platform can be classified as "tools" or "games", and tend to be relatively low cost. There are many subcategories of tools but I would argue that the main distinction between a game and a tool is in its use. Does the app allow the user to access something, as in the case of news media outlets, weather information or dictionaries? Does it help the user complete a task, like a calculator or translator? Does it connect the user to another person or group of people, as in the case of social media or communication apps? These apps are used to accomplish what I would describe as an external task, in the sense that Juul's "quantifiable outcome" exists outside the app itself. Most apps in the category of "games" follow Juul's definition, with value placed on specific outcomes and emotional investment in the result. However, there are apps where information obtainment and retention is the main goal, effectively combining external tasks with a game structure. There are apps that use quizzes to help the user learn a language or recognize flags of the world, but the commonality between these subcategories of games is the goal, with emotional investment as stimulus. Yet, even in the case of educational games, the impetus behind a user's interaction with the game is to do something, or to retain certain information, *correctly*, and failure to do so results in repetition of a specific ability level until that particular task is completed.

*Biophilia* is unique in its ability to be both a tool and a video game, especially in regard to the meeting of music and gaming. Many of the apps use music in a manner opposite to the way music has been typically included in video games, where its normative function is more akin to a movie soundtrack. Arcade-style games and platform games use music to draw players into the game with sounds for positive and negative reinforcement (a *ding!* vs. a **thud** being an example of the typical association with high or ascending sounds as representing positive reinforcement, and lower or descending sounds representing negative), faster music to indicate that time is running out, and also provide different melodies to accompany different levels of play (most famously this can be exemplified by the now-classic music for specific worlds in any of the *Super Mario Bros.* games for the various Nintendo gaming systems).

As a video game, *Biophilia* could be more closely aligned with music-oriented games such as *Rock Band* or *SingStar*, in which the objective is, to an extent, correct "performance", though for the most part Björk does not give users the opportunity to be incorrect. Björk uses games as a way to elicit a new interpretation of her music through individual interaction, though there is no explicit objective or correct way to perform, and the only gain is personal. The audio within most of the apps can be changed based on choices made by the user (as in the previously mentioned 'Crystalline'). In each case, the audio track is based on the instrumental and vocal sounds and programmed beats that make up the particular song for which the app was created, but the arrangement of sounds can be different each time, depending on how the app is used. In essence, the visual effects have become the notation, while the choices made during "play" become an act of re-composition, though the word "composition" itself presents challenges that will be examined later in this chapter.

I will use the song and app for 'Solstice' to look more specifically at the *Biophilia* apps and interactivity. In the introductory material to 'Solstice', Björk reveals that she drew inspiration for the song from a poem written by a friend. The poem, which then became the lyrics to the song, compares the solar system to lights on a Christmas tree. This idea inspired the visual format of the app, which Björk then combined with the image of a pendulum, owing her decision to the concept that "the four seasons are because of the tilt of the earth".[6] Björk commissioned a team of scientists form the Massachussetts Institute of Technology, led by Andy Cavatorta, to build a new instrument with which she would perform the piece (she commissioned several new instruments for *Biophilia*, including a pipe organ played using a PlayStation controller). The finished product was a set of four "gravity harps": "pendulums which each pluck a round harp at the bottom of their swing".[7] The harps each rotate so that specific strings are sounded by the plectrum fixed at the bottom of the structure, depending on which string needs to be plucked to emit the correct sound.

Björk's desire to present a physical representation of the musical process is also evident in the app design. The concept of a pendulum is one of the main visual constructs of the 'Solstice' app. When a user opens the "play" option in the app menu, the default setting is something called "Song Mode", which means that the harp accompaniment from the recorded version of 'Solstice' is pre-loaded into the app.

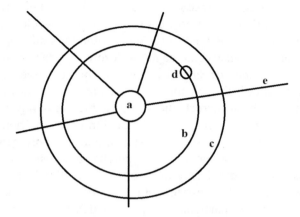

*Figure 8.1* Diagram of 'Solstice' app, "solar" view option

Users first see a central red circle (a) with lines of varying lengths coming out of its sides (e). The lines, functioning like strings on a harp, can be red, orange, green and blue. A larger circle (b) surrounds the smaller inner circle, and a small dot (d) moves along this circle, like a planet on its path of orbit. As the planet moves past each string, the string vibrates as if plucked, and a tone plays, the pitch of which is based on the length of the string. The strings in the app are representative of the physical strings on the gravity harps created in order to play the song, while the orbiting planet represents the plectrum that the harp strings hit on the pendulum's swing. During the orbit of the planet that "plucks" the strings, the centre circle rhythmically changes colour, following a pattern of red, orange, green, then blue. As this centre circle changes colour, only the strings of corresponding colour are played. This top-down view is called "solar", but there is a second view option, called "tree".

Tree view morphs the pendulum structure into a side view of the lines, with the different colours stacked like an evergreen tree. This reflects the song's lyrical reference to a Christmas tree, and the stacked colour arrangement makes the colours easier to visualize independently of one another. For example, the larger orbit path of a different colour (c, shown in both Figures 8.1 and 8.2) can have its own separate "plectrum" (d¹) following the path of orbit and playing the individual strings as it moves. In this way, each of these concentric circles functions as an individual pendulum, and when the user clears the field and builds from scratch, any number of circles can be created in any of the four colour options. The structural components of the app, specifically in relation

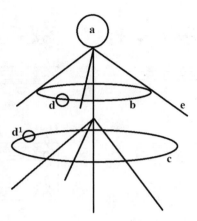

*Figure 8.2* Diagram of 'Solstice' app, "tree" view option

to their function as elements of composition, will be discussed further, but first the app's visual relationship to music must be considered.

As a tool, this app can function as a way of visualizing musical analysis. In her written analysis accompanying the app, Dibben uses the term counterpoint to discuss the musical patterns produced by the pendulums, defining it as "the term used to describe the relationship between two or more voices or instruments that share the same harmony but have different rhythm or contour".[8] The patterns made by the pendulums, while existing on their own independently regulated paths, fit together to become something new. The visual display in the app allows users to reconsider ideas about song structure and methods of composition through the viewing of counterpoint as independent circles that remain part of the same structure. The app menu also offers an option called "score" that is an animated scrolling view of the musical score for 'Solstice' shown in time to the audio track of the recorded version of the song. Upon consideration of both the "score" animation and the pre-designed "Song Mode" of the app, I realized that, in "Song Mode", the four coloured concentric rings correspond to the four repeating measures of the instrumental accompaniment to the song. I will now refer to these bars as **A**, **B**, **C** and **D** (Figure 8.3).[9]

The colour options within the app actually represent a structural component of Björk's composition (the "measures", in a traditional setting), and users can incorporate this method in order to visually distinguish between different melodies they create. "Song Mode" only plays one colour/melody at a time (as the centre spot cycles through the four colours), reflecting the arrangement

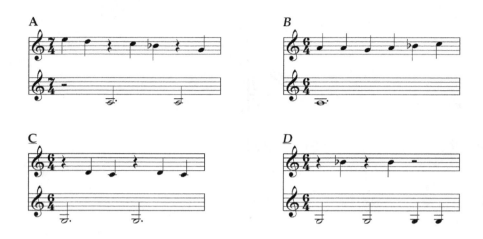

*Figure 8.3* Notated measures of recorded 'Solstice' instrumental accompaniment

of Björk's accompaniment, but when creating their own melodic arrangement the user has the option to allow all of the colours to play at the same time.

After the initial load of "Song Mode", the user can clear the screen and create a unique harp part from scratch by pulling these coloured "strings" out of the centre circle one by one. The user chooses the string's tone by listening to the notes play as they are dragged; the outward dragging motion creates a descending cascade of notes that can be heard one by one if the user drags slowly enough.[10] Through this process, users have the opportunity to choose a tone based on their own listening experience, even if they are unfamiliar with the concept of a string's length being relative to pitch. The user can then swipe the orbiting circles into motion (the speed of which varies depending on the speed of the swipe), and the newly-created part will play with Björk's original recorded vocal line over it. It is as if users were "composing" a new accompaniment to Björk's vocals. However, due to the musical limitations imposed upon the user, the choice of the word "composing" may not be quite accurate. The user is able to choose a pitch for each particular string, but they do not have a full chromatic scale to choose from. Instead the choice is limited to a group of six notes from the Phrygian mode on A (A, B♭, C, D, E and G, in four octaves), all of which are part of the original cache of notes used in the recorded instrumental accompaniment to 'Solstice'. A user can exercise creativity, but within the frame that Björk has set. A better name for this process might be improvisation, due to the similarity between the limitations Björk places on the user and the process followed by musicians in instances of directed improvisation. Björk has chosen this six-note scale as the template, but it remains up to the user to do what they will with the materials offered to them. External limitations like the template do not entirely negate the act of creating, be it an act of composition or of improvisation. A more important question may be to ask what to call the user: performer, composer, player, improviser, listener? The user plays all of these roles at one point or another while using the app. "Collaborator" might be most appropriate, but that term assumes a proprietary quality that is not necessarily included in the categorization of *Biophilia* as an album by a single artist; for the purposes of this chapter, "user" will have to suffice.

The user can experiment with counterpoint by using the different colours as tools for melodic organization. Björk's recorded harp part begins with the pattern (as per Figure 8.3):

**A** *B B* **A** *B B* **A A** *B B* **A** *B B* **A A** *B B* **A** *B B* **A**

Note that the **B** measures are always in groups of two.

This is followed by the entrance of the **C** and **D** bars:

**C** *D D D D D D D* **C** *D D* **C** *D D* **C** *D D* **C**

This second grouping of measures does not initially seem to be as structured as the first section of the piece, but halfway through the section it develops a structure that mirrors the grouping of the measures in the first section, with one bar of **C** followed by two bars of **D**. The app's use of colour along with the separate paths of orbit as structural tools allows the user to experiment with large-scale visual organization while still providing the opportunity to choose individual pitches. Not only can the user see the string lengths as a way of visually differentiating pitch, but there is also the option to use the colours as a way to develop a larger structural form for what has been created. The user can use a colour to recall a specific melody (or "bar") that they have created, and then those melodies can be placed in a specified order using the colours. In this manner, a user who does not read music could use this app to purpose-fully create a structured composition based on visual pattern recognition.

This method of non-traditional musical education is being put to use in schools via the Biophilia Educational Program. The program describes their use of the *Biophilia* App Suite as an effort to "break up conventional teaching modes by merging music and science together". The website also notes that the program is "particularly well suited for children with ADHD, dyslexia and other learning disabilities". On the now defunct website *Holy Moly*, William Mager (2011) wrote about his experience using *Biophilia* as a person who has been deaf since birth, specifically the "animation" section of the app suite, noting that the differentiated scrolling visual stimuli, combined with sound vibrations from the iPad speakers, provided an experience that was "beautiful, lyrical and haunting".

Given *Biophilia*'s educational agenda, and that each song is based around a specific musical topic, it is appropriate for Björk to have composed relatively simple pieces of music to be used with the app suite. When listening to the audio tracks, it is not difficult to pinpoint the element of each song that Björk chose to feature. 'Moon' opens with a mechanically repetitive line that becomes the basis for its sequencer app. The arpeggiated bass line in 'Thunderbolt' is visually represented in its app as lightning. Each song having a specific educational feature not only simplifies the learning process for the user, but also makes the music of *Biophilia* stand apart from Björk's existing body of work. For example, it would be difficult to narrow 'Hyper-Ballad' (*Post*, 1995) down into a single musical feature in order to incorporate it into an app. The same could be said for her later work, such as 'Earth Intruders' from *Volta*, released in 2007, or the music-box emulating bell tones of *Vespertine* (2001). This differentiation is not meant to be seen as a value judgement of the albums in Björk's catalogue, but perhaps an opportunity to view the audio-only version of *Biophilia* as possessing space that would normally be filled by the multisensory stimulus of the app suite.

## Musicological Interaction and Critical Reception

If the apps function as the vessels by which the user engages with Björk's music, Nicola Dibben's analyses aptly mirror the parallel efforts within the field of musicology. Björk's explicitly stated musicological intentions have been discussed above in terms of how they may have affected her compositional process, but it is also important to consider how reading Dibben's essays may affect the process of listening and engaging with the music and apps they accompany. These analyses are a stylistic differentiation for Dibben, as well as for Björk. The minimalist writing style of the prose mirrors Björk's songs in *Biophilia* – gone are the titles and capitalization of the peer-reviewed article – though the structure and presentation of the essays were likely influenced by overall design elements to retain a sense of continuity and bring the essays into the larger aesthetic of the *Biophilia* project (which included specific colour palettes and specially designed fonts) (Dibben, 2013: 692). In any case, the writing style has been appropriately adapted (both in its visual presentation and its content) for the *Biophilia* audience, many of whom may not have previously engaged with a musicological text. Dibben explains specific musical terminology in general terms that a broad audience can understand. In the 'Solstice' analysis she writes, counterpoint is the term used to describe the relationship between two or more voices or instruments that share the same harmony but have different rhythm and contour. by using only the voice and a single line played by pendulum-harp Björk emphasises this linear dimension of music (from one note to the next in time) instead of its vertical relationships (notes which sound together) [sic].[11]

Dibben's stylistic simplicity functions in a similar manner to Björk's musical style throughout *Biophilia*. By presenting theoretical information about music in a basic manner, users are able to learn potentially new concepts about music (as Björk intended), but are not specifically directed to a single interpretation of their engagement with the app.

Returning to the earlier question of whether an influence of musicology would affect the way a user might interact with the *Biophilia* games, it is certain that an educational background in music would influence gameplay once the musical objective has been explained, but it is not a prerequisite for any of the interactive programs in *Biophilia*. Rather, Björk and Dibben are making an important musicological statement in terms of audience and tone: musicology can be an accessible tool for musical education, and it can be an aid for a listener to learn more about what is being heard without having previously studied music. The non-traditional scholarship presented in *Biophilia* delivers up front what normally takes time to be processed and reflected on by scholars typically uninvolved with the project's creation. While peer-reviewed journals and scholarly articles are a necessary and stimulating part of existing musical research, collaborations between musicologists and artists could potentially spark a new genre of "simultaneous" musicology.

Dibben's essays allow writing about music to be concurrent with music writing; they invite musicology into the project, rather than waiting for it to be a response. It can be assumed that Björk had access to the drafts before publication in the app, and the process of interaction must certainly have shaped the result. The essays do not critique Björk's work like a review, or analyse the nature of its post-release effect. They offer an interpretation of the musical elements that Björk wished for the piece to highlight, including aspects of music theory and analysis as well as explanations for why each particular app was designed in a particular way.

Criticism of *Biophilia* has varied on the subject of Dibben's contributions. *The Guardian*'s Alexis Petridis (2011) states in his review of *Biophilia*, "once you've read the essays, there's virtually no room for the listener to put their own interpretation on the songs, which at a stroke cancels out a portion of the pleasure of listening". This criticism makes several assumptions: one is that users will read the essays before any sort of interaction with the music; another is that they will read the essays at all. There is no suggested order to the explorative process in the *Biophilia* suite. More troublesome, however, is Petridis's assumption that the average user cannot use external information to further develop individual ideas about a song.

Petridis's view implies that after reading Dibben's analyses the listener is no longer able to form their own interpretation about the songs accessed through the app suite. Yet one of Björk's explicit purposes of producing *Biophilia* was to help users understand specific theoretical concepts of music in a non-traditional setting. Dibben's essays encourage the listener to pick out specific motifs or perhaps to be attentive to an aspect of the song that may have otherwise gone unheard. The Romantic idea of an ideal interpretation of music without any "distraction" invites discussions of musical autonomy that are especially inapplicable to a project like *Biophilia*, where the entire point is for the music not to be autonomous, but to coexist with other stimuli, yet most reviews of *Biophilia* inevitably find their way to this very subject. Reviewers typically discuss the general project with the apps and then turn to the music as if it were a separate entity from the app suite. The BBC's Mike Diver (2011) writes, "Thankfully, *Biophilia* serves as wonderfully as a 'standard' album as anything else". David Fricke (2011) at *Rolling Stone* notes that, "soul easily trumps software", and Mark Pytlik (2011), writing for indie rock's most notoriously hard-to-please reviewers, Pitchfork Media, asks if Björk is "piling conceptual materials on top of her music in an effort to give it extra depth". The deconstructive nature of this reception is based in habit, and until there are more examples of mixed-media projects in wide release, popular music reviewers will likely continue this practice. *Biophilia* challenges users to think about the definition of the pop album, including whether this project can even be categorized as such. If *Biophilia* is something that exists outside the traditional framework of a music album, it seems impractical to attempt a critique based on criteria held for a separate medium of artistic output.

## The Future of Play

Though some music reviewers have attempted to analyse the cultural impact of *Biophilia*'s audio track without the apps, the media discussion about the impact of interactive music has proved to be one of the most interesting parts of the project. Digital music has revolutionized the music industry in countless ways, but the effects of digital music consumption have not always been beneficial to the previously held practice of creating and releasing an "album". iTunes libraries fill up with single songs and "shuffle" functions have made the once painstaking process of creating a mix tape possible through the click of a mouse. Album release dates are challenged by industry leaks resulting in illegal downloads. The availability and, perhaps more importantly, the portability of digital music has made it a constant in daily life. iPods and smartphones provide aural stimulus on the commute to work or while jogging. This access to digital music is not entirely negative, since it is now also possible for music to reach a wider audience, and for that audience to be exposed to more different types of music than ever previously possible. Yet it does become overwhelming to sit down at a computer and have to browse through thousands of songs to find something to listen to. Scott Snibbe, a computer-based artist known for creating early interactive apps for iOS and one of the many collaborators on the *Biophilia* project, refers to this type of interaction with music as a "casual relationship" (Dredge, 2011). He believes that music digitization causes people to miss out on "falling in love" with music, and that the concept of "non-interactive" music "was a phenomenon of the recorded music era", convincingly pointing out that sheet music was the nineteenth-century version of an app (ibid.). Snibbe's division of music into "interactive" and "non-interactive" genres is thought-provoking, begging the question of whether music becomes interactive exclusively through play.

The *Biophilia* experience is not a casual one. It may not encourage a user to sit and listen to the entire album from start to finish, but it does bring a greater level of personal attention to elements of Björk's songs through its interactivity. Björk has harnessed the all-consuming nature of video game culture and applied it to music. As Seth Schiesel (2011) wrote in *The New York Times*, "The real magic happens when you press 'play'. That doesn't tell the machine to play the song; it means it's time for you to play the song."

Other popular musicians are diversifying methods of releasing their music. Beck Hansen's album, *Song Reader*, was released entirely in sheet music format on December 11, 2012. At the time of the album's release, Beck did not record any of the songs and encouraged people who bought the music to record their own versions of the songs and post them on YouTube. In his preface to *Song Reader*, published in *The New Yorker*, Beck shares his thoughts on the project:

> The opening up of the music, the possibility of letting people work with these songs in different ways, and of allowing them a different accessibility than what's offered by all the many forms of music available today, is ultimately what this collection aims for. The songs here come with piano arrangements and guitar chords – as well as parts for brass instruments, in one case, and ukulele chords, in others – but personalizing and even ignoring the arrangements is encouraged. Don't feel beholden to what's notated. Use any instrument you want to. Change the chords; rephrase the melodies. Keep only the lyrics, if desired. Play it fast or slow, swung or straight. Take a song and make it an instrumental or an a cappella. Play it for friends, or only for yourself. These arrangements are starting-off points; they don't originate from any definitive recording or performance. (Hansen, 2012)

A YouTube search for "Song Reader" on January 22, 2013, yielded about 39,000 results – just over a month after the release of the sheet music. With this method of release Beck essentially gave up the right to control the way his compositions were heard by the general public. It can be argued that this method, encouraging consumers to play the compositions rather than to hear Beck's version, brings greater familiarity with each piece, in the same way that a pianist's relationship with a sonata might change after learning and performing the work. It would be an oversimplification to refer to this as a greater familiarity with a piece, for it is a different kind of relationship altogether. Later in 2013, Hansen began to play his own live versions of the *Song Reader* material, a process that did not negate the existing individual versions recorded by fans, but rather cemented the concept of a performance of a song being a "version" of the piece, rather than having the artist's version functioning as a recorded Urtext.

Major pop artists are also experimenting with interactive albums. In August 2012, Lady Gaga wrote on her "Little Monsters" website (an online social network for die-hard Gaga fans) that her new album, *ARTPOP*, would be released as an app. Rather than focus on educational interaction, Gaga's project is a combination of musical and social interaction:

> ARTPOP will be released as an IPAD, iPhone, mobile and computer compatible application (WORLD) that is completely interactive with chats, films for every song, extra music, content, gaga inspired games, fashion updates, magazines, and more still in the works! I will also be able to upload new things to the APP all the time, the same way I upload to twitter and [Little Monsters]. (2013)

Gaga's twist on Björk's app concept is considerably broader than *Biophilia*, due to both the social aspect of *ARTPOP* and Gaga's plans for continuous content addition after its initial release. It seems overwhelming in its content, to the point where the concept of "the album" has been reimagined as a social centre for Gaga fans. In fact, the scope of Lady Gaga's project may have been too broad – over a year since its release, the app component to *ARTPOP* (including "Petga", Gaga's version of the "Mother" app) has received considerably less attention than its recorded and live elements, and several of the planned apps have missed their scheduled release dates.

Rap artist Jay-Z has also had difficulty with the release of his 2013 album *Magna Carta . . . Holy Grail* via an exclusive app deal for Samsung customers. While approximately 1.2 million people installed the Android app granting them early access to the album, within a month of its release a privacy advocacy group had asked the U.S. Federal Trade Commission to investigate the app after an accusation that the software was "unnecessarily invasive"

(Michaels, 2013). In the case of *Magna Carta . . . Holy Grail*, the app component to the album seemed to function more as a delivery service rather than an interactive tool or game, while Gaga's *ARTPOP* was focused on a social media element. Neither attained the level of interactivity or aesthetic completeness of the *Biophilia* app suite, but in both cases the apps were not on equal footing as the rest of the merchandise.

Beck's sheet music release also has a social element, but on both a digital and a personal level. The artist's request for people to share their home recordings on YouTube has created a comparative, even competitive, element, whether intentional or not. By sharing a recording of one of the pieces from *Song Reader*, a user becomes open to criticism – and possibly learns first-hand what it is like to be at the mercy of the opinions of strangers. In a sense, this element of *Song Reader* is an interactive game of who can get more views. A user can gauge whether or not their attempt was "successful" by reading the opinions of others.

There is a distinct lack of this type of social interaction in the *Biophilia* app suite. A social component provides an opportunity for another person to become a user's partner or opponent. *Biophilia* includes a feature for saving work (for example, users can save created harp parts in the "Solstice" app), but does not offer opportunities to share the work with other *Biophilia* users. While single-player games still exist, the combination of video gaming and widespread access to the Internet has allowed users to not only play with other users who are physically present and using the same console, but with users around the world. The platform exists, and most new games (especially in app form) have integrated social elements, even if they are for single player only. The option to link a gaming app to Facebook or Twitter in order to share high scores creates a competitive atmosphere in which the result of sharing is an immediate connection to other players of the same game. With *Biophilia*, Björk's intention is for users to develop their own musical knowledge, and the lack of sharing options removes any chance for a competitive environment to develop.

Yet the potential for components of game culture remains in all interactive music. Playing music is both enjoyable and challenging, it can be done alone or in a group, and its results can be for personal use or public domain, sharing an interpretation and exposing it to criticism – in a sense, competing with other interpretations of that same piece. *Biophilia*'s interactive features may cover a broad range of musical, educational and game-like qualities, but that immersive quality may be the essential key to bridging the gap between these two types of play.

## Notes

1. Samantha Blickhan is a PhD candidate at Royal Holloway, University of London. She holds undergraduate degrees in Vocal Performance and English Literature from the University of Iowa, and a Masters in Musicology from the University of Oxford. Her PhD thesis examines visual representations of sound, with a particular focus on the notation and palaeography of medieval song, and also considers modern methods of interaction with music notation in the fields of research and teaching.
2. Though the statement is not read by Björk, the attribution of the album and app content is copyrighted to her name, and for the purposes of this chapter all content that is not specifically attributed to another author will be cited as the intellectual property of Björk Guðmundsdóttir.
3. The genre variance extends beyond Björk's own output: Pulitzer Prize-winning composer Kevin Puts's *Symphony No. 3* ('Vespertine') (2003) was inspired by Björk's 2001 album of the same name.
4. Nicola Dibben, Analysis of 'Sacrifice', in *Biophilia* (2011).
5. Nicola Dibben, Analysis of 'Crystalline', in *Biophilia* (2011).
6. Introductory matter to 'Solstice', in *Biophilia* (2011).
7. Nicola Dibben, Analysis of 'Solstice', in *Biophilia* (2011).
8. Dibben, Analysis of 'Solstice'.
9. The differentiation in font style is intended to represent the different colours of the corresponding circles in "Song Mode".
10. This sound is similar to that produced when dragging notes over the score in the Sibelius or Finale notation software packages.
11. Dibben, Analysis of 'Solstice'.

## References

Björk (2011) *Biophilia*. One Little Indian/Well Hart.

Burton, C. (2011). "In Depth: How Björk's 'Biophilia' Album Fuses Music with iPad Apps." *Wired*. July 26. http://www.wired.co.uk/magazine/archive/2011/08/features/music-nature-science (accessed September 7, 2014).

Cavatorta, A. (2011) "Gravity Harps for Björk." Personal blog post. July 2. http://andycavatorta.com/2014/08/01/gravity-harps/ (accessed November 12, 2011).

Dibben, N. (2013) "Visualising the App Album with Björk's *Biophilia*." In *The Oxford Handbook of Sound and Image in Digital Media*, edited by C. Vernallis, A. Herzog and J. Richardson, pp. 682–704. New York: Oxford University Press.

Diver, M. (2011) "Björk Biophilia Review." *BBC Online*. http://www.bbc.co.uk/music/reviews/5zq4 (accessed September 10, 2014).

Dredge, S. (2011) "Scott Snibbe Talks Björk's Biophilia, Apps and Interactive Music." *The Guardian Music Blog*. October 21. http://www.theguardian.com/technology/appsblog/2011/oct/21/scott-snibbe-bjork-biophilia-app (accessed September 10, 2014).

Fricke, D. (2011) "Biophilia." *Rolling Stone*. October 11. http://www.rollingstone.com/music/albumreviews/biophilia-20111011 (accessed September 10, 2014).

Hansen, B. (2012) "A Preface to 'Song Reader.'" *The New Yorker*. November 12. http://www.newyorker.com/culture/culture-desk/a-preface-to-song-reader (accessed September 12, 2014).

Juul, J. (2005) *Half-Real: Video Games between Real Rules and Fictional Worlds*. Cambridge, MA: MIT Press.

Lady Gaga (2013) *ARTPOP*. Relative Wave/TechHaus/Streamline/Interscope Records.

Mager, W. (2011) "Touch the Music." *Holy Moly: Music Reviews*. July 29. http://www.holymoly.com/music/reviews/bjorks-biophilia-brings-music-back58397 (accessed September 9, 2014). Archived as https://web.archive.org/web/20120306215315/http://www.holymoly.com/music/reviews/bjorks-biophilia-brings-music-back58397

Michaels, S. (2013) "Jay-Z's Magna Carta Holy Grail App Under Investigation." *The Guardian*. July 17. http://www.theguardian.com/music/2013/jul/17/jay-z-magna-carta-app-under-investigation (accessed September 13, 2014).

Nonesuch Online Journal (2011) "Björk's 'Moon' Single and 'Biophilia' App Now on iTunes." *Nonesuch Online Journal*. September 7. http://www.nonesuch.com/journal/bjork-moon-single-biophilia-app-now-itunes-2011-09-07 (accessed September 9, 2014).

Petridis, A. (2011) "Björk: Biophilia – Review." *The Guardian Online*. October 6. http://www.theguardian.com/music/2011/oct/06/bjork-biophilia-cd-review (accessed September 9, 2014).

Pytlik, M. (2011) "Björk: Biophilia." *Pitchfork.com*. October 13. http://pitchfork.com/reviews/albums/15915-biophilia/ (accessed September 10, 2014).

Schiesel, S. (2011) "Playing the New Björk Album, and Playing Along, with Apps." *The New York Times*. October 24. http://www.nytimes.com/2011/10/25/arts/video-games/bjorks-biophilia-an-album-as-game.html?_r=0 (accessed September 10, 2014).

## Website

Biophilia Educational Program. http://biophiliaeducational.org (accessed September 12, 2014).

# 9 Palimpsest, Pragmatism and the Aesthetics of Genre Transformation

## Composing the Hybrid Score to Electronic Arts' Need for Speed Shift 2: Unleashed

*Stephen Baysted*[1]

Like music for film and television, video game music is not a wholly artistic endeavour. It is a commercial-artistic one and the commercial factors impacting on the composer are numerous and profound. Unlike film and television music, there are many attendant technical considerations and imperatives that impose strictures upon the form, constructional devices and musical vocabulary available to the composer. And as with all music composed for the screen, it is always critically important to keep in mind that its function is primarily to serve the wider ambitions of the production rather than to determine them.

This chapter chronicles the compositional process of the *Shift 2: Unleashed* (2011) video game score from conceptualization to completion. We will explore the underlying aesthetic objectives of the music, the commercial tensions inherent in the production of a "Triple-A" game franchise and their impact on creative musical interventions. We will also investigate how the score functions as a cohesive, unifying force governing the player's emotional responses. The score takes as its starting point ten chart-topping rock and pop songs which are renegotiated and re-imagined as affective "cinematic" musical experiences. The score is, and remains, unique in its genre. But in order to understand the process we need to wind the clock back to the development of its prequel: *Need for Speed: Shift*.

In September 2009,[2] *Need for Speed: Shift* was released worldwide by Electronic Arts Inc. on three platforms.[3] It was the sixteenth iteration of the bestselling game series in the history of the medium, with more than one hundred and forty million copies sold globally and grossing in excess of $2.5bn in revenue to date.[4] *Shift* signalled a significant change in direction and emphasis from more recent iterations of the *Need for Speed* series,[5] from illicit nocturnal street racing culture in the "arcade" mould to real world circuit racing "simulation," and thus taking it from a more casually oriented game to one that demanded greater skill and investment from the player.[6] And by investment we should not only consider the time taken to become a proficient player, but also the financial implications of steering wheel setups, racing seats and other specialist controller devices that the enthusiast might purchase, and the use of which the game should support, even invite. *Shift* also marked a strategic fragmentation of the franchise, with three further non-competing *Need for Speed* titles being launched in 2009 and 2010.[7]

The development of *Shift* was undertaken by London-based developer Slightly Mad Studios and EA Blackbox based in Vancouver.[8] I was both Audio Director (thus ultimately responsible for all of the sound in the game) and part of the team of composers. *Shift* attempted to rekindle the flame of the early history of the game series by re-focusing on a more authentic driver experience, and in particular, the racing driving experience. The press release at launch explains the underlying motivation:

> "With *Need for Speed SHIFT*, we set out to create a racing game that pushes the genre and delivers something never before seen in a Need for Speed title," said Patrick Söderlund, Senior Vice President at EA Games Europe. "By focusing on the driver's experience through the first-person view, we are able to capture the high-speed intensity and gripping emotions of racing."
>
> Players are thrust into the loud, intense, and athletic experience of racing a car from the driver's perspective through the combination of perception based G-forces, the hyper reality of the cockpit view, and the all-new brutally disorienting crash dynamic. *Need for Speed SHIFT* features an accurate, accessible physics-based driving model that allows you to feel every impact, every change of track surface and every last bit of grip as you push yourself to the edge. (EA, 2009)

Even accounting for the customary marketing hyperbole of press releases, as new feature sets go, this "hyper realistic" cockpit view was indeed innovative for the series (if not racing games more generally) and borrowed much, conceptually at least, from the first-person shooter genre, especially with regard to the manner in which the player is deliberately disorientated when impact is made with other cars or immoveable trackside objects. The graphical detail of the cockpit had been modelled with the utmost fidelity and this also meant that the player was encouraged to abandon the customarily favoured and default "Chase" or "Third-Person" view of previous iterations of the series and indeed many other (arcade) racing game series.[9]

*Shift* was to be a racing simulation game, but not in the conventional sense. To be sure, the cars and racing circuits were accurately modelled in 3D from manufacturer and license-holder blueprints, laser scans and other commercially sensitive methods, and the vehicular sounds were recorded from real racing cars on the track or on chassis dynamometers wherever possible. But the physics engine was intended to be accessible rather than the last word in fidelity; the phrase bandied around during the development process was "pick up and play". A useful, though potentially pejorative phrase has been coined by players to describe this kind of simulation: "simcade" (a conflation of simulation and arcade).

*Shift* was both a critical and commercial success, not least in the domain of audio, where it was nominated for two Motion Picture Sound Editor's Golden Reel awards and a Game Audio Network Guild award. The vehicular sounds in particular were notably more aggressive and "distorted" than in previous iterations and indeed in other racing games. As Charles Deenen, the then *Need for Speed* Franchise Audio Director recalls,

> we were always under the assumption that cars in games should sound like "enhanced" real cars, and that we shouldn't deviate from that. But there was a new development team we were working with [Slightly Mad Studios] who said "We like it distorted". I was like "We can't distort the car sounds. It's too unrealistic". Turned out the development team was right. The perception for most people in the world was that this was what a car sounded like, because they were accustomed to hearing clipped audio on YouTube. So we did another focus group, and asked people which one they preferred: clean, normal car sounds or clipped ones from YouTube. All nine people said "YouTube". We were like oookay . . . ("Sam", 2014)

Sound and music played an important role in the game and, in particular, in the menu system. The original score itself placed a greater emphasis on sound design elements – heavily processed racing car recordings and pit to car communications – than more conventional musical material. The result was a novel, impactful and immersive sonic experience rather than a musical one, though the strategic use of musical drones did help to anchor the ambient elements to a musical frame to a limited degree.[10] Like all recent iterations of *Need for Speed*, *Shift* included a range of licensed music that had been sourced by the Electronic Arts music supervisory team based in Los Angeles.

*Shift*'s sequel, *Shift 2: Unleashed* (2011), pushed the franchise further down the road of simulation than ever before; indeed it is fair to say that to date it is still the most authentic evocation of competitive motorsport in the entire *Need for Speed* series.[11] There are, I would suggest, three reasons for this: Slightly Mad Studios, founded by Ian Bell, were renowned for their work in this area and when *Shift* was launched they continued to develop *Shift 2* without EA Blackbox but with some production assistance from EA DICE in Sweden;[12]

Patrick Söderlund (now Executive Vice President, EA Studios) is a talented and committed racing driver himself and was very active in an executive production capacity throughout development; and as the franchise had been tri-furcated two years previously, a more focused and more authentic racing simulation could be developed, liberated from too many compromises that would normally afflict a title that aimed to have universal appeal. Throughout development an emphasis was placed on fidelity and authenticity in all domains of the game: graphics, physics and audio; the "Authenticity Trailer", released two months before the game was launched, highlights the lengths the development team went to in order to ensure that racing was faithfully simulated. The trailer features interviews with racing drivers from a variety of motorsport disciplines and it shows how the game development process was informed by data and feedback from real racing teams that lent the whole enterprise credibility.[13] In the case of audio, the focus on authenticity meant that a decision was made early on to position the game firmly in the camp of the racing simulation, and for the first time in many years, a *Need for Speed* title would not have licensed music playing during actual gameplay. We will return to this point presently as it is one that defines the genre musically and conceptually, and will repay more detailed discussion.

The underlying aesthetic of *Shift 2* was determined soon after development commenced in 2009. It was to be "the driver's battle" and as such it was a logical progression from the work – especially on the first-person aspects – already undertaken in *Shift*. The game aimed, primarily, to simulate the visceral nature and intensity of competitive motorsport by immersing the player graphically, physically and sonically in the simulated world of the driver. The "Teaser Trailer" released in November 2010 managed to capture the tenor visually and sonically for the game and showed off the innovative night-time racing effects; we explored many musical avenues for this trailer but eventually decided that an entirely sound-effect-based audio landscape would be more impactful.[14] In the game, the player views the world exactly as the racing driver sees it and in order to faithfully replicate this, a new camera mechanic was devised: "Helmet Cam". In addition to the first-person g-force and impact effects pioneered in *Shift*, *Shift 2* would take this one stage further and mimic the tendency for drivers to rotate their heads towards the apices when steering the car into corners. It would also prove an extremely useful viewpoint where the "drifting" game mode was concerned, given the fact that drivers spend much of their time looking through the side windows as the car skids sideways around a circuit. The idea of exposing the player to a visceral and intense experience would pervade every aspect of the game, including the synchronized audio design of the User Interface (UI) and the experiential chronological sequencing of the music. As in *Shift*, the boundaries between audio and music would again be frequently blurred and often traversed, but unlike *Shift*, music was to play a central role in the immersive experiences of the player.

## The Process

Although game development commenced in earnest in 2009, musical development did not gain any particular traction, or indeed momentum, until June 2010, some ten months prior to the game's scheduled release. It is, of course, entirely customary for music to be composed towards the end of a game's production schedule, except in those cases where its functionality is unorthodox or its implementation is dependent on complex code, above and beyond the feature-sets of commonly used middleware such as FMOD or Wwise. Happily, *Shift 2* did not require too much in the way of elaborate programming to be undertaken for its music to operate, but there would prove to be other, far greater, challenges to overcome in order to complete the project.

It was clear from marketing strategies communicated from executives to us in meetings in London that it would be a non-negotiable requirement to include licensed music from artists who were popular with a 15 to 25 year old audience – the particular demographic that the game was targeting. At that juncture, individual artists and bands had not been identified by the marketing team, but any licensed music that would be included in the game would need to have broad international popular appeal given the planned worldwide release. To be sure, it was not immediately apparent how the use of popular song form material would be compatible with the underlying aesthetic of the game: "the driver's battle". Indeed, from a composer's perspective, when one conjures up images of the cut and thrust of professional motorsport, intense battle scenarios played out at night between ferociously competitive drivers and the visceral, brutal nature of racing cars travelling at immense speed, myriad stylistic exemplars from film (rather than popular music) readily present themselves. Moreover, the menu system in the game had already been "temped" and populated with film music clips as a means of giving producers an indication of the musical direction the music department wished to take.[15]

Fortunately, as mentioned above, the artists had not yet been selected and it was eventually left to Charles Deenen and me to determine the genre of the music to be licensed. This was to prove a crucial and decisive factor in how the unique musical concept was conceived. Charles came to my studio in the UK in early June 2010 and we spent two days discussing how we would tackle and resolve the apparent impasse that had been reached. We understood only too well that we would have to use licensed music, but we both wanted to produce an original and innovative "cinematic" music score – cinematic in scope, musical vocabulary and production value – that would enhance the player's experience and be aligned with the wider aesthetic ambitions of the game itself. Two primary questions thus presented themselves at that point: how could music function, non-diegetically, to enhance the player's experience and depth of immersion when, in the simulation genre, music is never interactive and is very rarely heard during sequences of gameplay?[16] Secondly, how could popular song material from an array of bands be transformed into a score that functions as a cohesive, unifying force affecting the player's emotional responses?

In response to the first question, during gameplay in a racing simulation, vehicular sounds should always take precedence over musical ones and it is customary not to have music playing whilst racing at all.[17] There are many reasons for this, not least that including music would undermine realism. There are attendant deep-rooted acoustical reasons too: it is incredibly difficult for sound designers to balance car sounds with music. Whilst there are technical strategies to assist with this process, most are unsatisfactory and lead to frustrating compromises. The primary issue is that the frequency ranges of the majority of car sounds overlap problematically with many core orchestral instruments' ranges. This leads to both sound and music competing for the same audio territory and the problem is exacerbated by the player's need to hear certain audio cues – for example, tyre sounds – so that corner entry speeds can be judged. Given that the player is not subject to g-forces, they must be presented with carefully balanced aural cues to be able to judge the limits of traction and grip at all times. In an arcade racing game, this is of course less of an issue from a gameplay perspective since the physical representation of the car's interaction with the world is not aiming to be an accurate one.

Clearly, then, the menu system would be the sole interface for the gamer's musical experience. In terms of enhancing immersion both in a gameplay and a musical sense, the menu music would need to preface, prefigure and prepare the player for the world of gameplay; it would need to be intimately bound up in the very business of motor racing. Van Elferen has shown how the player, through what she terms "game musical literacy", is able to make the leap between compositional vocabulary and the underlying structural and narrative elements to arrive at a heightened sense of involvement in the game:

> Combining the audio-visual literacies of film and television music with ludoliteracy, game soundtrack design appeals to a specific game musical literacy. Through intertextual references to audio-visual idioms from other media, game soundtracks deploy player literacy for their immersive effect: it is because gamers recognise certain composing styles that they are able to interpret gaming events and feel involved in gameplay, game worlds and game plots. (Van Elferen, 2016: 36)

As we will see in a moment, harnessing sounds from the auditory experience of motorsport would serve to further intensify the player's sense of involvement and ultimately their sense of immersion.

We explored how players would be exposed to musical representations of racing in the menu system and we carefully plotted their musical journey from their very first playthrough to a world championship victory. The elaborate three-dimensional Graphical User Interface (GUI), which enabled the player to navigate through the game, would prove to be both an invaluable tool and a metaphorical thorn. The GUI comprised a series of carefully designed 5.1 audio elements – literally bursts of car sounds, "whooshes", percussive impacts and pit-to-car radio communications – which accompanied its on-screen rotational movement. This movement was triggered randomly by the player and as a result these 5.1 audio elements, which overlaid the menu music, had enormous potential to interfere with it; there would be no opportunity to synchronize the two in musical terms. Consequently we were forced to explore how the visceral and symbolic elements of the sound design might also be deployed to enhance gameplay and musical immersion. If we were to systematically superimpose additional layers of processed "pit-to-car radio" transmissions and race-day atmospherics over the music, the sonic experience on the journey between menu music, GUI audio and gameplay might appear more fluid and linear on the one hand and a little more musically coherent on the other. The use of such extra-musical material was not new – I had already incorporated engine sounds, tannoy announcements and pit-to-car radio elements into my score for GTR composed during 2004, but such systematic connectedness between game states was indeed an innovative departure in this genre.

All of our musical work and impact on the player would therefore need to be accomplished in the menu system and in preparing the player for racing. Unusually for the racing game genre, the music's primary objective and function would be a narrative one: it would seek to describe the "real" racing driver's emotional and psychological journey and at the same time represent and enhance the concomitant experiences of the game player through well-understood processes of aesthetic response. During the race build-up phase, our intention was to represent the varying emotional states of the racing driver in music: excitement, fear, stress, apprehension, determination and so on. We discussed what such music might sound like. Would it be slow or fast? Would the tempo and meter be irregular? Would there be many juxtapositions of material which would represent their jumbled sequence of emotions? We eventually landed upon the idea that any such music might have a certain surreal, ambient and expansive quality to it, and for want of a more appropriate term, "surreal" became the working brief for the menu music that preceded gameplay. If music that prepared the player for racing was difficult to describe and define, then happily, the music that would be triggered as the player crossed the finish line was more straightforward to characterize. If the player had won the race, then an emphatic, celebratory, euphoric and "epic" style of music would be triggered (crowd sounds were overlaid in order to enhance the sense of celebration and context); if the player had lost, then we determined that music which had been extensively post-processed, brutalized with filters, bit-crushed and distorted (both sonically and musically) would be triggered. Additionally, we would also plan to make use of the licensed music tracks in their original form. We had succeeded in adumbrating a musical plan, albeit *in embryo*.

Our three provisional musical genres – "Surreal", "Epic" and "Brutal" – would quickly need to be prototyped and the entire concept, which was a risky one, approved by the Executive before we could move forward with composition and commissioning. Although at this point it was eight months prior to game release, and under normal circumstances such a time span would be more than adequate, we were also required to license music and that is frequently a complex, convoluted and protracted process. As it would turn out, the manner in which we would want to use this licensed music would add an extra layer of complexity to the licensing process.

We decided that we would attempt to renegotiate and reframe any music that we licensed and transform it into suitable material for our musico-narrative ambitions. This meant that we would need to find songs that were anthemic and ones that had especially strong melodically-focused choruses. This ruled out many popular music genres and seemed to point inexorably and almost exclusively to one in particular: rock music.[18] We worked closely with the music supervision team in Los Angeles to source music from bands that would be popular with the target demographic as well as giving us the best possible opportunity to reframe them successfully; if memory serves, we evaluated over forty possible songs and for budgetary reasons we were seeking to whittle these down to just ten.

The first track that we pursued and used for prototyping during July 2010 was 'Night of the Hunter' (2009) by Thirty Seconds to Mars. This song has a strongly defined conventional musical structure – intro, bridge, pre-chorus, chorus, middle eight – and its powerful, melodically-driven chorus proved to be an ideal test bed for musical development. The prototyping process involved commissioning demos from a range of composers (myself included) and each one was tasked with producing three versions of the track which would correspond to each of our musical genres: Surreal, Epic and Brutal. The game would eventually require in excess of one hundred minutes of music to be used variously in the menu system, the in-game full motion video content (non-interactive video clips) and as material for the Marketing Department to use in their trailers and television advertisements.[19] Whilst *Shift 2* did have a comparatively large music budget for racing simulation games, there are always limitations and it is worth pointing out that licensing music that is both current and popular from successful artists can be an extremely costly enterprise. As a result we would be aiming to license ten tracks in total and it was, of course, not just a happy coincidence of economy that we were planning to compose three versions of each song.

During August, much of our time was spent sifting through music and assembling the composition team.[20] In practice, because of the way in which game development works, we only had sixty days in which to complete the entire musical content; both the licensor approval process that was required and the game "content lock" in December saw to that. Figure 9.1 shows, in particular, how the final months of *Shift 2* development were used and demonstrates, in general terms, that they are very rarely focused on content creation, but rather on the practicalities of delivering and bringing a finished boxed product to a worldwide market.

| June 2010 | Music concept devised |
| July | Demo prototyping |
| August | Band search |
| September | Production: phase 1 |
| October | Production: phase 2 |
| November | Licensor approval |
| December | Music mix; game content lock |
| January 2011 | License contracts finalized |
| March | Game release |

*Figure 9.1* The development process of *Shift 2: Unleashed* (2011)

The early sketches and the prototyping process allowed us to shape and refine the musical concept and, indeed more importantly, determine the musical vocabulary and its frames of reference. It also assisted us in our search for suitable music to license as we now had a better sense of which types of song would be more likely to work effectively. As part of each licensing deal that was concluded, we were provided with detailed "stems" for all songs. Stems are the individual tracks (or in certain cases sub-mixes) from an original recording session – in many instances sessions may be broken down into extremely detailed elements. This meant, in practice, that we were in an excellent position to be able to analyse and deconstruct each song, breaking it down into its most fundamental elements and identifying its "genetic fingerprint". Essentially the quest for each composer was to preserve any significant fragments of melodic, rhythmic or sonic material from each licensed track so that, once renegotiated and reframed, the original song, like the written-over layer in a palimpsest, would still be partially audible and recognizable to the target demographic – even if the end result had moved far beyond the ambit of the original in all musical domains.

Before we explore the compositional process in more detail, it is necessary to discuss some of the technical and operational idiosyncrasies of the menu system since they impacted directly and significantly upon the approach to the race build-up. Due to some rather complex technical limitations, especially on the previous generation of gaming consoles, involving principally, but not exclusively, system RAM and hard disk access, "streaming" music during the loading phase of the game proved to be extremely problematic. This meant in practice that it was not simply possible to play a single track, unbroken, throughout the passage from the menu system through to the point of gameplay. Figure 9.2 is a very simple flow chart detailing the different stages of "game state" between the game opening and gameplay itself.

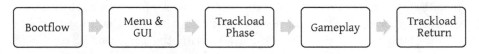

*Figure 9.2* A flow chart detailing the game states of *Shift 2: Unleashed* (2011)

"Bootflow" describes the phase during which the game opens, the initial introductory screens are displayed and the full motion video material is shown to the player. Once this phase has ended, the player is placed in the menu system where they are able to choose game modes, career objectives, vehicles, racing circuits and browse statistical information about their previous races. "Trackload Phase" is the stage during which all of the component elements necessary for gameplay are gathered together and compiled by the program. During Trackload, the player has no control or possibility of interaction; they are simply spectating at this point. It is important to note that the duration of the Trackload phase is essentially indeterminate because content will always differ between racing circuits, numbers and combinations of vehicles involved in the race and gameplay modes. Significantly, it also differs between platforms, with PCs generally being faster to load than the consoles. Having said that, PC Trackload times are also determined by the computer's CPU clock frequency and number of processing cores, hard disk type and speed, and the amount of available RAM. This inter-platform indeterminacy has, of course, a significant impact on any musical strategy too. "Gameplay" needs no explanation except to say that there are instances where there are two or more races in a series, so there is a hiatus between one race finishing and the next one loading, which needs to be accounted for sonically. Once again, that hiatus is of an indeterminate length depending on processing speed, disk access times and memory bandwidth. "Trackload Return" is the phase which takes the player from Gameplay back to the menu system. As in Trackload, the player cannot interact during this process and it is of indeterminate length – often on a powerful PC this phase may only last a matter of seconds.

As the player enters the menu system from the Bootflow phase, our design specified that a Surreal track type would be played, representing the varying emotional states of the racing driver in their preparation for the race. However, this track would need to be halted once the Trackload phase had been triggered by the player due, as mentioned above, to streaming and RAM limitations. It was impossible to predict how long the player would remain in the menu system and as such to what extent the music track would have unfolded by the point at which the Trackload phase had been triggered. Our musical objective would be to make any transition between Menu and Trackload appear to be as seamless as possible, but the issue was that, in all probability, the moment of transition would be most likely to occur at a musically inappropriate juncture. Another factor that we would need to contend with was that, due to audio memory budget restrictions, music played during the Trackload phase would have to be looped and those loops would need to be relatively short. Looping was also necessary because the Trackload phase was of indeterminate and differing lengths depending on platform and compiled content.

We experimented with a range of material for Trackload, especially with music unrelated to the menu track, since that seemed to offer a potentially more predictable solution. However, in practice, using unrelated material had two unfortunate side-effects: one was to undermine any sense of immersion that we had worked extremely hard to construct; and the other was to make the transition between Menu and Trackload jarring and awkward as two different pieces of music would then be juxtaposed in quick succession and at potentially musically inappropriate and incompatible points. After much testing we established that the most satisfactory solution would be to use a looped extract of the currently-playing Surreal menu music track and that the GUI sound design that was triggered on the launch of the Trackload phase meant that it masked the transition somewhat. It was not a musically ideal solution by any stretch of the imagination, but it was a workable one nonetheless. The same track would then be carried through to re-engage the player at the moment the finish line was crossed following Gameplay. If the race had been won, then the Epic version of the track would be played reinforcing the player's sense of achievement and euphoria; if the race had been lost, then the Brutal incarnation would be triggered. In each case, the player's journey would be accompanied by a single track set from menu, through Trackload to game completion and Trackload return. Additionally, if the player chose to continue watching a replay of their race, the original version of the track would be played. Although borne very much out of compromise and somewhat governed by technical constraints, this musical mechanism did ensure that the narrative arc of the music was as coherent as possible. And finally, once the player had returned to the menu system, a new music set would be initialized.

## The Score

Let us now turn to the compositional process itself and to the frame of reference and musical vocabulary that each musical genre demanded. While the number of stems available from each song recording session varied, the most important elements – isolated lead vocal parts – were present in all cases. As mentioned above, the objective was for the composers to conserve each licensed track's significant musical material so as to retain its identity through the diverse variations, with the aim of preserving recognition by the target audience. This project was aided by the target demographic's familiarity with the activity of remixing popular song form material and, more importantly, to the conceptual frame of remixes. For the Surreal and Epic versions, we decided that the hybridized "epic" orchestral cinematic language typified by Remote Control Productions, and from films such as *The Last Samurai* (2003), *Man on Fire* (2004), *The Dark Knight* (2008), *Iron Man* (2008), *X-Men Origins: Wolverine* (2009), *Transformers: Revenge of the Fallen* (2009), *Angels and Demons* (2009) and *Inception* (2010) would be the primary point of reference. The instrumental forces common to all the above examples are a blend of an extended symphonic orchestra (with frequently large or outsize brass sections),[21] large percussion ensembles often incorporating non-Western instruments, and sound design elements using a wide range of electronic sound sources from analogue and digital synthesizers to virtual instruments, sample-based sources (including orchestral samples), and lead and bass guitars. This somewhat eclectic (but by now familiar) mix of acoustic and electronic sources is strategically blended and most skilfully produced to create expansive, dramatic and contemporary-sounding film scores. The influence of these scores and their musical style extends beyond the ambit of film, reaching far into the world of television and games and has directly influenced contemporary film trailers. Somewhat ironically, "trailer music" has now become a commercialized musical genre in its own right and one that itself proved to be a major influence on *Shift 2* (Kelly, 2011).

The musical syntax of the Remote Control Productions style can be readily characterized by its relatively straightforward modal harmonic progressions, rhythmical ostinati like the now cliché – though seemingly not passé – "Batman" spiccato string figures,[22] extended and frequently heroic or triumphant melodies orchestrated for unison French horns and celli and doubled at the octave with violins and trumpets, all propelled by larger-than-life percussion ensembles and electronic effects. Of course there are far more facets to the music than those rather prosaic and superficial generalizations would suggest, but nevertheless, they do help us to swiftly understand the essence of their soundworld and how they tend to operate on a musical level. And crucially, this soundworld signifies a contemporary cinematic aesthetic to players, too, through the agency of what Van Elferen (2016) describes as musical affect and musical literacy elsewhere in this volume. The resultant scores are, in many respects, beyond reproach as exemplars of contemporary hybridized film music and many of them stand as highly effective, impactful, emotionally charged and epoch-making compositions in their own right outside the context of film itself. Because of the global audience reach of this music, and the scores' influence on other composers working in film through the ubiquitous use of temp tracks, Remote Control Productions in large part defines the "contemporary sound" of music for moving-image media.[23] But there are other elements to consider when discussing the "contemporary sound" in film and they are extremely important in the sense that the vocabulary of film music is being indelibly marked by musical genres and by songwriters, producers and composers from outside its conventional boundaries.[24] A parallel can be directly drawn between this and with what Karen Collins (2008: 129) describes as the intertextual relationship between games and the paramusical phenomena associated with popular music artists. It is also worth noting that Electronic Arts is *de facto* one of the most significant music production companies in the world with two of its own record labels, and that over the past twenty years the *Need for Speed* series has become a pop culture phenomenon in itself (Kawashima, 2013).

I now move on to discuss several aspects of the *Shift 2* score in more detail, namely tempo, meter, instrumentation, post-processing and production, and reharmonization. In broad terms, the ten Surreal versions – composed by Ramin Djawadi[25] and myself – have substantially slower tempi than either the originals or the Epic and Brutal versions. And in the majority of cases they also have different time signatures and metrical underpinnings. Compare, for example, the three versions of 'Night of the Hunter' and observe that whilst they are all driven by a rather emphatic rhythmical figuration – the Surreal version less consistently – the tempo, meter and patterns of accentuation differ substantially between them.[26] My Surreal version of 'Night of the Hunter', for example, is mostly in 6/4, interspersed with 3/2, whereas the others are strictly in common time. If we compare the original Biffy Clyro 'Mountains' (2008) with my Surreal version, one can identify substantial differences in meter and indeed in tempo (the original being 158 beats per minute, the Surreal half tempo at 79 bpm).[27] Not only was 'Mountains' an outlier in terms of its status as the only British song in the game, the fact that its meter alternates bar to bar in the verse between 4/4 and 7/8, that the chorus has a "half-tempo" feel and that the post chorus has a 2/4 codetta, made it a particularly challenging song to renegotiate. In the Epic and Brutal versions, the metrical differences from the original are less marked (though neither use 7/8, opting instead for a consistent 4/4), but their genres are radically different with the Epic building to a trailer-style choral-dominated climax and the Brutal version exhibiting an extensively post-processed and "glitchy" drum and bass vocabulary and sensibility.

In order to reduce the tempo for the Surreal versions, the vocal stems – as well as any other stem fragments being used – required slowing down. Until very recently, this process, whether undertaken in Digital Audio Workstation software such as Pro Tools, Cubase or Logic, or in dedicated sound editing software such as Wavelab or Soundforge, always introduced undesirable digital artefacts. Depending upon the particular algorithm used to "stretch" the audio, these artefacts usually manifested themselves as an extremely subtle, but for the composer infuriatingly noticeable, pitch modulation or amplitude modulation, and some of the rhythmical accuracy of the original would inevitably be lost in translation. Any rhythmical imprecision or intonational issues present in the live performances and captured during the recording process at the original tempo would be augmented and exacerbated as the audio was slowed down. As a result, one always found that additional editing and processing was required to make the stretched audio work satisfactorily in its new context. Obviously, the greater the stretching factor, the greater the probability of digital artefacts and imperfections being introduced and so as a composer one was constrained by relatively narrow tempo windows within which to work. It was simpler to modify the meter and thus effect a substantial deviation from the metrical identity of the original, rather than relying exclusively on tempo-changing processes.

In terms of instrumentation, I wish now to consider the cinematic use of guitars, solo voice and choral elements. As befits the racing game genre, and indeed televisual presentations of motorsport itself, the sound of overdriven electric guitars pervades the *Shift 2* score. In my Surreal version of 'Issues',[28] guitars feature prominently in the introductory section with a stretched and delayed melodic motif set against a processed piano saturated in reverb, synthesizer pads, delayed vocals from the original song and an embedded mezzo-soprano vocal line; this is perhaps the most ambient section of all of the Surreal versions. The ambient wash eventually gives way at 1:04 minutes to an orchestral build beginning with rising tenths at the bottom of the respective ranges on celli and double basses, which continues its unbroken upward trajectory to the climax at 1:49 minutes with the original vocal from the chorus. Guitars also feature prominently in my version of Switchfoot's 'This is the Sound' (2010) from their album *Hello Hurricane*.[29] An overdriven guitar pad effect opens the track which is replaced at 23 secs by a slowed-down original guitar stem awash with delay and reverb, and passed through a high pass filter and some aggressive equalization settings. This melodic and textural device becomes engulfed by the orchestra at 35 secs and eventually makes way for a section that features a heavily processed and stretched instance of the original vocal line. Guitars do return but only to be swamped again by the orchestra rising up – trailer style – to a climax, complete with an extended embedded portamento violin "riser" line and a typical eleventh-hour sharpening of the seventh of the mode at the cadence point to make it momentarily tonal and more dramatic, before a piano dominated coda which sinks away into a reprise of the opening guitar effect. In my Surreal 'Night of the Hunter' version, guitars are ever-present too – an overdriven guitar wash begins the track, and "power chords"[30] sit underneath the orchestral and choral textures to add a certain pungency and grit. Djawadi's Surreal mixes all have prominent guitar elements – whether composed or taken from the original stems and subject to additional processing.

Surreal 'Night of the Hunter', is perhaps the most vocally dominated version in the game and much use is made of the original and varied vocal stems, from the *sotto voce* of the lead in the opening verse (13 secs), through to the ensemble choral style of the "chorus" (22 secs), to the soaring descending countermelody (1:27 mins). Additionally, a range of choir samples were embedded in order to bolster the impact of the original chorus. The track also includes a live mezzo-soprano part which helps give shape and definition to the vocal parts (for example at 45 secs), and sits atop the crescendi into 1:23 minutes and 2:15 minutes. It is worth mentioning that this method of combining and blending a real instrument or vocalist with sampled instruments – especially where unison melodic lines are concerned – helps render the whole more convincing; the real instruments generally bring much needed expression and musicality to the samples and assist in making the sampled articulations more credible. The mezzo soprano and choir virtual instruments were used in Surreal 'Issues' (40 secs and 1:37 mins); Surreal 'This is the Sound' (1:27 mins onwards); Surreal 'Mountains' (33 secs and 1:33 mins) with prominent mezzo-soprano parts and choir at 2:04 minutes; and in Mick Gordon's Epic 'Mountains', the choir takes a central role throughout.[31] 'Night of the Hunter' is also substantially reharmonized, especially with regard to its dramatized opening section which helps to frame and intensify the slowed-down lead vocal taken from the chorus section of the original. It is fair to say that the majority of the original tracks were reharmonized to varying degrees and extents and this was due primarily, I would suggest, to the process of genre transformation in which the original required intensification or dramatization to suit its new context and role. It was not that the original songs were in any way deficient or ineffectual *per se*, simply that they were not particularly well suited in their original forms to the aesthetic vision of the game (the "driver's battle"); they had, after all, been composed and intended for an entirely different musical purpose and audience.

The emphasis on what was quite radical post-processing throughout the score is one of its defining sonic features. The original vocal performances are frequently passed through low-pass, high-pass or band-pass filters (and various combinations of them) and subject to deliberately destructive equalization settings (such as the "telephone" effect) to help distort the sound as well as disguise some of the digital artefacts described above. Other techniques, such as bit-crushing, rhythmical panning, reverse reverb-saturated vocal fades, extreme stretching and stutter effects, are in evidence too. Of course, there are instances of effects processes that now, some five years hence, seem a little passé – Izotope's Stutter Edit plugin, for example, would be deployed rather more sparingly now. It is important to observe that whilst not necessarily revolutionary in themselves, many of the processes used in the making of the score were not in widespread use in popular music genres at the time.

Production itself – and by that I mean the process of mixing and mastering the final compositions – was always intended to be an important part of the project and integral to our underlying aesthetic ambitions for it. In our initial discussions, Charles Deenen and I had identified the need for the music production to take on the same cinematic values as the music itself and to be mixed and mastered in such a way as to match, at once, the overblown intensity of trailer music and the expansive and impactful dynamic range characteristic of Hollywood film music. To that end, we engaged Grammy Award-winning film score producer Steve McLaughlin to mix and master the game score in 5.1 surround. Relatively aggressive compression and limiting effects were used during McLaughlin's mix in London in early December 2010 in order to obtain the trailer-style sound, and much detailed work was done at stem level to give the score a homogenous and coherent sonic signature, given that it had been composed by a team spread across three continents and four time zones.

Genre transformation is clearly not a straightforward process; it involves a root and branch renegotiation of the original artefact and a finely developed understanding – both conceptual and technical – of the destination genre's musical *modus operandi*. The transformation of rock songs into cinematic hybrid orchestral music presented numerous challenges. As we have seen, these challenges – many entirely outside the control of the composer – were further amplified by the technological constraints of the video game platform itself; the commercial imperatives that govern the production of "Triple-A" funded video games; marketing-driven factors including a focus on target demographics; the technical limitations of music technology; and the conventions and musical parameters of the target genre itself. In *Shift 2: Unleashed* then, we see a game score that is shaped as much by the game's underlying aesthetic ambitions as it is by pragmatism and the realities of commercial-artistic creative endeavour.

## Notes

1. Stephen Baysted is Reader in Film Composition at the University of Chichester. He is also Audio Director, Sound Designer and Composer for Slightly Mad Studios. His practice-based research has focused on questions of immersion, diegesis and genre, and has involved his work on *Need for Speed: Shift* (2009), *Shift 2: Unleashed* (2011) and *Project C.A.R.S.* (2015). Stephen's video game audio has been nominated for two Motion Picture Sound Editors "Golden Reel" Awards, a Jerry Goldsmith Award and two Game Audio Network Guild Awards.
2. Development began in early 2007.
3. PC, Xbox 360 and Playstation 3. iOS and PSP versions were released later.
4. Exact sales figures are difficult to determine, not least because they are already out of date, but a 2013 investor-oriented press release by Electronic Arts Inc. puts the number at 150 million (EA, 2013), whereas an article in *Variety* suggests 140 million (Graser, 2013).
5. See, for example, *Carbon* (2006), *Pro-Street* (2007) and *Undercover* (2008).
6. Tim Summers in *Understanding Video Game Music* (forthcoming) identifies five distinct subgenres of racing game and offers a more granular discussion than is possible here of the conventional ways in which music may be used within each of them. There is of course a further extra-musical distinction to be made and that is the way in which racing games (and their subgenres) approach the representation of real-world physics and the interactions of their vehicle models within their simulated physical world. In a "hands on preview" to *Shift 2 Unleashed*, journalist David Houghton proffers a further insightful distinction: "The bar has been raised for racing games over recent years. Speed and sexy car models just aren't enough any more. 'Racing simulation' doesn't just mean accurate braking distances and half an hour noodling around with engine tuning before each race. It means an affecting evocation of all the physical trauma, fear and excitement of rattling around a track at high speeds in a heavy chunk of explosive metal" (Houghton, 2010). Indeed this definition of "simulation" bears more resemblance to the concept of immersion as it is conventionally understood to apply in multimedia contexts.
7. *Nitro* (2009), *World* (2010) and *Hot Pursuit* (2010).
8. EA Blackbox had previously developed five *Need for Speed* titles: *Hot Pursuit 2* (2002), *Underground* (2003), *Most Wanted* (2005), *Carbon* (2006) and *Pro-Street* (2007).
9. See, for example, Roper, 2009.

10. Supplementary materials for this chapter are available via the publisher's website and the Ludomusicology UK Research group website. See Online Music Example 1.
11. It is worth noting that the first *Need for Speed* game released in 1994 was branded *Road & Track presents: Need for Speed*. *Road & Track* is a North American car magazine first published in 1947. *Road & Track*'s involvement in the game lent it a certain gravitas as a title that leaned towards being a simulation rather than an arcade game, although the gameplay did involve driving as quickly as possible through traffic on the public highway.
12. The core development team at Slightly Mad Studios Ltd had worked together from 2003 under the guise of Simbin AB and subsequently Blimey Games Ltd. Critically acclaimed simulation titles that were developed during these periods were *GTR* (2004), *GT Legends* (2005), *GTR2* (2006) and *BMW M3 Challenge* (2007).
13. See Online Music Example 2, Authenticity Trailer.
14. See Online Music Example 3.
15. For an insightful discussion of the role of the "temping" process in film post-production, see Sadoff, 2006.
16. In my score to Atari's *Ferrari Racing Legends* (2012) there is one instance of linear dynamic (and non-diegetic) music triggered when it is announced over pit-to-car radio during a particular gameplay scenario that your team mate has just been killed in an accident a few corners ahead of your current position. A "Lacrimosa" is played. See Online Music Example 4.
17. Cf. *Formula 1 Grand Prix* (1992), *Grand Prix 2* (1996), *Formula 1 Racing Simulation* (1997), *Grand Prix Legends* (1998), *Sports Car GT* (1999), *Grand Prix 3* (2000), EA Sport's *F1 2000, 2001, 2002* (2000–2003), *Grand Prix 4* (2002), *GTR* (2004), *GT Legends* (2005), *GTR 2* (2006), *BMW M3 Challenge* (2007), *Ferrari Racing Legends* (2012), *Assetto Corsa* (2014), *Project Cars* (2015).
18. Rock music has long been associated with motor racing; perhaps the most well-known instance is the BBC's coverage of Formula One which continues to use Fleetwood Mac's 'The Chain' (1977) as the show's theme music. This topic would certainly repay further research and investigation.
19. Additional music was composed for several trailers including, for example, *Dark Corners* and *Attack the Corners*.
20. Charles Deenen would act as music producer, with myself, Ramin Djawadi, Troels Folmann, Mick Gordon and New York-based music collective Heavy Melody Music working on the compositions.
21. See Hans Zimmer's score to *Inception* (2010) which features an unusually configured and expanded brass ensemble consisting of six tenor trombones, six bass trombones, four tubas and six French horns. A short documentary trailer details the composition and recording process: http://youtu.be/XciGUzo9b6Q.
22. See 'Aggressive Expansion' and 'Why So Serious' in Zimmer and Newton Howard's *The Dark Knight* score of 2008.

23. It is also worth pointing out that Zimmer composed the score with Lorne Balfe to Activision's *Call of Duty: Modern Warfare II* (2009) and with Balfe and Slavov to Crytek Studios' *Crysis 2* (2011).
24. Trent Reznor of Nine Inch Nails fame who collaborated on Harry Gregson-Williams's score to *Man on Fire* (2004) and has been pursuing a flourishing career as a film composer in recent years; and Junkie XL (Tom Holkenborg), the DJ producer who began his work in film music as Harry Gregson-Williams's assistant has subsequently collaborated with Hans Zimmer on a number of projects including *Man of Steel* (2013) and *The Dark Knight Rises* (2012). Junkie XL now enjoys a burgeoning film composition career and has his main studio in Remote Control in Santa Monica.
25. Djawadi himself worked with Hans Zimmer and James Newton Howard composing additional music to Christopher Nolan's *Batman Begins* (2005).
26. Online Music Example 5.
27. Online Music Example 6.
28. Online Music Example 7.
29. Online Music Example 8.
30. Chords with open fifths usually played across all strings. In some instances, a "drop d" tuning was used. "Drop d" refers to the practice of tuning the low E string to D a tone below.
31. Online Music Example 9.

## References

Collins, K. (2008) *Game Sound: An Introduction to the History, Theory, and Practice of Video Game Music and Sound Design.* Cambridge, MA: MIT Press.

EA (2009) "Need for Speed SHIFT from EA Races into Retail this September" [Press Release]. http://news.ea.com/press-release/archive/need-speed-shift-ea-races-retail-september (accessed March 14, 2015).

EA (2013) "EA Signs Multi-Year Agreement with X-Games Medalist and Internet Phenom Ken Block for Need for Speed" [Press Release]. http://investor.ea.com/releasedetail.cfm?ReleaseID=799755 (accessed March 14, 2015).

Graser, D. (2013) "Ford's Mustang Races to 'Need for Speed'." *Variety.* http://variety.com/2013/film/games/ford-races-to-need-for-speed-1200494284/ (accessed March 14, 2015).

Houghton, D. (2010) "Need for Speed: Shift 2 Hands-on Preview." *Games Radar.* http://www.gamesradar.com/need-for-speed-shift-2-hands-on-preview-beautiful-brutal-and-scary-as-fck/ (accessed March 14, 2015).

Kawashima, D. (2013) "Interview with Steve Schnur, Worldwide President of Music at Electronic Arts (EA) Video Games." *Songwriter Universe.* http://www.songwriteruniverse.com/steve-schnur-123.htm (accessed March 14, 2015).

Kelly, S. (2011) "Movie Trailer Music." *The Guardian.* August 25. http://www.theguardian.com/film/2011/aug/25/movie-trailer-music (accessed March 14, 2015).

Roper, C. (2009) "Need for Speed Shift: Review." *IGN.* http://uk.ign.com/articles/2009/09/10/need-for-speed-shift-review-3 (accessed March 14, 2015).

Sadoff, R. (2006) "The Role of the Music Editor and 'Temp' Track as Blueprint for the Score, Source Music and Source Music of Films." *Popular Music* 25/2: 165–83.

"Sam" [Anon.] (2014) "Interview: SourceSound – Charles Deenen & Tim Gedemer." *SpeakHertz*. October 6. http://speakhertz.com/7259/interview-sourcesound-charles-deenen-tim-gedemer (March 14, 2015).

Summers, T. (forthcoming) *Understanding Video Game Music*. Cambridge: Cambridge University Press.

Van Elferen, I. (2016) "Analyzing Game Musical Immersion: The ALI Model." In *Ludomusicology: Approaches to Video Game Music*, edited by M. Kamp, T. Summers and M. Sweeney, pp. 32–52. Sheffield: Equinox.

# 10 Isaac's Silence
## *Purposive Aesthetics in* Dead Space

### *Mark Sweeney*[1]

This chapter is concerned with a particular set of relationships between video game music, film music and modernist avant-garde music. In a case study of Jason Graves's soundtrack for the third-person science fiction survival horror game series, *Dead Space* (2008, 2011, 2013), I delineate a particular sound-world and trace its origins back, via Hollywood, to the aleatory avant-garde music prevalent since the 1950s.[2] Graves unsurprisingly drew on the rich heritage of science fiction and horror film scores. However, rather than simply imitating a received caricature of modernist music as used in horror films, he also studied the works of Polish avant-garde composers Krzysztof Penderecki, Witold Lutosławski and Henryk Górecki. Throughout its disparate history, this particular sound-world has always been defined as "other" to the security provided by the Western tonal tradition as characterized/caricaturized in neo-romantic film scores – to which two of these composers, Penderecki and Górecki, nevertheless significantly "reverted".[3] While it was in the context of Hollywood's science fiction and horror films that this aesthetic solidified its "scary" semantic associations, I argue that games such as *Dead Space* and its sequels have more in common with the aesthetic paradigm's original intentions. This situation is particularly ironic given the wider avant-garde's often dismissive attitude towards mass culture.

In the first *Dead Space* (the primary focus of this chapter), the player's character, Isaac Clarke, is a silent protagonist – he does not speak and we do not ordinarily see his face. Given the widespread acknowledgement of the importance of "immersion" as a primary goal for the video game medium (see Chapter 3 of this volume), this narrative device is of particular interest as it supports a symbiotic relationship between player and avatar.[4] The acoustic void left by Isaac's silence is filled by both music and sound effects – sonically, sometimes indistinguishable from one another. The blurriness of this distinction problematizes the distance between sound effects and music, and goes hand-in-hand with Graves's research into avant-garde aleatory experimentation. Furthermore, the use of a dynamic music system that (re-)composes the soundtrack in real-time to fit the action on screen both supports and negates various aleatory principles.

## Selecting Sound-Worlds

When his vessel crash-lands into the spaceship it was sent to assist, Isaac Clarke becomes separated from his two colleagues and finds himself a lone engineer on the USG *Ishimura* (a huge mining ship orbiting the planet Aegis VII), fending off "necromorphs" (alien-infected animated corpses) whilst attempting to repair the ship's systems and find a way to escape to safety. Isaac is given the dangerous and difficult repair tasks, while his friends offer profuse guidance over the intercom. The only hints provided about Isaac's backstory are the brief and relatively vague allusions to Isaac's girlfriend, Nicole, working on board the *Ishimura* as a medical officer prior to his arrival. Her presence provides an additional motivation for Isaac's actions, as well as a pretext for his involvement in the rescue mission. As the story progresses, Isaac receives messages from Nicole, helping him uncover a conspiracy to use the *Ishimura* as a vehicle for obtaining a powerful artefact – the "Marker" – from the planet colony Aegis VII. It transpires that the Marker pacifies the "hive mind" of the necromorphs, and keeps them under control, but it also can manipulate Isaac's state of mind with powerful hallucinogenic effects. By the end of the game, Isaac discovers that Nicole committed suicide prior to his arrival and that the transmissions he thought were coming from her were actually from the Marker.

Isaac's role loosely parallels Ellen Ripley's character in Ridley Scott's sci-fi horror *Alien* (1979), although direct comparison makes the taciturn Ripley (played by Sigourney Weaver) appear loquacious. The antagonistic relationship between Scott and the film's composer, Jerry Goldsmith, was, despite their own misgivings, a productive one, as it resulted in an interesting dialectic of musical styles: the essentially neo-romantic vision preferred by Goldsmith for the film in juxtaposition with (or perhaps complementary to) the extended instrumental techniques borrowed from the avant-garde, or what he referred to as "the obvious thing: weird and strange, and which everybody [else] loved" (McIntee, 2005, 38).[5] The result is neither a complete synthesis, nor a strict dichotomy, as the neo-romantic music comes to the fore to support the epic narrative, and the modernist music predominates in tension-building or violent sequences.[6] Consciously or not, this duality of musical styles was replicated by Jason Graves in *Dead Space*, who had worked with Goldsmith in the past.[7] However, Graves has also claimed that as part of his preparation, he studied a selection of modernist avant-garde music, just as Goldsmith himself had done for the pioneering score to *Planet of the Apes* (Franklin J. Schaffner, 1968) (see below). For Penderecki, Lutosławski and Gorecki – three composers Graves paid particular attention to – the resultant sound-world was a by-product of a technical, aesthetic and, in the end, philosophical process (see Naumenko, 2008 and Balawender, 2010). As we shall see later, more often than not it was the "means" of sonically assembling the score, rather than the "ends" of the particular musical outputs, that are significant.

The *Dead Space* games are structured by a pendulum effect of non-interactive cutscenes punctuating gameplay. The interactive gameplay sequences are themselves carefully paced as tension-building exploration leads to moments of intense combat action. The two types of music (neo-romantic and modernist) map onto this form; the neo-romantic music is predominantly heard in cutscenes and pre-scripted sequences, while the dynamic modernist music is most noticeable during normal gameplay. However, this opposition is not a simple aural distinction as both sound-worlds are frequently integrated together to produce a coherent style (see below). While the basic plot arc of *Dead Space* echoes that of *Alien*, there are further parallels to be made between the sequels, *Dead Space 2* (2011) and *Aliens* (James Cameron, 1986). Both move away from the personal, internalized focus in the originals towards a more general action-orientated group dynamic where the protagonists return to face the alien enemy, but this time, backed up by a squad of marines. This change shifts the emotional and psychological elements of the horror significantly, and goes hand-in-hand with the *Dead Space 2* writers' decision to unmask Isaac, give him a voice, and more explicitly "characterize" him. The change certainly generated a great deal of debate amongst the gaming community.[8] Graves, who was re-employed as the composer for both sequels, was left with a dilemma as to how to write for this newly balanced narrative. In the first instance, he inevitably had to reflect the larger stakes (society as opposed to individual):

> The original *Dead Space* was very claustrophobic, and the music had a very chaotic, out-of-control sound to it. I wanted the music for *Dead Space 2* to sound bigger and more focused than the original. So the score makes use of more instruments in the orchestra to convey that larger-than-life feeling. (Naumenko, 2011)

But simultaneously, he had to maintain and further develop Isaac's internal struggle:

> Isaac definitely has a more identifiable character arc in the sequel. I used a string quartet, which is the antithesis of the huge, churning orchestra, to portray Isaac's vulnerability and character arc as he progresses through the game. (Ibid.)

Graves developed new material for the sequel, such as a leitmotif for Isaac (D-E-A-D), but retained much of the original distinctive sound-world – a form of musical branding essential to preserving the identity of the series. His final press release for the game clarifies the two distinctive musical areas that characterize the individual within the epic narrative:

> The score really runs the gamut as you play through the game. There are much bigger and scarier pieces along with quieter, more personal moments to counterbalance them. I wrote for string quartet to portray Isaac's vulnerable side. It's quite the emotional arc, but of course still done in a very *Dead Space* way. (Naumenko, 2011)

This is reminiscent of the duality found in Goldsmith's *Alien* score between the romantic "epic" and the modern "horror", although neither the game nor the film treat orchestration or style as exclusive categories. Both attempt to unify the opposing sound-worlds into a particular stylistic fusion.

In *Dead Space 2*, Graves readopts the nineteenth-century dichotomy of public and private musical spheres, embodied in orchestral and chamber music respectively. Indeed, although some players preferred the music of the first game, others found that the greater weight on the more familiar neo-romantic music in the sequel(s) provided relief from the unrelenting modernist music.[9] Furthermore, it seems that while many players were content with the modernist music as an underscore to violent gameplay, some said they felt that it was not as enjoyable to listen to outside the context of gameplay and so preferred the more obviously "epic" music. These opinions indicate that while there were some disagreements, it is clear that a balance was sought and largely achieved: the "inward turn" to Isaac's subjective psyche is balanced with an "epic texturing" of neo-romantic music – the outside world and larger social struggles of the narrative (Summers, 2016). This provides aesthetic relief and moral security, grounding the game around values that attempt to stabilize its otherwise precarious, uncertain and violent character.

## The Sound of Avant-Garde Modernism

While the neo-romantic sound-world employed by Graves across the series is familiar from Goldsmith's score, the origins of the modernist sound-world he utilizes for the internal psychological narrative and for the horror aspect of the genre is perhaps less so. Given Graves's claim that he studied aleatory avant-garde works, an understanding of the contexts in which *they* were written is particularly relevant to *Dead Space*. Two works often cited as pioneering examples of aleatory music are Stockhausen's *Klavierstück XI* (1956) and Pierre Boulez's Third Piano Sonata (1958), both generally categorized as modernist and avant-garde. The structure of the first of these is relatively simple and reflects

Stockhausen's interest in experimenting with the sonic properties of music. The pianist is instructed to glance randomly between the nineteen different sections of music to determine the order in which they should be played as he/she goes along, only finishing if one group is reached three times. Tempo and dynamic indications are given at the end of each section, to be employed in the next, whichever it may be, ensuring a degree of musical continuity. Stockhausen deliberately sets his project aside from earlier experiments with mobile form, such as Henry Cowell's *Mosaic Quartet* (1935), or the indeterminate chance pieces by John Cage, instead, claiming that his work

> is nothing but a sound in which certain partials, components, are behaving statistically . . . As soon as I compose a noise . . . then the wave structure of this sound is aleatory. If I make a whole piece similar to the ways in which this sound is organized, then naturally the individual components of this piece could also be exchanged, permutated, without changing its basic quality. (Cott, 1973: 70)[10]

Stockhausen's use of aleatorism on the structural plane – as mobile form – is supposed to be a mirror of the statistical randomness he finds in individual noises. *Klavierstück XI* is therefore to be thought of as a metaphor for sound itself. This may be considered a true modernist project since its quasi-scientific experimental aim is to be an investigation of the objective qualities of sound. Temporally, the experience of form is partially contingent on the listener's knowledge of the score. While all experience is linear in an immediate sense, as will be the final product of a mobile-structure, multiple performances of the piece reveal the work's non-linear structure. By applying aleatory procedures to both form and sound-world, Stockhausen ensures that the musical experience is consistent with his experimental intentions.

Boulez's *Third Piano Sonata* offered a critique of Stockhausen's experiment. Crucially, Boulez recognized the trap of assuming that chance – and the musical forms that relied on it (indeterminate and aleatory music) – was antithetical to the "automatisms" of total serialism. He discovered that, as Paul Griffiths puts it, "leaving any aspect to chance produced exactly the same effect as being forced by some scheme: the composer's presumed liberty of action was compromised" (Griffiths, 2010: 105). Thus, both total serialism and indeterminacy involve automatisms that jeopardize "freedom" in one way or another. (For this reason, these works can be described as modernist, because they push an "objective" abstract "language" over the communicative language of a subjective author.) Boulez's *Third Piano Sonata* offers five "formants" ("Antiphonie", "Trope", "Constellation-Miroir", Strophe" and "Séquence"; only numbers two and three were formally published) which the performer is asked to order in advance, as if preparing a route on a map. In his essay

"Sonate, que me veux-tu?" (1963), Boulez likened the role of the performer to Theseus in the Labyrinth. The image is evocative of Isaac's journey around the dark corridors of the *Ishimura*, but it is also provocative in the sense that the player follows narrative threads through the game's non-linear maze-like form, creating a unique linear audiovisual experience. Boulez drew heavily on literary criticism, work by James Joyce, and the poet Stéphane Mallarmé's concept of "perpetual expansion" derived from *Un coup de dés*.[11] Significantly, Boulez – characteristically of post-war French intellectuals (Barsky, 1998) – initially rejected Cage's "indeterminacy", but Cage claims that once Boulez had discovered Mallarmé, he began his own investigation and developed his own terminology, rebranding indeterminacy as "aleatory".[12] Boulez's 1957 essay, "Alea", offered a compositional framework in which chance is restricted in order to maintain creative control, a feature that distinguishes it from Cagean chance both procedurally and intellectually (Boulez, 1964).

The relationship of the avant-garde to its audience is most famously encapsulated in the title of Milton Babbitt's notoriously arrogant essay "Who Cares if You Listen?"[13] Likening research in music to research in science (and specifically, theoretical physics), Babbitt accepted art music's isolation from society as an inevitable consequence of its increased complexity. He subsequently believed that serious contemporary avant-garde music was necessarily elitist and required institutional (university) support, as it was beyond the everyday concerns of society. It is possible to detect an overly rational bitterness in much avant-garde writing as the need for composers to justify their work – and funding – became increasingly necessary. In *Rationalizing Culture*, Georgina Born's study on Boulez's own "Institutionalization of the Musical Avant-Garde" at the state-funded IRCAM, Born adopts Susan McClary's well-known phrase to characterize writing of the period as a "rhetoric of survival" (Born, 1995: 1–11; McClary, 1989: 62). The title of Born's book thus has a double meaning in that rationality itself was the key issue (understanding and "practising" culture by objectifying it), but that also, rationalizing, or "legitimizing", culture became necessary in an unprecedented way. (Of course, the avant-garde efforts to legitimize themselves and their work remain highly contentious.)[14] Babbitt's claims lose sight of music's role as a performative art and communicative language, and his almost childish equation with science is clearly flawed since in that discipline, social justification and utility are paramount in spite of mass incomprehension, which is often expected.

Penderecki's career path is characteristic of this Zeitgeist. His first compositionally "mature style" (during the 1960s) experimented with extended string techniques and the dialectic between very specific instructions and indeterminate graphic notations. Perhaps his most famous work, *Threnody to the Victims of Hiroshima* (1960) is scored for 52 string instruments and in it,

Penderecki applied the idea of tone/chord clusters to textures, developing them into a more large-scale aesthetic style often referred to as "sound mass composition". The indeterminate notational elements (the score is written with symbols rather than traditional musical notation), alongside the original title of 8'37" provide overt clues to artistic intentions that became manifest when in 1994, Penderecki explained that:

> [The piece] existed only in my imagination, in a somewhat abstract way. When Jan Krenz recorded it and I could listen to an actual performance, I was struck with the emotional charge of the work. I thought it would be a waste to condemn it to such anonymity, to those "digits". I searched for associations and, in the end, I decided to dedicate it to the Hiroshima victims. (Penderecki cited in Tomaszewski, 1999)

Without undermining the validity of these extra-musical associations, which, it should be noted, were only given weight by the composer after he had successfully moved in a very different direction,[15] the fact remains that the origins of the work were undoubtedly heavily influenced by Cage. It seems that Penderecki originally had little sense of how the final result would actually sound, or how an audience might respond to perceived semantic "content". The evidence suggests he was rather more concerned with abstract experimentation – the use of new *determining* notations for aleatory techniques. Any emotional responses or meaningful interpretations were by-products of an experiment with sound and musical structure. That said, it is also true to say that the majority of aleatory/indeterminate music was composed as "other" to the accepted classical canon. Breaking away from tonality and its associated rhythmic and formal structures by definition means "otherness". In an interview, Graves refers to Goldsmith's *Alien* as the textbook horror soundtrack, but suggests that the "original roots of every horror film score that's ever been written" can be found in Penderecki, not least due to the use of *Polymorphia* (and other works) in Stanley Kubrick's cult classic *The Shining* (1980).[16] (There is a small irony in the fact that Goldsmith himself had turned to Penderecki for inspiration for *Planet of the Apes*.) However, when referring to *Threnody* specifically, Graves shows little awareness of the composer's original intentions, remarking only on the impact of the music.

There are several string techniques and notational elements employed in *Threnody* that were of use to Graves. Penderecki outlined his new notations in detail at the start of the composition (Figure 10.1).[17]

| SKRÓTY i SYMBOLE | ABBREVIATIONS AND SYMBOLS | | SIGNES D'ABREVIATION ET SYMBOLES | ABKÜRZUNGEN UND SYMBOLE |
|---|---|---|---|---|
| ordinario | | ord. | | |
| sul ponticello | | s. p. | | |
| sul tasto | | s. t. | | |
| col legno | | c. l. | | |
| legno battuto | | l. batt. | | |
| podwyższenie o ¼ tonu | raised by ¼ tone | ┼ | hausse la note d'un quart de ton | Erhöhung um ¼ Ton |
| podwyższenie o ¾ tonu | raised by ¾ tone | ♯ | hausse la note de trois quarts de ton | Erhöhung um ¾ Ton |
| obniżenie o ¼ tonu | lowered by ¼ tone | ♭ | abaisse la note d'un quart de ton | Erniedrigung um ¼ Ton |
| obniżenie o ¾ tonu | lowered by ¾ tone | ⅾ | abaisse la note de trois quarts de ton | Erniedrigung um ¾ Ton |
| najwyższy dźwięk instrumentu (wysokość nieokreślona) | highest note of the instrument (indefinite pitch) | ▲ | le son le plus aigu de l'instrument (hauteur indéterminée) | höchster Ton des Instrumentes (unbestimmte Tonhöhe) |
| grać między podstawkiem i strunnikiem | play between bridge and tailpiece | ↑ | jouer entre le chevalet et le cordier | zwischen Steg und Saitenhalter spielen |
| arpeggio na 4 strunach za podstawkiem | arpeggio on 4 strings behind the bridge | ↑ 𝍇 | arpège sur 4 cordes entre le chevalet et le cordier | Arpeggio zwischen Steg und Saitenhalter (4 Saiten) |
| grać na strunniku (arco) | play on tailpiece (arco) | ⊥ | jouer sur le cordier (arco) | auf dem Saitenhalter spielen (arco) |
| grać na podstawku | play on bridge | ↑ | jouer sur le chevalet | auf dem Steg spielen |
| efekt perkusyjny: uderzać w górną płytę skrzypiec żabką lub czubkami palców | percussion effect: strike the upper sounding board of the violin with the nut or the finger-tips | 𝄐 | effet de percussion: frapper la table de dessus du violon avec le talon de l'archet ou avec les bouts des doigt | Schlagzeugeffekt: mit dem Frosch oder mit Fingerspitze die Decke schlagen |
| kilka nieregularnych zmian smyczka | several irregular changes of bow | ⊓ v | plusieurs changements d'archet irréguliers | mehrere unregelmäßige Bogenwechsel |
| molto vibrato | molto vibrato | ∿∿∿ | molto vibrato | molto vibrato |
| bardzo wolne vibrato w obrębie ćwierćtonu, uzyskane przez przesuwanie palca | very slow vibrato with a ¼ tone frequency difference produced by sliding the finger | ∿∿ | vibrato très lent à interval d'un quart de ton par le déplacement du doigt | sehr langsames Vibrato mit ¼ - Ton-Frequenzdifferenz durch Fingerverschiebung |
| bardzo szybkie i nierytmizowane tremolo | very rapid not rhythmicized tremolo | ⤸ | trémolo très rapide, mais sans rythme précis | sehr schnelles, nicht rhytmisiertes Tremolo |

*Figure 10.1 Threnody* – Abbreviations and symbols

These symbols can be seen scattered across the semi-graphic (but nevertheless precise) score in Figure 10.2.[18] The instrumental divisions are further subdivided, and Penderecki indicates the exact number required in each. The total forces required are 24 violins, 10 violas, 10 cellos and 8 double bass.

*Figure 10.2 Threnody* – Extract 1

There is no time signature – instead the music is played in "real time" with sections delineated by their duration in seconds (see 18" and 20" at the bottom of the score in Figure 10.3). The first 12 violins in Figure 10.3 are assigned a specific note (the chromatic scale attached beneath the top stave). Violins 13–24 are likewise assigned a different set of notes. These are combined as chord clusters on the stave, notated as thick lines that cover a complete spectrum of notes. Thus, a second violin cluster joins the first sounding a minor third below.

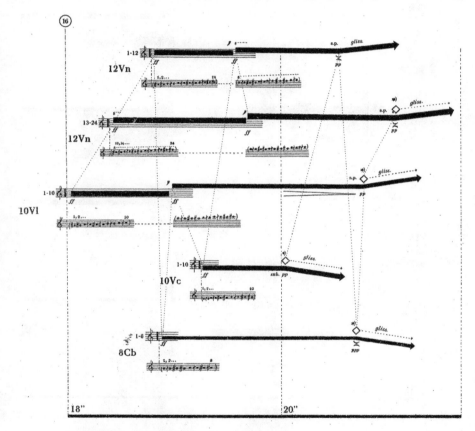

*) flażolety kwartowe / Flageolettöne / flageolet tones / harmoniques

*Figure 10.3 Threnody* – Extract 2

The clusters can move up or down as indicated by the arrows, but they can also expand in compass. The extract in Figure 10.4 shows how the upper and lower violin parts delineate the outer limits of the cluster as it expands and contracts.

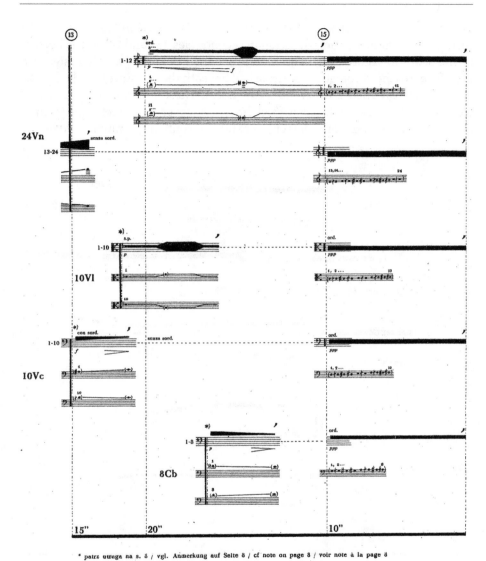

*Figure 10.4 Threnody – Extract 3*

The music dovetails between impactful cluster chords and sparser textures, a structure that parallels the dramatic pacing of *Dead Space* (discussed above) as much as it does any horror movie. It is worth noting that most of these technical and notational features of *Threnody* – the ones also employed by Graves to produce his score (see "Composition and Implementation" below) – actually leave very little room for "chance". The aleatory aspects come predominantly from conceptualizing musical components as broader brush-strokes. Penderecki's notations hardly fulfil Cage's desire to free sound from the tyranny of the composer. In fact, in attempting to reduce notational ambiguities, the additional precision produced by his advanced notation has more in common with totalist serial works.

Much of the music in *Dead Space* appears derivative of Penderecki, not just in terms of sound-world, but through the composer's creative process. Through the use of *Polymorphia* in *The Shining* and *The Exorcist* (William Friedkin, 1973), this sound-world became a clear sign for a particularly alien and frightening otherness, a learned cultural trope. But the extreme sounds generated by such experimental writing in an atonal idiom were always at odds (and therefore other) to even the most extreme reaches of romantic music – reaffirming, as it always does, tonality and hierarchical organization *by the very act* of stretching it to its limits. The gendered image of classic Hollywood film scores, heavily influenced by late-romantic concert and operatic repertoires as "over-emotional", has traditionally been juxtaposed with modernist music and its avant-garde opposition to mass culture.[19] Jeremy Barham explains:

> [C]omposers of scores for the psychologically, technologically or socio-logically dystopian visions of the following films – to varying degrees products of the early Cold War years and the socio-political unrest and gloom of the late 1960s and early 1970s – demonstrated viable new alternatives to prevailing neo-romantic scoring practices, whether through the use of pre-existent music or not:
>
> - Fred M. Wilcox's *Forbidden Planet* (1956) – pre-synthesizer "electronic tonalities" by Louis and Bebe Barron;
> - Alfred Hitchcock's *Psycho* (1960) – Bernard Herrmann's minimalist dissonant strings with which *The Shining*'s score has much in common;
> - Alain Resnais's elusive *Je t'aime, je t'aime* (1968) – Penderecki's evidently alien-sounding vocal writing;
> - Franklin Schaffner's *Planet of the Apes* (1968) – percussive, Varèse-like modernity from Jerry Goldsmith, who was reputedly influenced by Penderecki;
> - George Lucas's *THX 1138* (1970) – grating avant-garde electronic tone clusters by Schifrin;
> - Andrei Tarkovski's *Solaris* (1972) – Eduard Artemiev's harsh or brooding electronic sonorities and his similar treatments of Bach;
> - The aforementioned *The Exorcist*.
>
> ... more broadly, the use of Bach, for example, (for which read functional tonal harmony) as a universal signifier of humanity in films such as *THX* and *Solaris*, alongside atonal clusters as some kind of dehumanized

inverse involving technological oppression or psychological disturbance, initiated an approach that has since attained the status of reactionary cliché. (Barham, 2009: 138)

Barham also notes the irony in these developments when taking into account the famous 1947 Adorno–Eisler diatribe against the commercialization of music by Hollywood. How much more incredulous would they have been to find a mobile implementation of this modernist music in video games? Noting Dahlhaus's remark that "audiences who detest Schoenberg's music in the concert hall will accept it without a murmur as background film music is as fundamental as it is depressing", Barham quotes Mayersberg's comparison of *The Shining* to post-war music:

> It seems technically brilliant and yet fundamentally heartless. It seems deliberately clever and yet remains enigmatic. Kubrick has tried to bridge a gap which has occurred in the language of film. How can you express dissonance and fragmentation, the essential features of our present lives, in a manner which respects traditional harmonies? Can disorder ever be expressed in an orderly way? (Mayersberg quoted in Barham, 2009: 139)

*The Shining*, says Barham, responds to Eisler and Adorno by "providing music which is more than a 'secondary piece of decoration' and which has 'its own logic and integrity' but going far beyond this to ground aspects of the filmmaking process in the explanatory, instinctive world of musico-poetic expression" (ibid.). However, Kubrick seemed to support the integrity of the music one minute by adjusting one particular sequence in order to fit it to the pre-existing Bartók, and subverting it the next by editing and layering the music with sound effects and other excerpts (sometimes from the same piece). The resultant collage is a new form whose musical components only retain traces of their own original forms. Since *Dead Space* is not reliant on recycled or quoted material, its music being composed to fit the dynamic game environment, it fares differently.

Figure 10.5 shows a transcription of a representative excerpt from the soundtrack, 'Welcome Aboard the U.S.G. *Ishimura*'. In the game, the cue commences at bar 16 as underscoring to the opening cutscene dialogue, just as the team approach the stricken vessel.[20] The cue later introduces many of the string effects and brass cluster chords of the game's modernist musical idiom before returning briefly to the calmer opening material. The second violin part of bars 1–7 includes an example of the growing string glissandi as it would be notated by Penderecki. One of the principal musical themes – a three-note string melody (bars 9–10) rising by step with swelling dynamics – is then introduced accompanying the first view of the *Ishimura*.

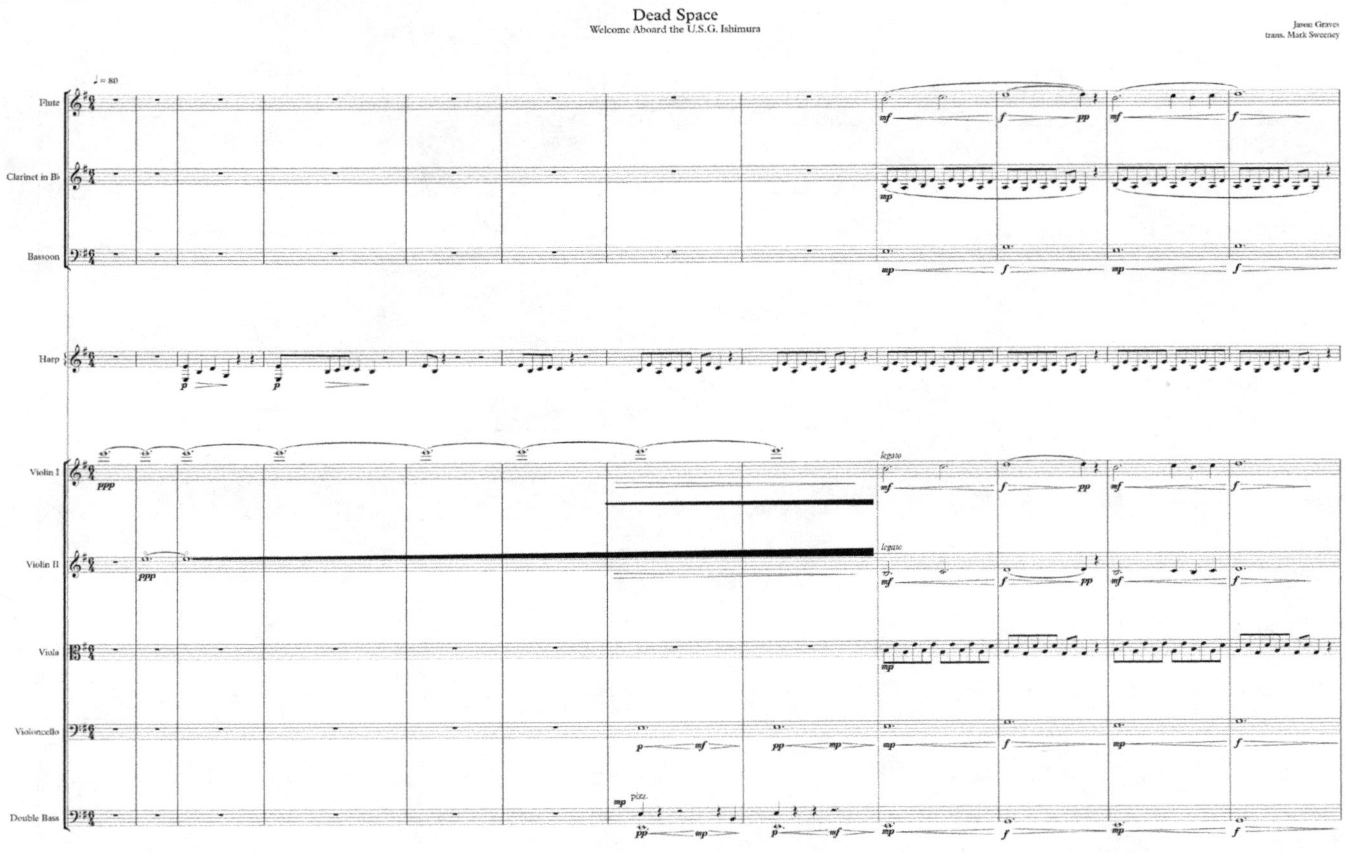

*Figure 10.5* 'Welcome Aboard the U.S.G. *Ishimura*' (extract) (continued on next page)

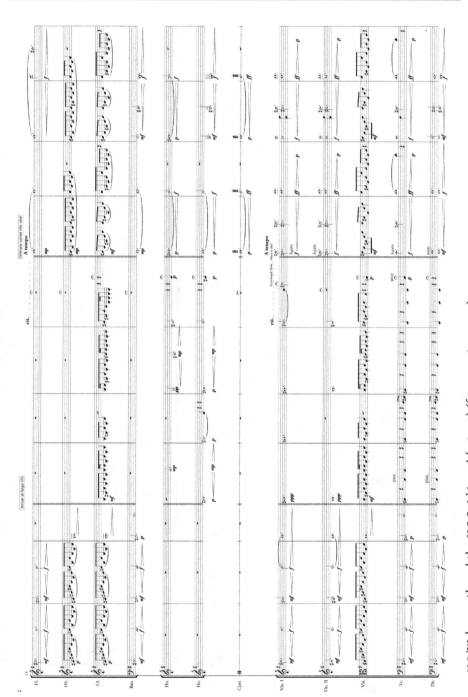

*Figure 10.5* 'Welcome Aboard the U.S.G. *Ishimura*' (extract) (from previous page)

The sense of yearning in the theme is heightened at bar 20 as the melody is converted into a chromatic rise, moving from a diminished chord on F-sharp to an augmented D-major chord instead of the original E-minor to G-major progression. The suspenseful fermata on the C-sharp in the first violins at the end of bar 19 occurs just as a crewmember asks the question, "Now . . . where is she?", referring to the *Ishimura*, shortly before the ship comes into view from behind an asteroid (see Figure 10.6), accompanied by the grander rendition of the string theme at bar 20. This demonstrates that the degree of synchrony between the musical score and the visuals (at least during cutscenes) is just as detailed as one would expect from a film score. It also shows the close integration of elements of both sound-worlds and the ease at which Graves moves from one to another, or combines them, utilizing the string glissandi almost as a leitmotif to represent the impending danger. Yet at the same time, this passage also starts the didactic work of attributing the different musical sound-worlds with particular narrative/gameplay functions: it teaches the player that neo-romantic music is heard when they are in a safe environment exploring the epic context of the narrative, but when the modernist music predominates, danger is near.

*Figure 10.6* The U.S.G. *Ishimura* comes into view (bar 20)

Graves's approach to such cutscene underscoring is no different from traditional film scoring. His integration of Penderecki's extended string techniques and advanced musical notations, in this context, is a means to an end – producing a soundtrack reminiscent of films such as *Alien*. Of course, this is in itself a sophisticated musical style entailing complex harmonies and detailed orchestration. For instance, in context, the dominant seventh chord on A reached at bar 19's *fermata* does not feel at all like a cliché despite its functional simplicity. The pull created by the use of diminished and augmented harmonies as both dissonances and their resolutions (Figure 10.7) creates a powerful sense of yearning tension and mystery. However, beyond the cutscenes, the ebb and flow of sequences of gameplay, exploration and cutscenes provide an additional layer of complexity.

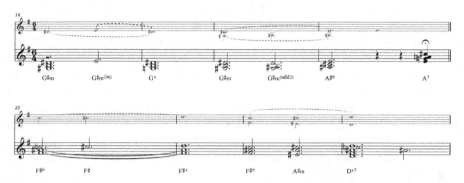

*Figure 10.7* Harmony progression, bars 16–23

## Composition and Implementation

Distinguishing between different types of musical cues in the game – be they simple pieces for cutscenes or dynamic music – is often more difficult than it might at first seem, since there are no readily-available scores, and the distinctions can only be made through careful listening.[21] Some fixed cues, for instance, could be composed to sound much the same as the modernist dynamic music heard during gameplay. Nevertheless, a clear distinction can be made between the neo-romantic and modernist sound-worlds. Much is revealed in interviews and developer diaries. After defining the parameters and musical style, Don Veca, the audio director, sent Graves a more detailed brief, including many audio clips of moments from his favourite soundtracks. According to various post-production interviews, Graves then recorded various musical elements (many were aleatory improvisations) with which to create a "sonic palette" (Curran, 2008; Music4Games.net, 2008). These elements included, for instance, numerous isolated string glissandi and various brass chords with which he could later create any number of chord clusters. From that point on, it was actually Veca who took on the predominant role of implementing the music within the game. During the actual gameplay, the music appears to have been arranged into four layers, each a stereo track representing a distinct "fear level": creepy, tense, very tense and chaotic.[22] This implies that the cues are already set sound files by the time the game engine can use them, and therefore the level of manipulation that the music engine can achieve must be on a higher hierarchical plane. Each layer is streamed in synchronization and then one or all are mixed "on-the-fly" depending on various game variables, such as the proximity of the necromorphs. So for each two-minute cue, there would actually be eight minutes worth of musical material available for sounding. This could be described as a "dynamic" or "interactive" music system (Collins, 2008: 139).

The thesis of Umberto Eco's *The Open Work* maintains that the distinction between poetics and aesthetics is of particular importance to the "open work", which he defines specifically as one with aleatory or indeterminate elements (either in sound-world or form), and broadly in contradistinction to all "traditional art" (Eco, 1989). Eco, while not wanting to displace aesthetic judgements altogether, attempted to rebalance contemporary criticism by laying emphasis on poetics – by which he meant a work's artistic purpose as opposed to the aesthetic value of the result.[23] This was particularly pertinent in the case of the open work because it was the indeterminate elements rather than any semantic content that formed an "epistemological metaphor" of modern society, as Eco saw it (Robey, 1989: xiv). In other words, the process of abstract formal experimentation was itself a basis for value judgements prior to any extra-musical associations later wrought. This adds weight to the idea that these conceptual origins matter. The cynic's cry that Graves's own experimentation was merely a means for gaining academic kudos and therefore amounted to little more than a publicity stunt might thus be held at bay. The opposite suggestion that this experimentation was only a means to achieving a particular result – that the process was necessary to create the scary sound-world required – is fallacious because it is neither technically necessary nor cost effective.[24] The programming requirements, alongside the need for multiple recording sessions, incurred an "unnecessary" expense.

Understanding exactly which musical elements are pre-composed and which are left flexible therefore matters a great deal, at least from Eco's perspective. The first stage in Graves's compositional process is remarkably similar to the indeterminate experimentation found in *Threnody*. But with this, Graves seems to be developing a "sonic palette" of materials with which to compose the score. Subsequently, the aleatorism of this initial experimentation is averted or "fixed", perhaps because Graves also knew in advance (apparently Penderecki did not) that he wanted to exploit the semantic content now attached to the resultant sound-world. Regardless, the story is complicated further when the score born out of this sonic palette is configured in layers and made interactive. As Graves/Veca had a specific dramatic goal to achieve, they produced four layers that the game engine can move freely between. It is important to remember that some of the music in the game is not interactive, but pre-composed for cutscenes or particular dramatic moments, as highlighted above. This is when most of the neo-romantic music occurs, framing or punctuating the interactive layered system that is left to accompany the core gameplay elements. While *Threnody* demonstrates an antagonistic relationship between aleatory and totalist serial techniques (perhaps ultimately leaning towards the latter), *Dead Space* arguably achieves a more integrated dialectic. From this perspective, both works could be described as postmodern, with multiple subjectivities found in their polystylistic aesthetic. There is some irony in this, as both aleatorism and serialism were born out of a modernist mind-set – both were initially employed as a means to "purify" the musical language, making it objective – although the former is paradoxically well suited to postmodern epistemology.

The semantic content Penderecki seemed initially oblivious to was sought after and exploited by Graves and Veca because it had picked up a powerful, and now practically inescapable, association with an otherness peculiar to horror and sci-fi film genres. (Penderecki's own associations with the horrors of Hiroshima, in turn, may have contributed to these connotations.) The contrast of tonal and atonal language, regular phrasing and rhythmic instability, melodically led textures and disjointed, chaotic ones, all aid in defining each other.

## Neo-Romantic Narrator, Modernist Psycho-Analysis

It is worth considering the extent to which the music in *Dead Space* might function as Isaac's emotional voice, or another distinct "narrator". Carolyn Abbate's famous argument that music can only rarely be said to function as narrative rests on the premise that narrative is signalled through the use of an external voice – a narrator. Abbate posits that in *The Ring*, Wagner undermines his Schopenhauerian view of music as an "untainted and transcendent" discourse by employing both textual and musical narrative voices that "ring false": "polyphonic narration" (many narrators speaking "with and across the text"), she says, "undercuts the very notion of music as a voice whose purity is assured by virtue of its nonverbal nature".[25] Abbate's call to listen for prosopopoeia in music as a sign of the presence of a narrator is particularly useful in *Dead Space*, in which an autonomous musical software engine may arguably have its own degree of agency.

Often when Isaac is alone, the music could be said to express Isaac's fears, whether or not they are justified. The interactive music engine described above outputs one of four streams of music, each representing an incremental degree of fear and action.[26] The decisions the engine makes are contingent on a cumulative dramatic input variable, specifically the sum-total "fear factor". This number is based on the number of individual objects (usually the necromorphs themselves) present within a given radius of the player, and the objects' "fear emitters" – values attributed to the objects which represent how scary or threatening they may appear. The crucial point to note here is that the music engine itself, the musical voice one could say, has no way of testing the validity of the information it receives. The music engine does not verify whether the input is genuinely dangerous; it just reacts to the fear factor. Subsequently, the programmers can "trick" the system, and in turn, the player, by attributing fear values to inanimate objects. These may include metal panels on the walls, for example, that could be triggered to fall off as Isaac passes by, in turn causing the music engine to react in the same way that the player might – as if they were in real danger. This is an effective scare tactic given the number of real surprise attacks he suffers. The sudden events can be, and often are, tied to loud sound effects but other music is layered before and after that has the potential to warn the player of impending danger. Thus, the music engine itself is tricked into treating real threats, and red herrings fabricated by the programmers, in the same way, jeopardizing the engine's omnipotence. This brings into question whether this musical voice is an additional agent within the game world – some other narrative force (the Marker perhaps) that can manipulate the player – or part of Isaac's consciousness. It is unclear if it is deliberately misleading, or naïve.[27] In these ways, the question of music's agency and its capacity to act within a fictional or virtual world is further complicated by the use of software as an intermediary in the creative process.

In addition to being an unreliable narrator, there is also a fuzziness involved in delineating sound from music, diegetic from non-diegetic, and between what is in Isaac's imagination and what is real. The intermixing of "stab chords" (short stingers usually comprising loud and sudden individual chords or notes in isolation) alongside diegetic sound effects across the game series highlights the close relationship between meaningful sound effects and the musical score "proper" – a distinction seemingly unimportant in mixed-media contexts. The attachment of music to diegetic fear-emitters clearly parallels the way in which sound effects are usually connected to diegetic sources, further highlighting the similarities of treatment by the audio team. In a Cagean sense, Isaac's "silence" is not silence at all, but provides the sonic opportunity for the ambient sounds of his (and the player's) worst nightmares, both on a diegetic level, and through the music's non-diegetic emotive content. As Cage noted, ambient sounds, when people pay attention to them, can function as music in that they communicate certain meanings.[28] Certainly the efforts that the audio engineers go to in placing and balancing the plethora of diegetic sounds in video games are testament to the fact that they are a purposeful and meaningful contribution to the games' narratives. This would suggest that from Isaac's perspective, diegetic ambient sounds need not be orchestrated by some living agent to function as a form of language and carry meaning. Of course, the player knows that the ambient sounds have all been carefully prepared, but the idea applies just as well to the player's world as Isaac's. The implication of this line of thought is clear enough, although somehow still contentious: the transmission of meaning is not contingent on authorial human agency; the only active agent required is a "reader". Beyond the connection to Cage, the significance of this relationship between sound effects and the musical score is that it highlights that both, being meaningful, stand in opposition to any anti-expressive avant-garde ideology.

The lack of vocal communication in *Dead Space* creates a specifically auditory expressive void in the game's narrative. Like the sound returning as the air rushes back in when Isaac leaves the vacuum of space in damaged parts of the *Ishimura*, this is filled in various ways, but primarily through the music. It also highlights the special closeness of music to other forms of communicative sound within the video game aesthetic. Cage's own experience at Harvard in 1951 led him to observe that even in a soundproofed anechoic chamber, the sounds of one's own heartbeat, nervous system and circulation become amplified in the inner ear. Indeed, *Dead Space* echoes this idea when Isaac must pass through various depressurized areas of the damaged ship. Sound waves obviously cannot travel in a vacuum, so the sounds he hears as the pressure gates open are audibly and visually "sucked away" with the air leaving him in comparative quiet. Nevertheless, the sounds in his own suit are inescapable, and become all the more meaningful: his breathing becomes a charged expression of the inherent danger and precariousness of his situation. This is "embodiment" at its most literal, and reminds the subject of that very real and human preoccupation: mortality.[29]

Isaac's silence signals an acoustic void pertinent to understanding *Dead Space*'s position on the spectrum of mass culture and high art. Because Isaac does not communicate directly (at least in the first game), greater attention is drawn to other strands of signification. Graves employs two clearly delineated musical sound-worlds, the neo-romantic, which functions as a narrator of sorts, and the modernist, which underscores the player's gameplay, as if expressing Isaac's fears. While both of these can be traced back through Hollywood film scores such as Jerry Goldsmith's *Alien*, the latter has an additional complex history of alterity. Like the fusion of styles in *Alien*, the two sound-worlds are distinct but not conflicting. They are combined into a genre-defining musical world (sci-fi horror). Although Graves's interest in the techniques of the avant-garde seem to be significant only insofar as it enables aleatory notation and technique, his use of these musical ideas in a video game also problematizes avant-garde ideology. The unambiguously emotive function of this music can only be seen as a further rejection of the blank palette Penderecki himself eventually rejected. Yet at the same time, the ideas of non-linear structure that aleatory techniques prefigure – mobile form and dynamic music systems – are employed to create the underscore during gameplay. In this way, *Dead Space* goes further than *Alien* in realizing the aesthetic potential of aleatory music.

Music continues to function in the myriad of different ways it did prior to avant-garde anti-expressive ideologies. Furthermore, it seems that ideas generated from non-linear musical systems have supplemented rather than displaced aesthetic possibilities. The *Dead Space* series demonstrates the potential of games to surpass *The Shining* as a retort to Adorno and Eisler, and exemplifies the tensions felt across the video game industry in collapsing the space between art and mass culture.

## Notes

1. Mark Sweeney completed his D.Phil. thesis (entitled "The Aesthetics of Videogame Music") in Musicology at Hertford College, Oxford. His primary research interest is on aesthetic theory and video game music. He was previously lecturer in Music at St Catherine's College, Oxford.
2. The term "sound-world" is related to R. Murray Schafer's concept of a "soundscape". However, Schafer's term is all encompassing whereas sound-world tends to refer to a particular musical "style" (Schafer, 2004: 29–39).
3. Penderecki's post-1975 output is often characterized as neo-romantic, including his Second "Christmas" Symphony (1980), while Górecki's popular Third Symphony (1976) contrasts significantly with his earlier serialist works of the late 1950s and early 1960s.
4. On immersion in video games, and related terminology, see Calleja, 2011: 2.
5. See "Future Tense: Music and Editing", *The Beast Within: The Making of Alien* (*Alien Quadrilogy*, DVD disc 2; Los Angeles: 20th Century Fox Home Entertainment, Inc.).
6. It is also interesting to note that Scott replaced Goldsmith's original ending cue with an excerpt from Hanson's neo-romantic second symphony, though crucially, only at the very end of the film when the Alien is dead, and the avant-garde threat is neutralized.
7. In an interview, Graves refers to "studying under" Goldsmith and Christopher Young (Naumenko, 2008).
8. See forum threads such as maksut029, 2011. See also Suliman, 2011.
9. Forum thread: http://forums.aegis7.com/32-dead-space-3/6991-dead-space-3-music.html (accessed March 21, 2013, now defunct).
10. See also Griffiths, 2010: 105.
11. *Pli selon pli* (1957–1962) took these ideas further by setting Mallarmé on a larger scale, which also brought about other restrictions.
12. For a detailed account of Boulez's writings on his relationship to Cage and indeterminacy, see Whitney, 2000.

13. The original title – "The Composer as Specialist" – was discarded by the journal's editor, in favour of one more provocative. Babbitt, 1958: 38–40.
14. Despite the flaws of Born's important ethnographic study, it highlights certain tensions and paradoxes in avant-garde thinking. See Hinkle-Turner, 1999 and Anderson, 1997.
15. In the 1970s, Penderecki began moving towards what has been described as a "post-romantic" idiom. He explained that he was saved from the trappings of the avant-garde illusion of "universalism" when he "realised the Utopian quality of its Promethean tone". Quoted in Tomaszewski, 1999.
16. The film is perhaps better known for its use of Bartók and Ligeti, names notably absent in Graves's interviews. The latter is also especially relevant to the genre due to exposure in Kubrick's 1968 film, *2001: A Space Odyssey*. See also Probert, c. 2012.
17. Figures 10.1–10.4 are taken from Krzysztof Penderecki's score for *Threnody for the Victims of Hiroshima* (1960), Copyright 1961 (Renewed) EMI Deshon Music, Inc., used with permission.
18. A good indication of how these symbols sound can be found at http://www.youtube.com/watch?v=HilGthRhwP8 (accessed March 22, 2013).
19. Caryl Flinn describes classic Hollywood film music as "out of step" with the "contemporary music scene". See Flinn, 1992: 20–23. See also Franklin, 2011: 3–18.
20. Bars 1–15 provide an introduction on the soundtrack, but are not heard in the game.
21. Furthermore, the dynamic mixing of all of these audio elements creates a collage of sound that is often moved into the background so that the game's diegetic sounds – such as dialogue, gunfire or footsteps – can be easily identified.
22. In an interview concerning *Dead Space 2*, Graves suggests that as many as eight streams were available. See Naumenko, 2011.
23. Understanding the open work as the cornerstone for a new paradigm of modern aesthetics, Eco's take on the "intentional fallacy" precluded neither the validity of authorial intent, nor the problem of infinite interpretive possibilities. Traditional aesthetic theory established by Kant put forward the idea that beautiful objects appear "purposive but without purpose". However, this was primarily an issue about function, not intended meanings. See Scruton, 2001: 107–109.
24. This is reflected in Tim Curran's interview with Graves in which the composer states that the convoluted "off-the-cuff" production procedure he suggested to Audio Director, Don Veca, actually became the process used, in spite of its expense. See Curran, 2008.
25. See Abbate, 1991: xiv.
26. Graves talks about transitioning from one level to another (rather than mixing multiple layers incrementally) in Curran, 2008.

27. Ben Winters has also described a similar idea in the context of film music. See Winters, 2012: 39–54.
28. See, for example, Cage, 1973: 7–12.
29. The concept of embodiment in the context of music has been discussed from many different perspectives. Leman, 2008 offers a theory of music cognition in the context of developments in multimedia technology. The literature on video game music is growing too. See, for example, Grimshaw, 2008, and Lori Linday's recent work on embodiment in video games and other virtual environments (2013).

## References

Abbate, C. (1991) *Unsung Voices*. Princeton: Princeton University Press.

Adorno, T. and H. Eisler (1994 [1947]) *Composing for the Films*. London: Athlone Press.

Anderson, J. (1997) "Down with them: Value for Money or a Monstrous White Elephant?" Review of the book *Rationalizing Culture* by Georgina Born, *The Musical Times* 138/1848: 25–29.

Babbitt, M. (1958) "Who Cares if You Listen?" *High Fidelity* 8/2: 38–40.

Balawender, G. (2010) "I've Always Been Flattered by Anyone who Wanted to Listen to My Music Outside of the Game" [Jason Graves Interview]." *Gamemusic.net*. http:// web.archive.org/web/20130602231457/http://www.gamemusic.net/interviews.php (accessed March 7, 2016).

Barham, J. (2009) "Incorporating Monsters: Music as Context, Character and Construction in Kubrick's *The Shining*." In *Terror Tracks: Music, Sound and Horror Cinema*, edited by P. Hayward, pp. 137–70. London: Equinox.

Barsky, R. (1998) *Noam Chomsky: A Life of Dissent*. Cambridge, MA: MIT Press.

Born, G. (1995) *Rationalizing Culture: IRCAM, Boulez, and the Institutionalization of the Musical Avant-Garde*. Berkeley: University of California Press.

Boulez, P. (1963) "Sonate, que me veux-tu?" Trans. D. Noakes and P. Jacobs. *Perspectives of New Music* 1/2: 32–44.

Boulez, P. (1964) "Alea." Trans. D. Noakes and P. Jacobs. *Perspectives of New Music* 3/1: 42–53.

Cage, J. (1973) "Experimental Music." In J. Cage, *Silence: Lectures and Writings*, pp. 7–12. Middletown, CT: Wesleyan University Press.

Calleja G. (2011) *In-Game: From Immersion to Incorporation*. Cambridge, MA: MIT Press.

Collins, K. (2008) *Game Sound: An Introduction to the History, Theory, and Practice of Video Game Music and Sound Design*. Cambridge, MA: MIT Press.

Cott, J. (1973) *Stockhausen*. London: Simon & Schuster.

Curran, T. (2008) "Filling in the *Dead Space*." *Film Score Monthly* 13/10. http://www. filmscoremonthly.com/fsmonline/story.cfm?maID=1607&issueID=44 (accessed August 26, 2011).

Eco, U. (1989) *The Open Work*. Trans. A. Cancogni. Cambridge, MA: Harvard University Press.

Flinn, C. (1992) *Strains of Utopia: Gender, Nostalgia, and Hollywood Film Music*. Princeton: Princeton University Press.

Franklin, P. (2011) *Seeing through Music: Gender and Modernism in Classic Hollywood Film Scores.* New York: Oxford University Press.

Griffiths, P. (2010) *Modern Music and After.* New York: Oxford University Press.

Grimshaw, M. (2008) *The Acoustic Ecology of the First-Person Shooter: The Player Experience of Sound in the First-Person Shooter Computer Game.* Saarbrücken: VDM Verlag Dr. Müeller.

Hinkle-Turner, E. (1999) "Georgina Born: Rationalizing Culture: IRCAM, Boulez, and the Institutionalization of the Musical Avant-Garde." Review of the book *Rationalizing Culture* by Georgina Born, in *Computer Music Journal* 23/3, Recent Research at IRCAM: 118–20.

Leman, M. (2008) *Embodied Music Cognition and Mediation Technology.* Cambridge, MA: MIT Press.

Linday, L. (2013) "Sound, Embodiment, and the Experience of Interactivity in Video Games & Virtual Environments." Paper delivered at *Society for Cinema and Media Studies Annual Conference*, Chicago, IL, March 2013.

"maksut029" (2011) "Isaac should be muted!" *Playstation Trophies.* January 20. http://www.ps3trophies.org/forum/dead-space-2/89472-isaac-should-muted.html (accessed January 24, 2012).

McClary, S. (1989) "Terminal Prestige: The Case of Avant-Garde Music Composition." *Cultural Critique* 12: 57–81.

McIntee, D. (2005) *Beautiful Monsters: The Unofficial and Unauthorized Guide to the Alien and Predator Films.* Surrey: Telos Publishing.

Music4Games.net [Anonymous] (2008) "The Music of *Dead Space*: Interview with Composer Jason Graves." *Music4games.net.* October 24. http://web.archive.org/web/20120703093455/http://www.jasongraves.com/press/pdfs/M4G%20Dead%20Space%20Composer%20Interview.pdf (accessed March 7, 2016).

Naumenko, M. (2008) "Jason Graves Interview: Brutal, Visceral, Musical." *Game-ost.com.* http://web.archive.org/web/20150319095302/http://game-ost.com/articles.php?id=45&action=view (accessed March 7, 2016).

Naumenko, M. (2011) "Jason Graves Interview: The Same, But Different and Better." *Game-ost.com.* http://web.archive.org/web/20150319095207/http://game-ost.com/articles.php?id=87&action=view (accessed March 7, 2016).

Probert, J. L. (c. 2012) "Jason Graves." *This is Horror.* http://www.thisishorror.co.uk/interviews/jason-graves/ (accessed March 10, 2014).

Robey, D. (1989) "Introduction." In U. Eco, *The Open Work*, trans. A. Cancogni, pp. i–xxxii. London: Hutchinson.

Schafer, R. M. (2004) "The Music of the Environment." In *Audio Culture: Readings in Modern Music*, edited by C. Cox and D. Warner, pp. 29–39. New York: Continuum.

Scruton, R. (2001) *Kant: A Very Short Introduction.* Oxford: Oxford University Press.

Suliman, M. (2011) "The Two Voices of Isaac Clarke." *Mending The Wall.* February 14. http://web.archive.org/web/20110301154926/http://mendingthewall.com/2011/02/14/the-two-voices-of-isaac-clarke/ (accessed March 7, 2016).

Summers, T. (2016) *Understanding Video Game Music.* Cambridge: Cambridge University Press.

Tomaszewski, M. (1999) Liner notes to *Krzysztof Penderecki: Orchestral Works Vol. 1.* Trans. J. Rybicki and R. Whitehouse. Naxos 8.554491.

Whitney, K. (2000) "Determining Indeterminacy: Vision and Revision in the Writings of Pierre Boulez." DPhil thesis, University of Oxford.

Winters, B. (2012) "Musical Wallpaper: Towards an Appreciation of Non-Narrative Music in Film." *Music, Sound, and the Moving Image* 6/1: 39–54.

# 11 Remixed Metaphors
## Manipulating Classical Music and its Meanings in Video Games

## William Gibbons[1]

Video game scores are "modern day classical music", composer Tommy Tallarico opined in a 2013 interview. "The truth is", he continued, "we're just as relevant as Beethoven or Mozart and we're just as good" (MacNamara, 2013). As game music has gained traction through concerts such as Tallarico's touring *Video Games Live* show, radio programmes like Minnesota Public Radio's *Top Score*, and "best-of" lists of classical favourites from organizations such as Classic FM, touting game music as the "new classical music" has become a common mantra from composers and critics alike. But the hyperbolic fervency of Tallarico's claims in fact underscores the existence of a perceived rift between the cultures of classical music and video games. The spectre of "classical music", in other words, becomes a talisman to ward off lingering notions that game music – and games themselves – cannot rise to the level of art.

In an article on games as art, for example, the linguist and literacy scholar James Paul Gee associates the game *Castlevania: Symphony of the Night* (1997) with an actual classical symphony:

> moving through this game is like moving through a symphony where every "tone" (image) and combination of "tones" (images) creates moods, feelings, and ambiance, not primarily information (as in movies and books). The experience of playing the game is closer to living inside a symphony than to living inside a book. And the symphony is not just visual, but it is composed as well of sounds, music, actions, decisions, and bodily feelings that flow along as the player and virtual character ... act together in the game world. (Gee, 2006: 59)

Gee's choice of a symphonic metaphor here ties in neatly with the game's title, but its importance goes beyond rhetorical convenience. The symphony as a genre is (in the popular mindset, at least) a pinnacle of musical artistry – classical music at its most "classical". Connecting a video game to this tradition supports (by association, if nothing else) a claim to artistic merit, linking the uncontested cultural value of classical music to the artistically ambiguous space that games occupy. After all, what loosely unites the incredibly disparate music encompassed by the label "classical" is its perceived status as "art". The musicologist and composer Julian Johnson, for example, succinctly – if polemically – describes classical music as "music that functions *as art*, as opposed to entertainment or some other ancillary or background function" (2002: 6, original emphasis). Johnson's hardline views on this distinction have long been rare in academia, but they nonetheless remain widespread in popular conceptions of classical music. As I write this, for example, the first sentence of Wikipedia's entry on "classical music" identifies it as "art music in the traditions of Western music" (2014a). Following the hyperlink to "art music" yields a well-balanced (if fairly brief) article on the topic, but one predicated on the circular definition of art music as "music descending from the tradition of Western classical music". Significantly, the article opens with the informative note that "art music" is "also known as **formal music, serious music, erudite music**, or **legitimate music**", terms that obviously convey an elitist system of value judgments (2014b, emphasis original).

Video games, by contrast, are steeped in pop culture, whatever claims we might choose to make for their status as art. In the words of game theorist Jesper Juul, they are generally regarded as "lowbrow catalogues of geek and adolescent male culture" (Juul, 2005: 20). For many game scholars, critics and players, their very existence as *games* is inextricably linked to their role as entertainment, although that status need not preclude their having educational and/or artistic value as well, of course.[2] The philosopher Grant Tavinor, for example, ultimately comes to the conclusion that any video game must be "intended primarily as an object of entertainment" (Tavinor, 2008; 2009). By definition, then, these two media are mutually exclusive. Let me be clear: I do not mean to debate or even lend credence to these positions, which I find reductive and essentially meaningless.[3] But neither can we simply dismiss these stubbornly persistent attitudes; whether we agree or not, to a large segment of the scholarly and general population, classical music is "art", removed from the commercial and aesthetic requirements that are the trappings of popular culture, while games are "entertainment", dependent on those same requirements for their existence.

Conceptually speaking, in other words, classical music and video games seem unlikely bedfellows indeed. And yet classical music appears in games with surprising frequency, and has since the early days of the medium, as I and some other scholars, including Neil Lerner, have argued.[4] When it does, this simmering tension between art and entertainment that pervades many games reaches boiling point. There are a number of ways in which these tensions are made manifest in games, but none manifest the inherent musical differences and play of stylistic juxtaposition more readily than remixed classical music in games. By "remixed", I specifically mean classical music that is significantly altered from its original form stylistically, usually incorporating elements of popular music styles, and thus becoming a work of hybrid authorship.

In his book *Remix Theory: The Aesthetics of Sampling*, Eduardo Navas outlines three basic forms of musical remix, all of which apply to some extent in video games: (1) the "extended" remix, in which the length of the work is expanded; (2) the "selective" remix, in which portions of the original are omitted and/or new material is added; and (3) the "reflexive" remix, which "allegorizes and extends the aesthetic of sampling" (Navas, 2012: 65–66). The first two forms are obvious in their implementation: most video game remixes of classical music, for example, are designed to be looped infinitely, in effect creating ultimate "extended" remixes. Likewise, nearly all game remixes take only some sections, or, in most cases, only limited melodic and harmonic material from the sources, typically fragmented into short, immediately understandable sections. I know of no game remix, for example, that contains an entire "development" section of a symphony movement; it would, for one thing, simply be too long (and/ or not repetitive enough) to combine effectively with the pop-remix medium. By and large remixes of classical music in games excerpt memorable melodic motives ("hooks", so to speak) rather than lengthy sections, and, in the case of remixes of orchestral music, isolated instrumental timbres rather than the entire ensemble. At the same time, however, remixes routinely add new musical elements to the original works – most often in the form of percussion, but also frequently including new harmonies and added melodic lines.

Most interesting, perhaps, is the "reflexive" aspect, which I will deal with most frequently in this chapter. In this form, the remix assumes an allegorical content, simultaneously taking on two (or more) layers of meaning related both to the original version and its historical/cultural context, and to the styles and musical choices represented in the new, remixed version.[5] In other words, the work becomes both "old" and "new"; it is both the original work and something different. The works chosen for remixing in games tend to be well-known – what we might think of as a mainstream classical Top 40. We might assume that the use (and re-use) of a few familiar pieces of the almost limitless classical repertoire stems from a lack of music-historical knowledge on the part of game designers, composers and audio directors, and (particularly in the early days of gaming) that argument has some merit. But such a view sells short these often highly educated and knowledgeable professionals. That the classical music is recognized *as* classical (if not the particular piece, though that is also in some cases desirable, as we will explore throughout this chapter) is critical to the function of a remix, which, as Navas tells us, "will always rely on the authority of the original composition, whether in forms of actual samples, or in form of reference ... The remix is in the end a *re-mix* – this is a rearrangement of something already recognizable" (Navas, 2012: 67). In other words, a remix with an unidentified original form ceases to be a remix at all, and, more importantly, loses its ability to harness the cultural value attached to that original. Yet in these new settings, classical works simultaneously become something new. As the musicologist Mark Katz notes regarding digital sampling, "Any sound, placed into a new musical context, will take on some of the character of its new sonic environment" and through this type of manipulation music can be "decontextualized and recontextualized ... giving it new sounds, functions, and meanings" (Katz, 2010: 174; 154).

Aspects of this reflexive process applied to classical music have appeared in other media for decades. Popular musicians have long taken advantage of classical tunes, as Michael Broyles (2011) and Matthew Brown (2012) have recently explored with the music of Beethoven and Debussy, respectively. We may think, for example, of Walter Murphy and the Big Apple Band's novelty disco remix 'A Fifth of Beethoven' (1976) or Billy Joel's reinterpretation 'This Night' (1984), each of which take inspiration and much musical material from works by Beethoven. On the other hand, although classical music is a common feature in traditional narrative media such as film and television, with a few notable exceptions (most prominently the score to Kubrick's *A Clockwork Orange* [1971]) the music is kept close to its original form (see Gengaro, 2013 and McQuiston, 2013). We can understand remixed classical music in games as a melding of these two traditions: popular reinterpretations of classical music on the one hand, and narrative cinematic uses of classical music on the other. For the remainder of this chapter I will focus on exploring how these reflexive remixes function in a few case studies ranging from the early 1980s to the 2010s, including some examples more illustrative of the "popular music" tradition of remixing – focusing on the music itself as a kind of transgressive stylistic play – and a final in-depth exploration of the game *Catherine*, which considers how this type of remixing might factor into a game's narrative structure.

### Gyruss (1983) and FEZ (2012)

The practice of altering classical music to fit in games is nearly as old as the games themselves. In fact, before the mid to late 1990s *all* classical music in games was in some way altered, whether for practical or aesthetic reasons (or both). Game technology of the time often could neither accommodate the number of simultaneous pitches often required for pre-existing music, nor replicate the sounds of standard instruments, with the end result being a translation of classical works into the idiosyncratic "bleeps and bloops" of early game music. Notes might be omitted, forms altered to be more easily looped, and similar modifications might be undertaken to adapt classical music for the technological limitations of the time, but by and large game designers of the late 1970s and 1980s endeavoured to keep music as close to its original form as possible. Though not strictly speaking remixes, these adaptations nevertheless often create a somewhat similar effect. The resulting timbral juxtaposition removes classical music from its "artistic" pedestal to some degree and places it in close contact with popular culture, akin to playing Bach on a banjo (as one might find in Bela Fleck's similarly transgressive 2001 album *Perpetual Motion*). While most early instances of classical works in games stayed as close as the technology would allow to the music's original form, a few early games directly and obviously experimented with juxtaposing classical and popular musical styles, with one prominent example being *Gyruss* (1983).

A staple of 1980s arcades, the shooter *Gyruss* has enjoyed a long life on a variety of home consoles, ranging from the Atari 2600 and Nintendo Entertainment System to a re-release on Xbox Live Arcade in 2007.[6] Nearly any mention of the game elicits commentary about its main musical theme, Konami composer Masahiro Inoue's remix of the enduringly popular Toccata and Fugue in D minor, commonly attributed to J. S. Bach as BWV 565, which was also featured in a number of other games in the 1980s.[7] A comment in the *Gyruss* review from the gaming website *HardcoreGaming101* is entirely representative of the music's stature in the overall success of the game:

> Gyruss, one of Konami's more popular games in the early 80s, is a "tube shooter" similar to Atari's *Tempest* [1981], although it also borrows heavily from Namco's *Galaga* [1981] . . . It's an impressive bit of technology for 1983, since it uses sprite based graphics rather than vectors like *Tempest*. It's also notable for its fast paced arrangement of Bach's Toccata and Fugue in D minor, one of the first – and best – uses of music in an arcade game. (Kalata, 2009)

The piece is prominently placed in the game, being the first music the player hears after a silent title screen. The monophonic opening notes of the toccata accompany the start of the game's first stage with a sustained tone reminiscent of the original organ instrumentation, initially suggesting that the music will be a straightforward transcription (reminiscent of 'A Fifth of Beethoven'). After the initial phrase, however (about five seconds long), the music quickly skips to the ending chords of the opening slow section, after which we hear two measures of a drum intro before the melodic material continues, now clearly in a much freer and decidedly popular remixed form.

We might wonder why Inoue would choose Bach's work as the main music of *Gyruss*. Part of the answer may lie both with perceptions of Bach's music as a high point of "classical" music and as an exemplar of musical complexity. In the early 1980s games – particularly arcade cabinets – were in a state of constant technological development. Each arcade game was a unique combination of hardware with widely varying graphics and audio capabilities; game developers and programmers were always searching for ways to both maximize those capabilities and to demonstrate them in the most apparent ways to players, thus (presumably) attracting gamers. Music was a key part in that attraction process, as game-sound scholar Karen Collins and others have pointed out (Collins, 2008: 9). In the loud, crowded atmosphere of the 1980s arcade, it was often the sound above all that drew players to a particular machine. In that context, we can return to *Gyruss* from a new perspective. The remixed Toccata and Fugue became a kind of technological benchmark – a dramatic way to illustrate the game's advanced sound capabilities. In contrast with the sporadic and brief musical outbursts of *Galaga*, for example, *Gyruss* provided wall-to-wall musical sound *while* multiple sound effects sounded simultaneously: no mean task with 1983 game audio technology.[8] The choice of Bach added another dimension – not only could the game play music constantly, but it could play *Bach*, often perceived as the composer of some of the most complex and technically perfect music ever written. We can hear in the grandiose opening statement of Bach's music the echoes of similarly bold promises which *Gyruss*'s creators were making about the technical perfection of their game.

Intriguingly, the *Gyruss* Bach remix has enjoyed a long afterlife well into the twenty-first century, and has itself been remixed on several occasions: the original arcade version was updated and altered for the Nintendo Famicom and NES ports (1987 and 1988, respectively), an electronic remix called 'Gyruss–Full Tilt' (by the DJ/composer JT.1Up) was included in the game *Dance Dance Revolution Ultramix 2* (2004), and the Xbox Live Arcade re-release (2007) featured yet another updating/remix of the original material. At what point, then, is Bach's music less the subject of the remix than Inoue's *Gyruss* music? Clearly it is nostalgia for the game rather than for the original organ work that motivates these new versions. This distinction highlights another (and I think largely beneficial) consequence of removing a classical work from its privileged status and bringing it into the realm of popular culture: it becomes inherently more fluid as (post)Romantic concepts of *Werktreue* (or "faithfulness to the work") give way to a sense of play. As Vanessa Chang points out in a study of musical sampling, "Rather than clinging to the myth of the composer savant, sampling maintains an ethics of inclusion that is social as well as musical, creating a tradition that involves the past without submitting to its structures and limitations" (2009: 156). As *Gyruss* (and the other games in this chapter) illustrate, remixing allows for a type of transgressive freedom and play that is often off-limits with classical music.

This type of musical play has continued long past *Gyruss* and the 8-bit era. In more recent years, however, remixed classical music has been a recurring feature in smaller niche games (often from independent studios) rather than in major studio releases. As audio capabilities advanced in the late 1980s and into the 1990s, the use of classical music in games seems to have declined in general, and when pre-existing music appeared it was typically adapted popular music. (We may also attribute this change to a number of non-technological factors, including increased budgets, more musically trained composers, and larger production teams.) Thus using remixed classical music in the twenty-first century conveys (or at least *can* convey) several concepts: an "independent" quality to the game that suggests its intellectual rigour by incorporating classical music, and (perhaps to a lesser extent) a kind of nostalgia for the 8-bit era, when classical music was more prominent in games.

The independent game *FEZ* (2012), a product of temperamental auteur game designer Phil Fish, is a case in point of both categories. *FEZ* is an homage to platformer games of the 8-bit era, with deliberately crude graphics designed to appear as two-dimensional pixels, despite actually being three-dimensional polygons (see Figure 11.1). The game's plot involves the traumatic introduction of a third dimension into this world, which players can access by rotating the screen – *FEZ* is thus literally adding a new dimension to a pastiche of nostalgia-inducing gameplay elements. As Chris Suellentrop of the *New York Times* writes:

> Mr. Fish is a Quentin Tarantino of 8-bit gaming, prodigiously quoting from the pop culture of his childhood (in this case, the Nintendo Entertainment System, rather than blaxploitation films). The oddly shaped blocks from *Tetris* can be seen everywhere in *Fez*: on the walls, on the ground, on signposts, scrawled on chalkboards, even in the constellations in the sky. Gomez, *Fez*'s protagonist, beams with joy, adorably, when he finds an important item in a treasure chest, much like Link, the hero of *Zelda*. But it is to *Super Mario Bros.* that *Fez* owes its greatest debts. For starters, there are mushroom levels, moving platforms on rails and an underground world that Gomez reaches by descending through a well that looks very much like a pipe. (Suellentrop, 2012)

The game's soundtrack, by composer Rich Vreeland (known as 'Disasterpeace'), is equally reminiscent of the 8-bit era, and, as critic Matt Miller pointed out in *Game Informer*, "drives home the '80s nostalgia vibe" (Miller, 2012). Its chiptune-influenced bleeps and bloops evoke but transform the memories of gaming in the 1980s, just as the graphics and gameplay do. It is not entirely surprising, then, that we find a piece of remixed classical music in the midst of the game's original soundtrack: 'Continuum', a remix of Frédéric Chopin's Prelude in E minor, Op. 28, No. 4.[9] A highly musically distorted opening – almost to the point of simulating problems with the computer speakers – evolves into a Vangelis-influenced synth arrangement before gradually reintroducing the distortion, ultimately culminating in a complete disintegration from music into static (noise).

*Figure 11.1 FEZ* (2012)

This remixed work thus evokes *FEZ*'s central notions of postmodern pastiche and nostalgia in both concept and timbre, but, moreover, the choice aurally illustrates *FEZ*'s efforts to transcend being viewed as pure entertainment. As Suellentrop's comparison of Fish to Tarantino also illustrates in the quotation above, *FEZ* is often regarded as a kind of "artgame"; in the same review the critic also refers to the game as "a *Finnegans Wake* of video games", for its impenetrable narrative and lack of clear direction. As in *Gyruss*, remixing the Chopin prelude in *FEZ* is a type of play, but here the use of classical music is also a subtle way of elevating the game artistically, coding it as a sophisticated and perhaps even "elite" type of game. (Notably, game magazine *Edge Online*'s review of *FEZ* observes that "Disasterpeace's mesmerising quasi-chiptune soundtrack suggests Holst's back catalogue put through a Mega Drive [Sega Genesis]" [Edge Online, 2012].) Ironically, the same techniques used in *Gyruss* to showcase the game's advanced sound hardware exude a retro-nostalgia in *FEZ*. Yet in both cases we find an illustration of musical play through stylistic juxtaposition and an appeal to classical music's artistic authority, whether to demonstrate technological or artistic achievement.

In both examples we have so far explored, the music has been separated from both action and narrative; it is, in other words, neither a part of their gameplay nor an outgrowth of their plots. That approach in incorporating remixed classical music allows the remix itself to remain in the background, enjoyable to players who appreciate the stylistic juxtaposition (or simply like the remixed version) while not creating a significant stumbling block to any players who might dislike either classical music or its alteration. In the following section, I explore a game in which the focus is clearly on the remixed classical soundtrack, creating a situation in which the complexities and juxtapositions of the relatively unusual phenomenon had to be addressed (if not necessarily understood) by both players and critics.

## *Boom Boom Rocket* (2007)

*Boom Boom Rocket* is a downloadable rhythm game released on the Xbox Live Arcade by Bizarre Creations, the makers of the highly popular downloadable shooter *Geometry Wars: Retro Evolved* (2005). Like *Geometry Wars* – which originated as a mini-game in the Xbox title *Project Gotham Racing 2* (2003) – *Boom Boom Rocket* is simplistic by design. Over a backdrop of a night-time cityscape, players complete sequences of rhythmically timed button presses on the controller in response to on-screen indicators, not unlike *Dance Dance Revolution* games, but using a controller in place of the dance mat. Correctly timed button presses trigger an on-screen fireworks display, a visual reward for successful gameplay (see Figure 11.2). Although the button presses are timed to correspond to elements of the music – metric structure, key changes, and so on – *Boom Boom Rocket* is in a sense less a "music game" than a "music visualizer" game; players contribute a visual accompaniment to the music rather than the music itself. This connection between music and the visual is made directly manifest by the inclusion of a non-interactive music visualizer mode, in which players simply watch the game creating a fireworks display based on any music track on the Xbox 360 hard drive.

The connection between music visualizers and video games is an old one, traceable back to the Atari Video Music system (1976), which connected to a stereo system and provided an abstract graphical accompaniment of the music.[10] Though the AVM system was not a "game" – there were no rules, or ways to score points, for example – its various knobs and buttons nonetheless provided an interactive aspect. As game scholar Ian Bogost has pointed out, "While primitive, Atari Video Music offers a sign of what would become the unique contribution videogames offer to music. Instead of listening, watching, dancing, or otherwise taking in music, videogames offer a way to *perform* it" (Bogost, 2011: 32, original emphasis). Bogost's observation that there is a kinship between the AVM system and games is an astute one, but I disagree that it allowed players to "perform" music in the sense that, say, *Guitar Hero* does. Instead, I would argue that it afforded listeners/players an opportunity to *interpret* music in a synesthetic fashion – an important distinction. Here

*Figure 11.2 Boom Boom Rocket* (2007)

players are not active participants in music-making, and their inputs have no effect whatsoever on how the music sounds.

In the absence of player avatars, narrative elements, a mimetic controller, or even changes in the game's colour scheme or backdrop, in *Boom Boom Rocket* the music assumes a central role, and is consistently the focus of player attention. Not surprisingly, the game features a soundtrack heavily influenced by electronic music styles – the relationship between electronica and the technological visualization of music is a longstanding one. The AVM system itself, for example, has been featured prominently as the backdrop of the synthpop band Devo's video for 'The Day My Baby Gave Me a Surprise' (1979), or seen at work on televisions in the background of Daft Punk's 'Robot Rock' (2005) video. In games, we may find a link between electronic music scores and music visualization in titles such as the shooter *Rez* (2001) and its prequel *Child of Eden* (2011), in which the actions in the game create the elements of its electronic soundtrack, or the techno-psychedelic imagery in games such as *iS: Internal Section* (1999), in which levels were designed based on the electronic soundtrack.[11]

What *is* surprising about *Boom Boom Rocket*'s soundtrack is that each of the 15 tracks in its soundtrack is also a remixed classical work (see Table 11.1). When the game was released, its soundtrack consisted of ten mainstream works remixed by composer Ian Livingstone, with each piece given a clever title alluding to its original identity; the musical styles of these remixes are largely focused on electronic dance music (EDM), but the game also includes the ska-influenced 'Rave New World' and the disco-funk 'Carmen Electric'. A downloadable "Rock Pack" (the only downloadable content, or DLC, released for the game) enhanced this stylistic range later in 2007 by adding five songs remixed by composer Chris Chudley (who had created the music for *Geometry Wars*) in a variety of rock styles.

*Table 11.1* Music tracks in *Boom Boom Rocket*

| Track Title | Source Composer | Original Source |
| --- | --- | --- |
| 'Smooth Operetta' | Delibes, Léo | 'Flower Duet', from *Lakmé* |
| 'Rave New World' | Dvořák, Antonin | Symphony No. 9, 'From the New World', IV |
| 'William Tell Overload' | Rossini, Gioachino | Overture to *William Tell* |
| 'Hall of the Mountain Dude' | Grieg, Edvard | 'In the Hall of the Mountain King', from *Peer Gynt* |
| '1812 Overdrive' | Tchaikovsky, Pyotr | *1812 Overture* |
| 'Valkyries Rising' | Wagner, Richard | 'Ride of the Valkyries', from *Die Walküre* |
| 'Tail Light Sonata' | Beethoven, Ludwig van | 'Moonlight' Sonata, I |
| 'Carmen Electric' | Bizet, Georges | Overture to *Carmen* |
| 'Game Over Beethoven' | Beethoven, Ludwig van | Symphony No. 5, I |
| 'Toccata and Funk' | Bach, J. S. | Toccata and Fugue in D Minor |
| **DLC 'Rock Pack'** | | |
| 'Sting of the Bumble Bee' | Rimsky-Korsakov, Nikolai | *Flight of the Bumble Bee* |
| 'Explode to Joy' | Beethoven, Ludwig van | Symphony No. 9, IV |
| 'Sugar High' | Tchaikovsky, Pyotr | 'Dance of the Sugar Plum Fairy', from *Nutcracker* |
| 'Eine Kleine Rochtmusik' | Mozart, Wolfgang Amadeus | *Eine Kleine Nachtmusik*, I |
| 'Cannon in D' | Pachelbel, Johann | Canon in D |

More so than in either *Gyruss* or *FEZ*, there is obvious humour at play in this music, illustrated most clearly in the song titles, but carrying over into the music itself (or perhaps vice versa), and there is a slightly subversive edge to both. The title 'Game Over Beethoven' of course invokes the 1956 Chuck Berry song 'Roll Over Beethoven', itself an exhortation for classical music to give way to popular styles; most of the rest of the titles suggest an updating, a replacing of "boring" classical elements with "edgy" modern ones: the generic descriptor "overture" is replaced twice, for example, once by "overdrive" and once by "overload". Some titles even carry a hint of violent rupture, particularly in the 'Rock Pack': Pachelbel's infamous 'Canon in D' becomes a "cannon", Beethoven's Ode "explodes", and Rimsky-Korsakov's bumble bee "stings". And yet, if Livingstone were utterly rejecting classical styles, why use the music in the first place? The end result in *Boom Boom Rocket* is both a celebration and a mockery of these classical works. Listeners (or, in fact, its creators) do not have to choose one interpretation or the other; as Katz notes, a newly created hybrid work "can be understood as derivative *and* novel, exploitative *and* respectful, awkward *and* subtle" (Katz, 2010: 160).

We may think, for example, of the pleasure that 1970s DJs took in introducing unusual elements into their works; Joseph Schloss points out that "many deejays are known to have taken a special delight in getting audiences to dance to breaks that were taken from genres that they professed to hate" (Schloss, 2004: 32). Certainly, to some extent audiences were aware of this playful goal: as one user-contributed review to the website *GameFAQs* notes,

> The songs – what I have played – are great and fun to listen to. And this is coming from a person who listens to rap and nothing else. Most of the music in this game is remixed Classical, and Classical bores me ... but not the music in this game. Why? I honestly don't know ... Another thing that makes this game fun for a person like me that enjoys Rap, RnB, and music of that nature is that the songs actually have somewhat of a beat (for the most part) and the fireworks flow with that. ("Cuzit," 2007)

*Boom Boom Rocket* illustrates perhaps more clearly than other titles the sense of pleasure derived from the transgressive act of remixing two seemingly incongruous musical styles.

Or – appropriately for a game based on fireworks displays – perhaps here we might fruitfully think of the cultural theorist Mikhail Bakhtin's notions of "carnival". Carnival is a time when traditional values are suspended, or reversed – a safe, playful space in which we can laugh at the most serious of matters. By looking at issues through a lens of humour, Bakhtin tells us, "the world is seen anew, no less (and perhaps more) profoundly than when seen from the serious standpoint. Therefore, laughter is just as admissible in great literature, posing universal problems, as seriousness" (Bakhtin, 1984: 66). By learning to laugh at these classical works in their new "goofy" setting, we can see them in a new light, visualizing the music (as the carnivalesque fireworks do) in a unique and revealing way. For Bakhtin, carnival was a way of breaking down the walls between the "high" and "low" arts through laughter. As literary scholar Renate Lachmann has pointed out:

> The inventory of carnival acts, symbols, and signs derives its meaning
> from this parodistic and profane inversion of canonized values, but also
> from the utopian dimension of the myth . . . The provocative, mirthful
> inversion of prevailing institutions and their hierarchy as staged in the
> carnival offers a permanent alternative to official culture – even if it
> ultimately leaves everything as it was before. (Lachmann, 1988–1989: 125)

If we place that sentiment in the both figuratively and literally carnivalesque
context of *Boom Boom Rocket* – which always suggests to me the spectacular
fireworks of Rio de Janeiro's carnival celebrations – we may begin to see some
underlying meanings emerge. Carnival is a "utopian" concept in that it highlights
the arbitrary nature of cultural hierarchies, and in doing so seeks to bridge
the gaps between them. We have already seen how the game connects with
longstanding attempts to find links between visual and aural art experiences,
showing us a relationship between two seemingly disparate experiences. In the
same way, these remixes poke fun at classical music not to denigrate it, but to
show us its affinity for, rather than difference from, the less "serious" popular
styles in which it finds itself. It may not be possible to permanently bridge
the gap between "art" and "entertainment" (or the "sacred" and "profane",
to think in Bakhtin's terms), but for a few minutes the fireworks of carnival
let us playfully explore the boundaries.

## *Catherine* (2011)

If *Boom Boom Rocket* seeks, however briefly, to tear down these distinctions,
the final game I discuss in this chapter depends on their existence to add
complexity to its already multi-layered narrative structure. *Catherine*, a release
from Atlus, the game studio best known for the gritty and deeply philosophical
Japanese role-playing game series *Shin Megami Tensei: Persona*, appeared on
the Xbox 360 and PlayStation 3 consoles in 2011. It also holds the somewhat
dubious distinction of being one of the most unusual games I have come across
in my game-related research (which at this point is no mean feat) both in its
narrative conception and in its blending of traditionally separate game genres.
*Catherine*'s premise is difficult to explain concisely: the player assumes the role
of Vincent, a 32-year-old slacker in the midst of a major life crisis. His long-time
girlfriend, the serious and professional Katherine, is constantly pressuring him
to improve his job prospects and get married, with a pregnancy scare early
in the game contributing to his stress. In the midst of his internal struggles
with responsibility, Vincent meets the young, attractive, fun-loving Catherine,
with whom he enters a second relationship (see Figure 11.3). After beginning
his affair, however, whenever he sleeps, Vincent finds himself transported to a
nightmarish dreamscape along with many other "cheating" men (all of whom

manifest as sheep). In the nocturnal realm, these men must continually solve puzzles to survive.

*Figure 11.3* Screenshot from a cutscene in *Catherine*. In this tense scene Katherine (right) finally encounters Catherine (left) in Vincent's apartment

*Catherine* is in many respects centred on the play of dualities, a choice evident even in its basic gameplay, which is divided into two starkly contrasting parts. In the day and evening, players guide Vincent through daily interactions with Catherine and Katherine as well as his friends, choosing how to respond in conversations, whether to reply to text messages, and so on. Each evening players find themselves at The Stray Sheep, Vincent's regular bar, where players can again speak to friends, order drinks, play a mini-game (based on block-shifting gameplay), and so on. This portion of the game is essentially a "dating-simulation" game, a (typically Japanese) genre focused on wooing various characters by performing in-game actions and completing tasks.[12] Elements of dating sims have been incorporated into other genres, as in the "romance" options available in many RPGs of recent years, including Atlus's own *Persona 3* (2006) and *Persona 4* (2008). *Catherine* has a number of features in common with dating sims, including a focus on binary choices, the existence of multiple endings (*Catherine* has ten possible endings covering a number of possible scenarios), a substantial portion of its gameplay being in an animated two-dimensional style, and the obvious influence of anime. In this portion of the game there is no need to hurry, or risk of "right" and "wrong" choices (unless the player is working towards a specific ending); the only point of the game is to advance the plot by juggling the relationships.

The dream sequences, however, are an entirely different story, and here the game deviates entirely from any pretences of being a dating simulation. Instead, players find another hybridization: a mixture of horror and puzzle games.[13] Though the nightmare realm has (for lack of a better word) a lobby area – where the player may converse with other trapped sheep, learn new puzzle-solving techniques, and purchase items – the bulk of the "night" portion of the game involves moving blocks to advance to higher levels, both literally and figuratively. Players must climb towers by pulling blocks to create stairs, a timed puzzle mechanic that provides the most traditionally "game-like" part of the experience of playing *Catherine*, complete with numerical scores, level names (3-1, 3-2, etc.), and an onscreen display revealing the number of remaining "lives", a location on the map, and other essential information. Each night culminates in a final "boss" confrontation in which Vincent must climb fast enough to escape from a macabre manifestation of some major concern from his waking life, such as a particularly terrifying demonic infant. Gone is the slow-paced, explorative tone of *Catherine*'s "dating sim" portion, replaced by an intensely nerve-wracking gameplay experience, in which a few small mistakes could end in a gruesome death followed by the game-over screen (which ominously reads "Love is Over") and being forced to repeat all or some of the night's puzzle.

*Catherine* thus becomes at its core a generic slurry – a combination of seemingly unmixable game concepts. Already we begin to see how this duality manifests itself on multiple levels throughout the game with an almost fractal repetition: dating simulation vs. puzzle/horror; day vs. night; the effervescent, blonde Catherine (dressed all in white) vs. the older, brunette, serious Katherine (dressed all in black); and so on, stretching seemingly into infinity. The game's musical score, by composer Shoji Meguro, not surprisingly reflects these polar differences by virtue of its own dualities. Music for the daytime and evening portions of the game (the "dating simulation" part, in other words) is loosely popular in style, favouring a piano-heavy light jazz idiom. Furthermore, this music is quite often diegetic; in the bar, for example, the player can use a jukebox to choose a particular track from a list of available tunes. As Vincent is carried to his dream world each night, however, the music for the loading screen and lobby area take on a much darker tone, with a dissonant string and piano sound evocative of horror films. Already we see one clear musical dichotomy, but more interesting for my purposes is the music that accompanies each of the puzzle sequences. With a few exceptions and repetitions, each of these levels is underscored by a different piece of classical music remixed into a variety of popular styles fairly typical of video game soundtracks – hip-hop, hard rock, electronic dance music, and so on. The pieces of classical music chosen for the game are all well-known selections, similar to those in *Boom*

*Boom Rocket* – works one might hear in any concert hall (see Table 11.2). Though initially this juxtaposition might be jarring to the player (as many aspects of *Catherine* may be), it quickly becomes clear that the combination of classical and popular styles is another of *Catherine*'s dualities, and one that has important ramifications for how we understand both the nightmarish night-time scenes and the game more broadly.

*Table 11.2* Classical music in *Catherine*

| Segment of Game | Original Composer | Original Source |
|---|---|---|
| Levels 1 and 2 | Holst, Gustav | 'Jupiter' and 'Mars', from *The Planets* |
| Level 3 | Beethoven, Ludwig van | Symphony No. 5, III |
| Levels 3 (boss), 4 (boss) and 8 | Mussorgsky, Modest | 'The Hut on Fowl's Legs' ('Baba Yaga'), from *Pictures at an Exhibition* |
| Level 4 | Bach, J. S. | 'Little' Fugue in G minor, BWV 578 |
| Level 5 | Dvořák, Antonin | Symphony No. 9, 'From the New World', I |
| Level 6 | Rossini, Gioachino | Overture to *William Tell* |
| Level 7 | Borodin, Alexander | Polovtsian Dances, from *Prince Igor* |
| Level 9 | Bizet, Georges | 'Farandole', from *L'Arlésienne* Suite |
| Final Boss | Chopin, Frédéric | 'Revolutionary' Etude, Op. 10, No. 1 |
| Victory of each level (not remixed) | Handel, G. F. | 'Hallelujah', from *Messiah* |
| Death (arranged, not "remixed") | Sarasate, Pablo de | 'Zigeunerweisen' ('Gypsy Airs'), Op. 20 |
| Break-Ups (in "real world") | Chopin, Frédéric | Piano Sonata No. 2, 'Funeral March' |

The play of dualities within *Catherine*'s use of classical music takes places on multiple levels, and I would like to briefly consider them from the most detailed to the most general, beginning with the selections of the individual pieces themselves. Because *Catherine* is more narratively focused than the other games we have explored in this chapter, the music is able to relate more directly to in-game events and situations. Some of the choices seem straightforward:

Handel's 'Hallelujah Chorus' (which is not stylistically remixed, but synthesized in a slightly inhuman-sounding fashion), for example, obviously symbolizes triumph, occurring at the end of each of the game's levels upon reaching the ending, and at the same time conveys a sense of the religious, the forces of "good", victorious over the "evil" nightmare (an idea also reflected in the angelic white feathers that begin to fall upon reaching a level's exit). Chopin's 'Funeral March' is slightly more complicated, representing not the death of an individual, but the death of a relationship. Uniquely among the remixed classical music, Chopin's music appears in the "real world" rather than the "dream world" in two scenarios: (ambiguously diegetically) in the bar after Vincent breaks up with Catherine, or at his apartment (non-diegetically) after Katherine breaks up with him, and in both cases remixed into a piano-jazz idiom evocative of the typical "daytime" music. In reflecting the ideas of "triumph" and "death", the 'Hallelujah Chorus' and 'Funeral March' conform to the semiotic markers established by their uses in countless films since the silent era, as well as television and earlier games. We might make a similar case for Chopin's well-known "Revolutionary" Etude, which underscores the game's final level. Vincent, in effect, revolts against the demonic forces responsible for his nightly torments, ultimately saving his life (and the lives of countless other men) in the process, matching the political overtones of the Chopin Etude.

Other musical selections, however, resonate much more subtly with *Catherine*'s central ideas by intertextually evoking other artworks with similar themes. The nineteenth-century French composer Georges Bizet's 'Farandole' – here remixed as a kind of stadium-rock anthem – is best-known today as a purely instrumental work, but it originated as incidental music for Alphone Daudet's play *L'Arlésienne*. In the context of *Catherine* the music may call to mind the plot of the stage work, in which a young man is torn between two women, one apparently sexually free (the titular "girl from Arles"), and the other more reserved. After eventually becoming (briefly) engaged to the "Arlésienne", he is driven mad by her involvement with another man and ultimately commits suicide by throwing himself from a high balcony. Clearly, this situation parallels Vincent's in *Catherine*: the male protagonist's struggle to choose between two diametrically opposed suitors, the centrality of infidelity as a plot device (although in *Catherine* the transgression is Vincent's own), and the threat of death by falling. The use of the violinist/composer Pablo de Sarasate's *Zigeunerweisen* for the game-over screens may function as a similar, and equally obscure, reference.[14] This time, the allusion is to Suzuki Seijun's 1980 Japanese cult film of the same name, in which Sarasate's piece features prominently on several occasions (including in the context of an ambiguous communication with the afterlife). Though the film's quasi-surrealist plot is nearly impossible to summarize, it deals with many of the same issues we find in *Catherine*, and in particular with complicated sexual relationships (polyamory, multiple instances of infidelity, and so on) and death. Moreover, as Japanese-studies scholar Rachel Dinitto has noted, *Zigeunerweisen* (the film) explores duality and "double vision" on multiple levels, a concept that extends to the same actress portraying two separate (and contrasting) roles as love interests. "In addition to the obvious doppelgänger effect", Dinitto continues, "Suzuki reuses or doubles images, scenes, dialogue, and sounds. These replications, be they false or true, tie the film together" (Dinitto, 2004: 46). Thus in both plot themes and narrative structure *Catherine* echoes Suzuki's film, using concepts of duality to frame a disparate, complex and occasionally unintelligible work.

In another method of reinforcing *Catherine*'s fundamental duality, Shoji Meguro seems to have been drawn to classical works that contain some type of internal dichotomy. For example, parts of the remixed version we hear of Rossini's *William Tell* Overture are "the storm" and the "ranz des vaches": the most dramatic and most pastoral moments of the piece, in other words.[15] Likewise, the remix of Holst's *Planets* incorporates elements of two movements from the large-scale work: Jupiter ("The Bringer of Jollity") and Mars ("The Bringer of War"), again juxtaposing two contradictory elements. In both the Rossini and Holst works, we find extreme contrasts in both the musical content of these excerpts and in both their musical and their extra-musical (i.e. "programmatic") content. Particularly intriguing in the latter type is the use of 'The Hut on Fowl's Legs', also known as 'Baba Yaga', from the Russian composer Modest Mussorgsky's tone poem *Pictures at an Exhibition*. 'Baba Yaga' is the only piece of music that appears several times in *Catherine*, twice accompanying "bosses" and as the soundtrack to level 8, a pivotal point in the game that is initially identified as the "Last Stage" (though there is, in fact, another level).

Baba Yaga is a figure from Russian folklore, a deeply conflicted character whose identity and motivations were always obscure: she could appear as either a beautiful young woman or as an old hag, sometimes helping travellers and sometimes hindering (or murdering) them.[16] Russian folklorist Joanna Hubbs has suggested that Baba Yaga is an embodiment of the feminine, and specifically of "feminine power": "the expression of realized potential fulfillment of the cycle of life associated with woman . . . In her the cycles of feminine life are brought to completion, and yet she contains them all" (Hubbs, 1988: 39, 37). Certainly we may find resonances with *Catherine* already, in both Vincent's fear of the advancing stages of a life (manifested in Katherine's possible pregnancy) and his inability to resist Catherine's "feminine power". But Baba Yaga's symbolism goes much deeper; though she may seemingly embody the "cycles of feminine life", upon closer inspection she is, like Vincent's nightmares, a monstrous perversion of the feminine and maternal. "She punishes the overcurious who would learn the secret of her paradoxical nature", Hubbs tells us. "Yaga is a mother, but a cannibal mother. She whose children are many . . . is also the hungry one who devours them" (Hubbs, 1988: 39). Vincent's "boss" encounters – many of which are accompanied by Mussorgsky's music – reflect similar ideas. In level 3, Vincent faces the "Immoral Beast", a lewd and Picasso-esque corruption of the human body itself evocative of the hut on fowl's legs, which is sometimes represented as "composed of parts of the human body, with legs for doorposts, hands for bolts, and a mouth with sharp teeth as a lock" (Hubbs, 1988: 38). Level 4's boss is "The Child", a disturbing manifestation of the responsibilities and demands of parenting. And level 8 finds Vincent (and Katherine) squaring off against a demonic version of Catherine, who tries to eat Vincent with her razor-sharp teeth, just as Baba Yaga consumes unwary travellers (and her own children). We might delve further into the connections between Baba Yaga and aspects of *Catherine* (one could easily, and probably should, spend an entire chapter doing so), but at this point it is clear that invoking Baba Yaga's legend in *Catherine* through Mussorgsky's music enhances and contextualizes our (and Vincent's) fears, reaffirming these visions as elements of something like a fairy tale – which is to say as a manifestation of lingering, if often subconscious, cultural concerns and obsessions.[17]

These examples from Bizet, Sarasate and Mussorgsky illustrate how the selection of a particular piece of music may deepen our understanding of a game's central narrative themes. But – to be totally clear – I do not expect that most players would approach *Catherine* with a frame of reference encompassing nineteenth-century French plays, the interpretation of Russian folklore, and Japanese cult films of the 1980s. (I do not, for that matter, think it is necessary for the game designers to have consciously intended the references.) Rather, if players catch a particular allusion it may deepen their understanding and appreciation for the game, and shape our interpretations of it. Players may even (as I did) catch one allusion and follow up by doing additional research, finding new depth in the gameplay from outside sources. The role of classical music in *Catherine* is not, however, limited to this level of understanding, and if we view its practice of remixing as a whole, we can see that the game is – like *Boom Boom Rocket*, *FEZ*, *Gyruss*, and nearly all instances of remixed classical music in games – quite revealing about the cultural values with which we imbue musical genres as a whole.

Classical music in media, including games, frequently signifies concepts such as "adult oriented", "familiar", "serious", "refined" or "complex". We may think, for example, of seemingly limitless uses of classical music in television advertising for luxury products, or as background music in upscale stores, restaurants, and so on. Less charitably, classical music often indicates that something is "old" or "boring", an outdated, out-of-touch, product that has outlived its usefulness (assuming it ever had any). Popular music, on the other hand, often identifies characters, products or situations as "youth oriented", "fun", "unpretentious", "exciting" or (again, cynically) as "superficial". Unlike the more obscure references to individual works we have already seen, the constantly reinforced dichotomous relationship between classical and popular musics, in terms of both musical style and intended audience, is something players will almost certainly have encountered long before picking up a controller to play *Catherine*.

In this particular circumstance, however, these long-held meanings take on new significance. The game's central duality, around which all the other dualities assume importance, is the contrast between Katherine and Catherine (an importance that stretches even to the game's title, which places the focus on the love interest[s] rather than onto the protagonist). The same ingrained semiotic markers we find with classical and popular music styles map quite neatly onto Katherine and Catherine, who – like the music itself – become jumbled in Vincent's dreaming mind. Katherine embodies Vincent's anxiety at the onrushing responsibilities of adulthood: his concerns over settling down, finding financial stability, and a nagging fear of becoming a boring adult. The vibrant and significantly younger Catherine, by contrast, seems to provide the antidote to these fears, offering Vincent a fun, if superficial, relationship that reinforces his youthful irresponsibility.[18] The music thus offers us another window into Vincent's troubled psyche, revealing – sometimes on multiple levels – his internal conflicts between adulthood and youth, or responsibility and freedom. We may choose to view the contrasting musical styles in any way we choose: the game gives us no suggestion of whether the original classical piece or its newly found popular style is more desirable, or which is the "dominant" or even "real" musical work. Unlike what we might think of as the (relatively) empty signifiers of *Boom Boom Rocket*, for example, through the narrative incorporation of the remixed music we find in *Catherine* we have the opposite problem: the music (like many aspects of the game) demands analysis, but offers an almost limitless supply of interpretations from which players can pick and choose their own meanings.

## Conclusion

Let me briefly conclude by suggesting one final level of meaning in *Catherine* and, to a greater or lesser extent, the other games we have explored in this chapter. Above any narrative function, we may read the remixed classical music as a commentary on the dualistic nature of these games themselves, and perhaps on modern gaming more generally. Whatever we may think of its aesthetic merits, *Catherine* remains a fusion of high-minded artistic aspirations and social commentary with low-art sensationalism and basic puzzle-style gameplay mechanics; it is Aristotle meets *Angry Birds*, Tennyson meets *Tetris*. It strives, in short, to be simultaneously "art" and "entertainment". Its soundtrack of forcibly juxtaposed classical and popular styles thus becomes a metaphor (or perhaps a synecdoche) for this larger conflict – a mirror of the precarious and arguably impossible liminal space many games like *Catherine* inhabit. This music, like the game, attempts to blend "art" and "entertainment", but its narrative effect ultimately relies on that combination remaining unconvincing. The music only makes sense if the player still perceives "classical" and "popular" musics to be one of the game's binary oppositions, like day and night, adulthood and youth, freedom and stability, Catherine and Katherine, and, perhaps, "art" and "video games". A last thought: tellingly, players in *Catherine* cannot have everything at once: there is no synthesis to the dialectic it presents, no perfect ending. Eventually, players must stop juggling and choose one of the two Catherines. If we read the entire game as metaphorical for the liminal state of games, what does that ultimate choice mean for us as players? Can *Catherine* and its remixed music exist simultaneously as art and entertainment – or must we, like Vincent, choose one path or the other? To echo Tallarico's claim with which I began this chapter: can a game score be "classical", and conversely, can "classical music" – remixed or not – ever be a game score? These games illustrate in unique ways the complex nexus of meanings inherent in any combination of classical music and video games, calling into question what for many players and critics may be deeply held assumptions about the cultural roles and value of both classical music and video games.

## Notes

1. William Gibbons is Assistant Professor of Musicology at Texas Christian University. He is the author of *Building the Operatic Museum: Eighteenth-Century Opera in Fin-de-Siècle Paris* (2013) and co-editor of *Music in Video Games: Studying Play* (2014). He is currently completing a new monograph, *Unlimited Replays: The Art of Classical Music in Video Games*.
2. Here we might think of the comparatively rare, if critically beloved, non-entertainment-based products that scholars such as Ian Bogost refer to as "artgames" (Bogost, 2011).
3. A number of scholars have argued against such reductive (and value-laden) terminology in recent years. Michael Long, for example, notes "The embarrassment academics daily confront when we halfheartedly recite categories of 'art' and 'popular' that we know are meaningless or wrong, and the extent to which we still regularly frame our own language in air, scare, or typographical quotes, suggests that if we could comfortably recategorize the objects of our discourse we would likely do so" (Long, 2008: 4). For a brief but insightful recent

overview of the terminological issues inherent in the term "classical music" (and its equally problematic synonyms "art music" and "cultivated music"), see Locke, 2012.

4. On classical music in early games, see Gibbons, 2009 and Lerner, 2013. Other studies of classical music in games include Cook, 2014 and Summers, 2014.

5. Here Navas draws heavily on the influential work of Craig Owens (1980a and 1980b).

6. A full list of ports is available at the Arcade History website, available online at http://www.arcade-history.com/?n=gyruss-model-gx347&page=detail&id=1063 (accessed July 15, 2014).

7. The Toccata and Fugue appeared in a number of games during (and after) the 8-bit era. I discuss its use in the NES games *Captain Comic* and *The Battle of Olympus* (both 1988) in Gibbons, 2009 and Plank-Blasko (2014) has examined more instances (including in *Gyruss*). I am grateful to Dana Plank-Blasko for providing me with a copy of her research.

8. Collins has noted the abnormal amount of sound hardware that went into the making of *Gyruss*, which included "as many as five synthesis chips and a DAC [Digital-to-Analog Converter]". The game seems, she notes, "to use at least two chips for sound effects, one for percussion, and at least one chip to create a rendition of Bach's *Toccata and Fugue in D minor*" (Collins, 2008: 19).

9. Chopin's music is surprisingly common in postmillennial games, and – very unusually – the composer himself is the protagonist of two titles: the Japanese role-playing game *Eternal Sonata* (2007) and the music game *Frederic: Resurrection of Music* (2011); the soundtrack for the latter is composed entirely of remixes of Chopin's music.

10. In more recent years electronic music visualizers such as the AVM have given way to software versions, most commonly on personal computers. Many media player programs (iTunes and Windows Media Player, for example) include built-in visualization modes, and there are a number of freestanding programs devoted to music-generated visual displays. Some game consoles have also included built-in (or downloadable) music visualizer programs, including the Atari Jaguar's *Virtual Light Machine* and the Xbox 360's *Neon*, both built into the consoles' media player functions.

11. On soundtrack-based level design in games, see Reale, 2014.

12. On dating sims, see Taylor, 2007 and Galbraith, 2011.

13. The blending of horror and puzzle genres in *Catherine* is not entirely without precedent. One might think, for example, of the popular PC title *The 7th Guest* (1993), its less-successful sequel *The 11th Hour* (1995), and other *7th Guest*-influenced titles such as *Phantasmagoria* (1995) and its own sequel *Phantasmagoria: A Puzzle of Flesh* (1996), each of which combined a horror story told in full-motion video (possible with new CD-ROM technology) with puzzles that would advance the plot. Significantly, however, for the most part the puzzles in these games were not timed, and there was no "action" element to the games. In a more humorous and not strictly "puzzle" vein, in 1999 Sega remade its popular arcade shooter/

horror game *House of the Dead 2* into *The Typing of the Dead*, an edutainment game in which players defeated zombies by quickly typing words on a keyboard. It has thus far spawned two sequels: *The Typing of the Dead 2* (2007) and *Typing of the Dead: Overkill* (2013).

14. The *Zigeunerweisen* is, like the 'Hallelujah Chorus', not stylistically remixed in *Catherine*, but its resonance with the game's narrative merit some mention here.

15. A "ranz des vaches" is a peculiarly Swiss type of folk tune, typically associated with Alpine cattle herders.

16. For an overview of Baba Yaga's history and interpretations, see Johns, 2004.

17. The literature on fairy tales as reflections of social pressures and/or fears is vast. Best known, perhaps, is Bruno Bettelheim's controversial 1976 book *The Uses of Enchantment*. More recently, see the several monographs on the topic by Jack Zipes, in particular Zipes, 2012: Chapter 4, on Baba Yaga. Significantly, we can trace much of the analysis of fairy tales to Jungian archetypal psychology, which is a recurring and obvious influence on Atlus studio's games, particularly the *Persona* series.

18. We may think here of Matthew Brown's suggestion (building on several studies) that adolescents turn to popular music "as a means of controlling their moods. It does so in several ways: by relieving them of tension or boredom, by distracting them from their troubles, and even by pumping them up for important social events" (Brown, 2012: 97).

## References

Bakhtin, M. (1984) *Rabelais and His World*. Trans. H. Iswolsky. Bloomington: Indiana University Press.

Bettelheim, B. (1976) *The Uses of Enchantment: The Meaning and Importance of Fairy Tales*. London: Thames and Hudson.

Bogost, I. (2011) *How to Do Things with Video Games*. Minneapolis: University of Minnesota Press.

Brown, M. (2012) *Debussy Redux: The Impact of his Music on Popular Culture*. Bloomington and Indianapolis: Indiana University Press.

Broyles, M. (2011) *Beethoven in America*. Bloomington and Indianapolis: Indiana University Press.

Chang, V. (2009) "Records that Play: The Present Past in Sampling Practice." *Popular Music* 28: 143–59.

Collins, K. (2008) *Game Sound: An Introduction to the History, Theory, and Practice of Video Game Music and Sound Design*. Cambridge, MA: MIT Press.

Cook, K. (2014) "Music, History, and Progress in Sid Meier's *Civilization IV*." In *Music in Videogames: Studying Play*, edited by K. J. Donnelly, W. Gibbons and N. Lerner, pp. 166–82. New York and Abingdon: Routledge.

"Cuzit" (2007) "Boom Boom Fun!" *GameFAQs*. April 17. http://www.gamefaqs.com/xbox360/937889-boom-boom-rocket/reviews/review-112746 (accessed July 18, 2014).

Dinitto, R. (2004) "Translating Prewar Culture into Film: The Double Vision of Suzuki Seijun's *Zigeunerweisen*." *Journal of Japanese Studies* 30: 35–63.

Edge Online [Anon.] (2012) "Fez Review." *Edge Online*. April 11. http://www.edge-online.com/review/fez-review/ (accessed July 18, 2014). Archived as http://web.archive.org/web/20131221064902/http://www.edge-online.com/review/fez-review/

Galbraith, P. (2011) "Bishōjo Games: 'Techno-Intimacy' and the Virtually Human in Japan." *Game Studies* 11/2. http://gamestudies.org/1102/articles/galbraith (accessed March 9, 2016).

Gee, J. P. (2006) "Why Game Studies Now? Video Games: A New Art Form." *Games and Culture* 1: 58–61.

Gengaro, C. (2013) *Listening to Stanley Kubrick: The Music in his Films.* Lanham, MD: Sacrecrow.

Gibbons, W. (2009) "Blip, Bloop, Bach? Some Uses of Classical Music on the Nintendo Entertainment System." *Music and the Moving Image* 2: 40–52.

Hubbs, J. (1988) *Mother Russia: The Feminine Myth in Russian Culture.* Bloomington and Indianapolis: Indiana University Press.

Johns, A. (2004) *Baba Yaga: The Ambiguous Mother and Witch of the Russian Folktale.* New York: Peter Lang.

Johnson, J. (2002) *Who Needs Classical Music?* Oxford and New York: Oxford University Press.

Juul, J. (2005) *Half-Real: Video Games between Real Rules and Fictional Worlds.* Cambridge, MA: MIT Press.

Kalata, Kurt (2009) "Gyruss." *HardcoreGamer.net.* http://www.hardcoregaming101.net/konamishooters/konamishooters2.htm (accessed July 15, 2014).

Katz, M. (2010) *Capturing Sound: How Technology has Changed Music.* Rev. ed. Berkeley and Los Angeles: University of California Press.

Lachmann, R. (1988–1989) "Bakhtin and Carnival: Culture as Counter-Culture." *Cultural Critique* 11: 115–52.

Lerner, N. (2013) "The Origins of Musical Style in Video Games, 1977–1983." In *The Oxford Handbook of Film Music Studies*, edited by D. Neumeyer, pp. 319–47. New York: Oxford University Press.

Locke, R. (2012) "On Exoticism, Western Art Music, and the Words We Use." *Archiv für Musikwissenschaft* 69: 318–28.

Long, M. (2008) *Beautiful Monsters: Imagining the Classic in Musical Media.* Berkeley and Los Angeles: University of California Press.

MacNamara, M. (2013) "The S.F. Symphony Gets its Video Game On." *San Francisco Classical Voice.* July 18. https://www.sfcv.org/article/the-sf-symphony-gets-its-video-game-on (accessed January 22, 2015).

McQuiston, K. (2013) *We'll Meet Again: Musical Design in the Films of Stanley Kubrick.* New York: Oxford University Press.

Miller, M. (2012) "Fez: Change Your Perspective." *GameInformer.com.* April 11. http://www.gameinformer.com/games/fez/b/xbox360/archive/2012/04/11/change-your-perspective.aspx (accessed July 18, 2014).

Navas, E. (2012) *Remix Theory: The Aesthetics of Sampling.* Vienna and New York: Springer.

Owens, C. (1980a) "The Allegorical Impulse: Toward a Theory of Postmodernism." *October* 12: 67–86.

Owens, C. (1980b) "The Allegorical Impulse: Toward a Theory of Postmodernism, Part 2." *October* 13: 58–80.

Plank-Blasko, D. (2014) "From the Concert Hall to the Console: The 8-Bit Translation of BWV 565." Paper presented at the North American Conference on Video Game Music, Youngstown State University, January 18, 2014.

Reale, S. B. (2014) "Transcribing Musical Worlds; or, is *L.A. Noire* a Music Game?" In *Music in Videogames: Studying Play*, edited by K. J. Donnelly, W. Gibbons and N. Lerner, pp. 77–103. New York and Abingdon: Routledge.

Schloss, J. G. (2004) *Making Beats: The Art of Sample-Based Hip-Hop.* Middletown, CT: Wesleyan University Press.

Suellentrop, C. (2012) "A New Game Delights in Difficulty." *New York Times.* May 16. http://www.nytimes.com/2012/05/17/arts/video-games/the-video-game-fez-is-complex-by-design.html (accessed July 17, 2014).

Summers, T. (2014) "From *Parsifal* to the PlayStation: Wagner and Video Game Music." In *Music in Videogames: Studying Play*, edited by K. J. Donnelly, W. Gibbons and N. Lerner, pp. 199–216. New York and Abingdon: Routledge.

Tavinor, G. (2008) "Definition of Videogames." *Contemporary Aesthetics* 6. http://www.contempaesthetics.org/newvolume/pages/article.php?articleID=492 (accessed March 9, 2016).

Tavinor, G. (2009) *The Art of Videogames.* Malden, MA: Wiley-Blackwell.

Taylor, E. (2007) "Dating-Simulation Games: Leisure and Gaming of Japanese Youth Culture." *Southeast Review of Asian Studies* 29: 192–208.

Wikipedia [Anon.] (2014a) "Classical Music." *Wikipedia.* http://en.wikipedia.org/wiki/Classical_music (accessed July 17, 2014).

Wikipedia [Anon.]. (2014b) "Art Music." *Wikipedia.* http://en.wikipedia.org/wiki/Art_music (accessed July 17, 2014).

Zipes, J. (2012) *The Irresistible Fairy Tale: The Cultural and Social History of a Genre.* Princeton: Princeton University Press.

# Index